THE STANDING MEDITATION

THE STANDING MEDITATION

NATE RIFKIN

EXCEL IN THE MODERN WORLD
USING AN ANCIENT PRACTICE

WOOD OX
PUBLISHING

This book does not replace the advice of a medical professional. Consult your physician before making any changes to your diet or regular health plan. I have changed some names to protect individuals' privacy. To maintain the anonymity of the individuals involved, I have changed some details.

The information in this book was correct at the time of publication, but the Author does not assume any liability for loss or damage caused by errors or omissions.

These are my memories, from my perspective, and I have tried to represent events as faithfully as possible.

PAPERBACK: 978-1-7358259-5-3
EBOOK: 978-1-7358259-0-8

First paperback edition January 2021.

Edited by Stephen Singular and Dina J. Rifkin
Cover art and layout by Cindy Curtis
Illustrations by Dylan Satterfield

Wood Ox Publishing
601 16th Street C#439
Golden, CO 80401
www.WoodOxPublishing.com

www.NateRifkin.com

For Dina, I'm so grateful to walk this path with you.

CONTENTS

CHAPTER ONE

DARKNESS

I hated myself. I hated that I was alone. I hated how I became a loser drenched in so much debt that I was terrified I'd end up homeless. My thoughts were like a faceless darkness drilling pain deep into my mind. *How could I escape this? Would I need to die?*

Ever felt like that?

I did. Then I found daylight.

I found a way to relieve my worst emotional pain. I freed myself from debt, built wealth, and fell in love with an amazing woman. We're now married.

But you've heard this story before. "My life sucked and now it's perfect. I did it and you can too!" We've all seen this from the world of self-help.

Ever gotten seduced into that world?

I devoured self-help for years. After I set goals, thought positive, and visualized what I wanted, feeling like I was shooting up joy into my bloodstream, the high wore off and I had nothing to show for it but how frustrated and confused I felt as my dreams shattered.

I got desperate enough to try that law of attraction stuff. The only thing I manifested was more debt. I also tried meditating, which made me feel hazy and restless. All the techniques that were supposed to work…didn't work. I felt hopeless. Angry. *Betrayed.*

Ever been *there?*

That's when I felt like killing myself. I drank vodka every morning to drown the darkness.

But I was too stubborn to give up—there's a reason my mother called me "pigheaded"—and my persistence led me in a different direction. I found a practice from a spiritual tradition that's thousands of years old. I stopped the modern self-help tricks and started training in an ancient practice, beginning with one minute per day.

I was surprised by the results. The practice wasn't about changing my thoughts, yet my thoughts turned from hurtful to happy. I wasn't trying to imagine a different life, yet when my emotional pain healed, I erased my self-sabotaging behaviors and leaped into a new career.

I escaped the darkness. Even better, I *excelled*—I built wealth doing what I enjoy and married the woman of my dreams. The journey wasn't easy or pain-free, but I feel blessed that I got to walk it.

This book tells my story and how you can use this practice to transform your life.

"Hey!" the woman shouted as she crouched and lunged at me, limbs pumping and body weaving like a two-legged spider.

She closed the distance between us on the sidewalk and shot out her arm.

"What's this?" she growled. The black spots of her missing teeth looked like a pair of giant dice in her mouth.

Her hand clenched my inner thigh, like a toothless dog chomping me with its gums. As I lurched back, she scampered away cackling, *"I told you this was my sidewalk!"*

I was on the southwest corner of Broadway and Nassau Street in Englewood, Colorado, a regular stumbling ground for drug addicts. To the north, the buildings of downtown Denver floated and shimmered like a mirage. Heat pulsed from the concrete of the sidewalk, the asphalt of the road, and the cinderblocks of buildings, their dull red and grey paint chipping. A row of thirsty bushes squeezed through a bed of rocks beside the road. A nearby tree sprouted from another pile of rocks, shading the rubble.

For 40 hours per week—excluding a half-hour lunch and two 10-minute breaks—I stood on this corner waving a sign. Every workday morning, I shimmied into a costume that looked like a giant $100 bill. Ten times more than my hourly pay.

Because thousands of cars and trucks chugged by me daily, the smock got caked with a combination of exhaust fumes, sweat, and the occasional BBQ sauce stain from a co-worker who used the costume as a bib for his lunch. Hours of high-elevation Colorado sun baked everything into the fabric. Sunburns stung my skin; it felt like rubber. The "Stop" sign to my left cast an octagonal shadow. I ducked my head behind it for shade.

How the heck did my life end up here? And how much crack did that woman smoke before she grabbed me?

I could answer the first question.

Six years earlier, I dreamed of becoming a millionaire. I fantasized about dating gorgeous women. I was a dedicated student of self-help and I took action on everything I learned. Six years later, I'd grown a compost heap of entrepreneurial failures, broken friendships, and debt. *I'm such a loser.* My thoughts, like starving animals, turned on me, clawing at my brain. I wanted to put a bullet through my head.

Debt collectors hounded me. Each time my phone buzzed, I cringed and didn't dare touch it. Even after the ringing stopped, the phone murmured a beep for a voicemail, reminding me that the delusions I'd constructed about growing wealthy were crumbling. I played the message and heard a voice reading from a script, "This is an attempt to collect a debt..." I pressed the #7 button to delete the sentence before it finished.

My $10-an-hour wage wasn't enough to pay them or the IRS debt hanging over my head. In a few months, I would file for bankruptcy, which lowered my debt to "only" $50,000.

A couple of years earlier, I'd started a business selling nutritional supplements with two partners. One morning, I woke up in my Denver apartment, plopped in front of my computer, and typed my username and password for some of our online software.

The login information you entered was incorrect.

Huh? I slowly typed it again. Incorrect. Once more, this time watching my fingers on the keyboard. *Incorrect.* I tried logging into a different piece of software connected to the business. Same result.

My gut twisted. They had locked me out overnight. Typical of my sloppy thinking, I hadn't bothered to get listed on the corporate papers or bank account. With just a few taps on a keyboard, they'd guaranteed

I'd never see a dime of the profits. There weren't any shouting matches, demands or drama. I didn't even bother trying to sue.

That betrayal was the last morsel of rotting food to top off the financial compost pile I'd built. Which was why, instead of enjoying a prosperous career, I was a 25-year-old college dropout who worked as a living, breathing punchline on a street corner.

If you were one of the thousands of people who drove by me, you might have looked at me with a sad smile. Plenty did, including a couple of high school kids who stopped in front of me on the sidewalk as if viewing a zoo exhibit, shook their heads, and, deciding to talk to the animal, said, "I'm so sorry."

"Oh, don't be!" I replied.

Even though it appeared as if my outer world was burning down, my inner world was rising from the ashes. My dreams of riches were splattered on the sidewalk—but something was different inside me.

I felt the happiest I'd ever been...*in my entire life*.

My thoughts were encouraging, I buzzed with energy, and I smiled way more than in the past.

How could this be?

Because even in the midst of my challenges, I was practicing a unique way to rid myself of emotional gunk and re-write my mental programming, and it was working. Rather than the latest self-help fad, which always failed me, this secret was thousands of years old.

I was still getting used to my happiness. Since childhood, I'd been trapped in an ugly cloud of sadness, a perfect reflection of the household I was raised in. As I grew from an oddball pre-teen into an angry, gangly teenager, I got more and more consumed by my storm clouds. Sitting on therapists' sensibly beige couches for 55-minute rounds of

BSing didn't help. Maybe nothing could. As I grew into young adulthood, my silent scowl kept my pain buried, but it was festering.

A fresh start, I thought, when I applied to colleges and chose UMASS Amherst. However, when I arrived on the colossal campus and shuffled past excited students, including gorgeous coeds, I realized that feeling hopeful was foolish. As everyone around me looked brighter and happier, my thoughts grew darker, especially at night when I curled up on my dorm room mattress. So many other kids here. So many beautiful women. They're out having fun. They're getting laid. But not you. Who'd want you? I squeezed harder into the fetal position, tears soaking my pillow, choking down the noise of my crying so my roommate wouldn't hear.

A million fresh starts wouldn't change a damn thing if I was too shut down to connect with others—or myself. My inner world needed to change, but I didn't know how. After three miserable semesters, I dropped out of college with no close friends and, seemingly, no future.

In lieu of traditional education and support, I turned to the hyped-up world of self-help. Apparently by thinking big and fixating on cheesy stock photos of mansions, smiling couples, and secluded beaches, fixing my life was a matter of mental photoshop.

I learned doctrines like *just imagine what you want* and *write down your intentions* and, in direct contrast, *be in the present moment.* I bought everything hook, line, and sinker—with the hook firmly embedded in both my wallet and my confidence.

I set all kinds of goals. Some were to hit certain levels of strength and muscular development. Others were to hit certain levels of income. I can't remember all the different goals I wrote down and committed to, but I'll never forget the result: I failed to achieve a single one.

As instructed, I sat and visualized every scenario I wanted to unfold in my life, almost undulating with emotion as I delighted in every crisp detail. I talked to myself in the mirror with the same fervor and conviction as a coach in a Hollywood movie halftime speech. Who cares if the neighbors heard me ranting? Maybe they'd get inspired too! Then I took whatever action, with the deluded belief that I'd attract duffel bags stuffed with cash and McMansions galore—as if wielding the same powers of manifestation as that creepy kid from *The Twilight Zone* who turned his parents' friend into a jack-in-the-box. But the universe behaved much like the voicemail of potential dates in those days—I left messages, but never heard back.

I also learned some spiritual practices from books—including the standing meditation this book is based on—but I barely tried them with any effort.

Setting goals, dabbling in spiritual practices, and visualizing success gave me brief glimpses of purpose, like bobbing my head out of the ocean to briefly glimpse the sunshine. But I sank back underwater just as quickly. I worked hard and thought positively, but my poor choices and self-sabotage still stuck to me like a Pit Bull's clamped jaw.

All I had to show for my faith and effort were my credit cards declining, no friends, and dateless weekends. More than once, I planned my suicide. Instead, I began making a mixed glass of vodka as my morning medicine. First, I poured the vodka, usually three fingers, then grabbed an energy drink can from the bulk package I'd buy online. The alcohol helped me float above my pain and sadness, and numb my nose to the stench of where my life was going.

At the time, I had a mentor who was a world champion athlete, multi-millionaire, entrepreneur, author…just the kind of guy I admired and wanted to be like. So, I'd invested the equivalent of a house down payment for his group coaching.

He saw I that was suffering, despite all my efforts. But he didn't give me a motivational pep talk or demand I double-down on my goals. He showed me something completely different: a form of meditation he used to bring everything in his life together. He didn't invent it, as this secret had been taught from person to person for thousands of years. After learning it, he went from broke to millionaire. It came from something called Daoism (pronounced DOW-ism), a spiritual tradition stretching back millennia.

At this point, I was no stranger to meditation. To me it felt like sitting in a chair and fighting off waves of impatience while thinking about not thinking. Hardly life-changing stuff. Plus, I was growing jaded toward anything that had a whiff of woo-woo, which seemed to be either "harness the universe's power to attract what you want" or weekend courses in "aligning with your spirit vibration's highest truth…blah blah."

This training is different. The following story, possibly legend or possibly true, shows how.[1]

Roughly 200 years ago, in a village in China, robbers regularly raided caravans full of grain, sometimes killing the merchants who drove the caravans.

The robbers were deadly martial artists and the local judge realized the criminals couldn't be stopped by ordinary means. The judge secretly hired a powerful martial artist named Master Kuo Yun Shen to stop them.

Master Kuo assembled a group of his own martial artists and one night they confronted and killed the gang of robbers, but one robber escaped. He went before the judge and demanded that Master Kuo be executed for his crime.

The judge had Master Kuo arrested, but there was a problem. Master Kuo could testify against him, saying, "This is what you hired me to do, your honor."

At the trial, the judge motioned the bailiff to escort Master Kuo into a private room. The judge met him there and said, "The robber is demanding justice for you murdering his gang. I can't reveal that I hired you and I can't go easy on your sentence, either. If you keep quiet about our deal, I won't have you executed. Instead, I'll sentence you to three years in prison. But both your hands and feet will be shackled the whole time. This way, you'll serve only three years, but because you're chained up, it will still appear harsh."

Master Kuo agreed. The judge brought him back into the main chambers and announced his sentence. At first, the robber was angry. *Just three years in prison?* Then the robber realized something. Because Master Kuo's hands and feet would be chained the whole time, he couldn't practice his martial arts.

The robber, himself a deadly fighter, decided he'd wait the three years and, when Master Kuo was released, the robber would kill him—thus giving the robber a legendary reputation.

Master Kuo was thrown in a small cell. His hands and feet were chained together. He couldn't throw a single punch or kick, but Master Kuo didn't simply sit in his cell. He stood and held his body in a certain way to enhance its energy. Upon his release, Master Kuo was confronted by the robber. For three years, the robber had trained himself in martial arts; now they squared off and fought. After three years of standing still in a small cell, Master Kuo defeated the robber.

As I listened to the story, I was getting a glimpse into another reality. I didn't want to be a martial artist, but to transform my mind's shackles into resources, so I wasn't imprisoned by confusion, frustration, self-sabotage, powerlessness, and self-hate. True or not, the story contained a real lesson. Master Kuo had found a powerful way to meditate and get stronger. I wondered if this could help me.

After learning the standing meditation, I returned home. At this point, I was living in Boulder, Colorado. A couple of years earlier, I'd dropped out of college, started my own business, moved to Boulder, and lived a spartan lifestyle—a cheap futon with a metal frame resembling a public trash can, a chair, and a particle board desk. One plastic dish, one fork, and one cup that I hand-washed over and over. I left every item where I last used it; my condo was a museum of joyless efficiency. No decoration except for a list of goals and a vision board I later shoved into the recycling bin. And, a brown wall-to-wall shag carpet, even in the bathroom, holding enough microbes to become a sentient being.

My only decent furniture was my bed. Every day, after I lurched out of it, I practiced the standing meditation and wondered if I were quietly absorbing some esoteric power from an unknown source. For the first few weeks of standing in one place with my knees slightly bent and my arms suspended in front of my chest, it seemed less like a meditation and more like a diabolical punishment out of a junior high gym class, my legs feeling like chestnuts roasting on an open fire.

As the weeks went by, my shirts started feeling different, because my shoulders grew a little wider from relaxing. No surprise there. But how I felt *did* surprise me. Something buzzed through my body, like the first warm wave from a good cup of coffee. My mental chatter began turning from a hurtful critic into an encouraging ally. I felt a *little* better. Could this actually help me?

I kept practicing the standing meditation. One evening, something shocking occurred.

Outside the screen door of my condo, as I stood to do the practice, crickets chirped a gentle chorus. Some nights, I heard nearby trees rustling in the wind like gentle brooms, but tonight they were silent. I deepened my breathing as I adjusted my body's position. Within a few minutes, my entire body buzzed with warmth, like being dipped into a soothing hot tub. It felt as if a glowing sun had ignited within me, emanating light throughout the dark room. I basked in what felt like a state of bliss. Then I eased onto my futon.

"Whoa!"

What just happened? I didn't know. But as I sat, I couldn't help but smile. It was as if, for the past few months, the standing meditation had been chipping at my sadness, and this evening, an iceberg-sized chunk fell away.

As more weeks went by, I felt happier. My hope returned. People began looking at me with their heads cocked, commenting that "something was different" about me, even though I hadn't told them I was doing any kind of meditation.

The more I practiced, the more confidence radiated through me. I'd given up on trying to think positively, but my thoughts were now more loving and helpful. For most of my life, I'd regularly—almost daily—lose myself in vivid imaginings of how I was a failure and would always fail.

No bully or cruel person could possibly match the intricate, precise scenarios I'd constructed where, over and over again, I'd see myself as a loser. But as I practiced the standing meditation, those awful mental spirals became rarer.

Behaviors that used to sabotage me began to evaporate. I lashed out less and became more reflective. More clear-headed. The practice didn't wipe away all my problems. In fact, my life was about to enter a multi-year, hurricane-like healing crisis, but the standing meditation made me strong enough to face the challenges. Instead of panicking when my business partners cut me out, I came to recognize that I was now removed from a toxic relationship.

For years, my budget-balancing consisted of dropping unopened credit card bill envelopes onto the carpet as if the shag would absorb them with the same efficiency as other spills. When that didn't work, I'd pile other mail on top, burying the bills like a bad memory. I had a tsunami of credit card and IRS debt. I'd slouch in my chair, imagining calls from my landlord. "Your rent is, uh, a bit late so I was wondering..." Then would come angrier phone calls. Then an eviction notice would get taped inside my screen door. Then a sheriff would drill the deadbolt so they could grab me and drag me to the street.

The standing meditation practice, however, helped yank me out of my financial drowning and gave me the good sense to swim to shore.

It wasn't a magic wand for making money or for absolving my past money misdeeds. Early in 2012, I filed for bankruptcy. I walked to my north Denver bankruptcy meeting, commonly called "341" after section 341 of the Bankruptcy Code. After the judge questioned me about my tax payments, I went home almost free and clear of debt. I was forgiven all my credit card debt and some tax debt. However, more than $50,000

IRS debt was, in bankruptcy lingo, "non-dischargeable debt" and still stalked me like a vulture.

I also got a job spinning signs and moved to the cheapest place I could find, so I could save money, pay off the IRS, and begin to build wealth.

As I struggled to rebuild my life, the lessons from the meditation and the Daoist tradition it comes from cradled me like helping hands to organize the rubble of my existence. I fundamentally believe that (to get a little more woo-woo) it reconfigured my energetic field to enhance my physical, mental, emotional, and spiritual health, and opened possibilities otherwise locked away.

I decided to dedicate my life to practicing this form of meditation and learning everything I could about it. Daoism is a spiritual tradition believed to have started with China's Yellow Emperor, around 3,000 BC.[2] The ancient Daoists used rigorous experimentation and spiritual inquiry to discover "...that all things in the world were composed of the same energetic vibrational substance, constantly moving and interacting."[3] They found that we can harness the power of this energetic substance to enhance our health and spiritual development. The methods for practicing this energy cultivation have been kept secret*—plus they're hard to do—so very few devotees exist today.

After a decade of immersing myself in these Daoist teachings and experiencing profound changes from them, I decided to share my experience with as many people as I could by writing this book.

*Secrecy was kept for a few reasons. Daoist meditation and energetic cultivation has strong ties to martial arts and ancient martial artists were careful about teaching their training methods for fear of strengthening future opponents. Plus, many people skilled in energetic cultivation have made a living by teaching it, so they didn't give their knowledge freely. Finally, many of the practices were often withheld until students proved their dedication to the training, which took many years.

In the following pages, I'll show you how to perform the standing meditation, which is called the Immortal Post. I'll give you all the general guidelines for the Immortal Post, as well as the tricky details I learned through hard-earned experience. I'll also share the Daoist lessons I used to put my life back together and, ultimately, to thrive. I'm also going to quote from a book called the *Dao De Jing* (also spelled Tao Te Ching), often translated as *The Way and its Power*. Although it can't be confirmed, most people believe it was authored by a Daoist philosopher named Laozi.* The paradoxical lessons in this short book are timeless.

This Daoist practice of standing meditation saved my life. It got rid of my self-sabotage and sadness, when nothing else did. It helped me build my career, when so much else failed for me. It made me a better man. I'm now writing this as a married man, living with the love of my life in our beautiful home in Golden, Colorado, and I'm the happiest I've ever been.

But what you're about to read is as much a warning as it is encouragement. Even with Daoist meditation helping me along the path, I still fumbled into stupid decisions, buried my face into my hands and cried, screamed, and wandered into enough dead ends to fill, well, a book.

As the saying goes, "the journey of 1000 miles begins with a single step." Sometimes you'll sprint, saunter or march forward on this journey, and other times you'll crawl or seem to sit still. But as long as you're on the path, you're home. Daoism won't remove the challenges from your journey. It removes the weakness preventing you from pulverizing those challenges. I'm not going to ask you to embrace Daoism as *the*

* Also spelled Lao Tzu or Lao-Tze.

answer, but I do ask you to give the practices you're going to learn an honest chance. Test them as you walk your own path and discover how your life transforms. To quote Morpheus from The Matrix, "...all I'm offering is the truth. Nothing more."

CHAPTER TWO

COPING WITH PAIN

When I was seven years old, my brother and I were playing a computer game in our den. He was almost twelve, practically an adult in my eyes. Usually, he played the game and I perched on a chair silently cheering him on. The den was next to the garage and our front yard rose all the way to the room's only tiny window, making it feel more like a basement. In the summer, the den was a dank cave-like refuge from the heat. In the winter, it was a shiver-inducing meat locker.

Behind the house was a geriatric river with a willow tree fallen halfway across it. A hurricane had swatted it down. The tree's root mass, big as a truck engine, was now a hunk of mulch for wasp nests. In summertime, I stepped along the trunk and over the river, like a cat burglar crossing a ledge, placing my feet more and more carefully as the trunk tapered into a branch. Halfway across the river, I'd stare at the dark, fishless water. Every season, like a fallen soldier lifting a trembling hand for help, the tree sprouted leaves. Eventually that stopped, and the river swallowed the bones.

As I got older, I spent less time around trees and more time in that den, glued to the television, computer screen, or both. One day, our mother called for my brother and me and we jumped up the stairs and peered around the corner to the living room, where my mom and dad sat, like two strangers in a waiting room.

Even though my brother and I were paying attention with our heads, our bodies began their contortions—stretching back down the stairs. My mother stuck her chin out and gave a pronouncement like a judge delivering a verdict:

"Your father and I are getting a divorce."

"Okay!" we both replied, darting back downstairs to continue our game. If it were a sitcom, there'd be tearful, meaningful moments or hugs of reassurance. We were a silent movie, with no captions or wild gesticulations, just a household of perpetual awkward silence, with tension rising when someone spoke. Our family was so disassociated and distant that, to my brother and me, a divorce announcement registered only as an annoying pause from gaming.

I've often heard that children are very aware of their family dynamics. Television seems to portray children as precocious, but I was clueless about what was going on around me.

My father, after getting home from his work as a physicist, would sit in the living room alone, furrow his brow, and listen to classical music. On weekends, he did woodworking projects in the basement, alone. The shriek of the table saw, muffled by the closed door, was like the house's elevator music. Sometimes, he'd take me to the playground and I'd run around alone. He'd usually get bored and walk across the street to the library and I'd eventually have to find him.

My father was never demeaning and rarely aggressive but, to a six-year-old, the silent, brooding giant in the corner was plenty scary. Decades later, I discovered my father didn't want to participate in raising children. So, instead of encouraging me, he did his best not to acknowledge my existence. His silent presence got downloaded into my and my brother's brains like an operating system, closing us off to other people. My brother grew more silent and withdrew more every day. My program of silence wouldn't kick in until I was a teenager. But according to my dad, I was explosively angry, even as an infant. I shrieked, cried, argued, and fought.

My mother maintained the house, while taking care of my brother and me. She was usually pissed off at us—mostly me. Even "shut up!" got too laborious for her and she'd just shout "Shut!" at me.

Although it seemed normal at the time, I was marinating in a household of miserable people. Whatever love or affection that had existed between my parents was doused long ago. There was no touching in our family. I didn't want to be touched, couldn't be consoled. Any touch triggered one of two programs in my brain: Run or fight.

Starting when I was five, my mother drove me to various therapists to fix the family. So much talking, nodding, awkward silence, and mom staring at me with eyes pleading for me to explain why I was such a rotten kid. The therapist rambled, as if analyzing how a train is slowly wrecking.

One therapist convinced my mom to get me a teddy bear to cuddle when I felt angry or overwhelmed. We soon stepped out of the Burlington Mall with me hugging Furry, and I became known as the weirdo in the 2nd grade who *carried around a teddy bear.*

Sometimes, while my mom saw a therapist at his home office, I sat in the living room outside and raided his mini-fridge. I dug through the cans, snaking my arm past the ones labeled diet, and sometimes got the thrill of finding an Orange Slice.

My mom was too dissociated to recognize how angry and hostile she was. Instead of treating my father with respect, she made sniping comments about how poor of a job he did raising my brother and me. She told me that my father's co-workers stopped carpooling with him because of his social awkwardness. I can still hear the way she'd drawl, "Your father-r-r." Usually, these comments were to point out the genesis of my behavior problems. She didn't understand that by insulting my role model, she was also programming me to think that any romantic relationship with a woman would be hostile.

Then came the moment when she called my brother and I into the living room. Our parents divorced and dad moved out. One day he was there. Next day, he wasn't. At seven, I translated the divorce into another example that I'd always be alone, never having a happy family. And I'd never be happy because I was unlikable and damaged.

Before the divorce, money wasn't on my radar. After, money became like a haunting bully. Once, my mother and I stood in a gift shop. From the shelf I pulled a notebook with a sturdy black cover and flipped through the blank pages. I wanted to draw on them. I asked my mother for the notebook. She looked at the price, then glared down at me. "Are you really going to use this? And not just draw on a few pages?"

I nodded. She bought the notebook and I drew on every page, filling them as fast as I could with stick figures, racing to the last page so I could make good on my promise—nothing had gone to waste.

Money, the invisible giant, got final say in where we went, what we ate, and how miserable we felt as we did it. Anything nice came with performance anxiety—I felt compelled to pretend to enjoy it.

When I grow up, I'm going to get rich. Then I'll feel comfortable spending money.

My saving grace was that my father never said a bad word about me. Even though my mom sometimes did, I disliked her enough that her words didn't seem to seep in. While I grew up in an emotionally binary environment—either anger or nothing—I absorbed a useful rationality from my dad. My mother, with all her faults, could still be encouraging. She tried to fix the broken family, but had no good resources.

Neither parent coddled me. They weren't monsters, but because of how I perceived and behaved, I often thought the world was monstrous.

In school, I got punished for fighting.

"Nathaniel has behavior problems."

My only way to interact in my comfort zone was to lash out. Yet school assignments were easy. In art class, I was good at drawing angry faces. Just carve three lines down the forehead, converging at the nose bridge. One time, we paired up to make model cities out of Styrofoam, paper, and tongue depressors. I partnered with another behavior problem kid. We mixed Elmer's glue with green paint, poured it everywhere, and said the city's nuclear power plant exploded. *Meltdown Metropolis.*

Before weekends, I asked my mom to call other families to see if anyone wanted to do a playdate. I was too scared to call. She flipped through a little red, staple-stitched booklet with my classmates' phone numbers. She dialed and dialed. Everyone was always busy.

My only close friend was a kid named Jeff whose mother gave him alcohol before he was a pre-teen. Every morning in the summers, without fail, Jeff galloped across the street and rang our doorbell.

One early evening when I was eleven, Jeff came over. Mom was going to drive us to the movie theater to see *Starship Troopers*. But he came over too early. My mom asked why.

Jeff said to her, "My stepmom told me to come over early because you wanted to go to Macy's."

That wasn't true. The stepmom probably made something up to get Jeff out of the house. Lately, Jeff had been complaining about his stepmom's weird behavior and my mom couldn't help but push herself into the situation. She got the stepmom on the phone and accused her of lying.

"Bring my son home to me," the stepmom said.

"He's not your son and you don't treat him like one," my mom said, hanging up on her. As Jeff and I ran in circles screaming, my mom compulsively washed dishes. She said, "If the cops are going to come over, you always want your dishes clean!"

She herded us into the car and drove to the theater. Jeff's dad's car zoomed beside us and his dad pointed for my mom to pull over. She complied. He marched to our car, glaring down at mom like a cop about to issue a ticket.

"Do you have a problem?" he asked, hands on his hips.

Half a minute later, he drove away with my best friend and I went to the movie alone.

Jeff was forbidden from ever playing with me again.

As the years went by, other children made friends, learned social skills, and created wonderful memories. I was either bullied or the bully. More and more proof shoveled onto me like dirt that I'd always be alone. As a pre-teen, I grew my hair long.

"Cut your hair—you look like a f@&$ing girl!" other kids said.

I was too stubborn to cut it.

As a teenager, I shaved my head and sprouted the nastiest acne of anyone in my school. My back was covered by so many zits it looked as if I had a medieval plague, but I managed to hide it. I couldn't, however, hide the concentration of acne on my forehead, as if aliens had carved a blood red crop circle on the front of my skull.

Nothing got rid of it until I took a drug called Accutane. The doctor warned me about severe liver damage and birth defects if I got a woman pregnant. *Well, that's not happening.* The pills' bubble packets had outlines of a pregnant woman with an X over her. Accutane hasn't been sold in over a decade because it triggered so many lawsuits. Looking back, I was subconsciously programming my body to become as ugly on the outside as I felt on the inside.

In an 8th grade science class, a girl played a video on the classroom's TV. Her mom had filmed a home movie of the girl's birthday party—maybe she had turned six or seven. The camera panned across crowded tables of kids shouting and stuffing themselves with pizza, laughing between balloons, string, and glittery paper.

"Hey everyone!" the mom said from behind the camera. She kept panning the camera around the room until stopping at the last table. A kid sat alone at that table and stared ahead, eyes unblinking. Then he panned his head to face the camera.

As my six-year-old self bunched his forehead muscles harder, glowering deeper, scattered laughter rattled from the 6th grade class.

The mom said nothing and moved the camera somewhere else.

I got suspended twice in junior high school. A kid on the bus tried to trip me and stepped on my foot so I punched his face over and over. Suspension number one. In music class, I propped my feet on a kid's chair, resting my boots against his shoulder because I felt like being an idiot. He pushed my feet off, so I pushed him on the floor. Suspension number two. I apologized to him the same day, after school.

Like many angry people, I didn't know I was angry. I thought everyone else was an asshole. My grades reflected my disregard for studying and I sucked at sports. I was interested in writing, but lacked the discipline to produce much content.

Hanging out with my father on weekends gave me superficial comfort. We'd watch a movie.

My mom once said, "Your father probably chose to watch a movie because it was the cheapest way to spend time with you."

On Saturday, I sometimes tagged along with him the next day to run errands or read books at the local library. We didn't talk about deep things and I never thought to ask about the family or what we were enduring.

My brother was usually with friends or working. Before my first day of high school, I asked him, "Do you have any advice?" Without looking at me, he said, "No."

Living with my mother during the week was painful. She cut up her Prozac pills and arranged the slices on her bedside table, flakes of dust around them. She was trying to avoid the side effects, but still get some relief, which she never did. They numbed her and made her scared to leave the house, yet she still pushed herself to get jobs and provide for us. I became the clichéd kid who was alone at the field after football practice because she forgot to pick me up. While I waited for her to remember me, I practiced running and weaving between tightly planted trees.

I didn't understand what my mother lived through until I got older and the same self-hate plunged into my brain. As a teenager, I craved escape. Wandering from room to room in our house didn't inspire memories of happy laughter around the dinner table or family games in the living room. It was as stagnant as a used mop bucket.

The pain burrowed into my body, as I slouched and drew in my shoulders as if clamping down on the emotional larvae it had produced. My mom demanded, "Pull your shoulders back!" but to no avail. When I caught my face in the mirror, I saw my parents' scowls. When my mom and I argued, and rage pulsated over the top of my head and cascaded down my face, my mom would stare deep into my pupils, shake her head, and chuckle at me. Then she'd look away, deaden her gaze, and curl deep inside her skull.

By high school, I didn't punch anyone or get suspended because my lashing out transformed to lashing within. I swallowed my fear and grief deep enough that I didn't know it was festering in hidden regions of my brain (and, as I'd later learn, parts of my body). Instead of picking fights and getting in trouble, I pushed it down inside of me, as self-hate. The only emotions I showed were anger and sadness. You could almost see the dark cloud churning around me.

"There's three kinds of sex," Veronica said, ticking off her slim fingers. We were both sixteen or seventeen. Her birthday was the day after mine and I once tried to joke about me being her elder. But I could make 1,000 jokes and she'd never look at me the same way she looked when she talked about other guys.

"There's making love. There's sex. And there's f***ing," she said.

At that point, I'd kissed a girl. On a dare. When I was 12. But by high school, being normal and happy didn't seem like a stretch, but like hearing about some paradise on the other side of the world, something mythological, something you can't afford.

My classmates dated, got laid, gossiped, got gussied up for prom. Even their pain—the breakups, anxiety about college, and backstabbing by friends—made me jealous. I had a few superficial friendships, but nothing lasted.

In my senior year of high school, I read a self-help book that stated you can bond with someone when you ask, "How did that make you feel?" When a woman in my physics class told me about someone insulting her, I asked her the question.

"...I felt like that person was acting like an ass****. Why are you asking how I feel?"

This was one of many experiences where self-help failed for me, yet I'd keep returning to it.

I later learned that when people can't deal with their pain, they build something called a coping mechanism.

Think of victimhood. Or victimizing. Self-sabotage. Laziness. People-pleasing. Lack of awareness. These behaviors develop for a reason. As my teachers now remind me, "In the past, it was useful to you." "It" is the coping mechanism, once useful for your emotional survival or even your physical survival. You got angry because someone violated you. You panicked because someone attacked you. You developed a coping mechanism—like chronic anger or a tendency toward panic attacks—to make sure you could react instantly if the threat appeared again.

These coping mechanisms aren't always logical or even effective. They are your brain's flimsiest attempt at protecting you from perceived threats. The problem is when the threat goes away, the coping mechanism doesn't turn off.

Here's an example. When someone gets an emotional shock—like getting yelled at by a parent—they feel fear or grief. If the emotions don't get relief, they can fester into anger or despair.

If you don't process the fear or grief, you'll cope with it. One way to cope with fear or grief is by fighting against them—getting angry. Another way is to resign yourself to feeling fear or grief, which leads to despair.

Finally, the emotions crystallize into depression and denial. You become depressed when your anger turns inward. You try to relieve your despair by mentally blocking yourself from it. That's when the coping mechanism develops. By the time someone gets to this stage, they have shut away parts of themselves, like the scar tissue over a cut or burn on a hand. It's numb, so the hand is less sensitive, but also less functional.

My coping mechanism was to shut myself off from people emotionally, so I never grew close relationships. It probably formed in response to my parents' emotionally distant behavior and divorce. It protected me from the pain of loss and left me alone with the devil I knew: loneliness. Instead of feeling love around my distant father and angry mother, I felt fear, which boiled into anger and resentment, which I turned inward into depression. Then I developed the coping mechanism of forcing everyone to be distant.

If I felt threatened, my anger erupted. If my shyness didn't keep people away, my scowl would. Either way, my emotional walls got thicker. This coping mechanism may have helped me when I had to withstand a hostile mother and cruel classmates, but as a young adult it left me lost and hurt. A starving dog snarling at anyone, even if they offered food.

I didn't know what was wrong or how to ask for help. And even if

I did, few people would know what to do. When you create a coping mechanism in response to pain, you must shut down your awareness and disassociate. You cripple yourself in an attempt to avoid emotional shock. When you normalize abuse, your brain thinks of loving behavior as foreign, so it filters out any evidence of it. You can't see the potential of a loving relationship because your brain has cut off that possibility.

Many times, coping mechanisms show up in subtle ways, like someone snapping, "I don't want to talk about it!" or ending a conversation when a sensitive subject comes up. Coping mechanisms take the form of mental models about yourself and the world, showing up as beliefs like, "I'm not good at math," or "I always end up dating liars."

They can also show up as, "I don't care" and "I'm fine." If you had asked early-20s me about drinking every morning, or ignoring my bills, or not having friends, I'd have mumbled some variant of, "I'm fine."

This is why coping mechanisms are so difficult to dismantle, especially with self-help and Western models of therapy. Coping mechanisms make themselves unnoticeable, like how a mosquito pumps painkillers into your body as it sucks your blood. Pushing yourself out of your comfort zone can spur your coping mechanisms to dig in their heels, like how scratching a bite makes it swell and itch. Talking about your problems can ingrain your view of them, compelling you to cling to your coping mechanisms harder. Plus, as we'll cover later, coping mechanisms aren't just mental and emotional. They're energetic and help shape the world around you. When I became hostile, I always ran into other hostile people.

Beliefs, mental models, and coping mechanisms control the function of our brains, shape our bodies, and map out the trajectory of our future. Because of my belief system and coping mechanisms, I couldn't form relationships, romantic or otherwise. Later, I'd go broke while continuing to fantasize that I'd soon be rich and dating the woman of my dreams. When my fantasies mutated into real-life nightmares, I came close to killing myself.

Coping mechanisms are bad enough because they cut you off from joy, success, and fulfillment in life. In addition, they're not free of cost. They require massive amounts of energy to maintain themselves.

When you unravel your coping mechanisms, new worlds open up to you. You gain new perceptive abilities, new insights about yourself, and new reserves of confidence, calmness, adaptability, and creative thinking. This happens because you're coming home to your true self.

Sound silly? Consider this. Years ago, people would toss sage advice at me: "Just be yourself!" I'd always sneer back. *Bullsh&$. I'm already myself. I need to change myself because myself isn't getting the results I want.* The clearer, if less pithy advice, would be "Just be yourself without coping mechanisms."

Fortunately, coping mechanisms don't have to be permanent. When I worked with energy as the Daoists discovered, I changed my beliefs and models by unwinding my mind and body's original responses to shock and pain.

As I went from younger to older teen, my height kept increasing, but my weight did not. I'd say to the mirror, "You're a pathetic, ugly stick figure." Near the end of high school, I began pumping iron, determined to change.

Standing in the gym alone, a summer breeze whipping through

the double doors propped open by cinder blocks, and hoisting weights above my head was my Zen garden. The challenge engaged my mind, and the exertion triggered pleasure hormones that made my body feel alive, while cradling my twitching, burned out muscles like in a warm blanket. Lifting weights brought a taste of joy and fulfillment and my first glimpse of how to change my inner and outer worlds. Exercise didn't get me out of my emotional quagmire, but it made me feel temporarily better and gave me a sense of purpose.

As a senior in high school, I flipped through a copy of *Princeton Review: Guide to Your Career.* I scanned the salary ranges, which eliminated 95% of the jobs. Doctor was too much school. Didn't want to be a lawyer. Business owner and entrepreneur were the only two left. Their salaries didn't have an upper limit. *Fine, I'll go with that.* With enough income, I'd free myself from the clog in my throat when I wanted to buy something nice.

In 2004, I graduated high school. After the ceremony finished, a kid asked me, "How do you feel?"

I shrugged and stared as the other blue-gowned graduates whooped, hugged, hollered, and cried.

He sighed. "Do you…feel…*anything*?"

Yeah. I felt ready to leave that 18-year dumpster fire.

I fantasized that when I went to college, I'd peel off my old identity like a wetsuit. Even though I didn't know the term at the time, I believed I could end my coping mechanism of keeping people distant. Little did I realize that my sadness, anger, and disassociation, which birthed my coping mechanisms, were buried deeper than all my wishful thinking. Changing the scenery was just giving them a new place to ooze.

CHAPTER THREE

LOST

Two weeks into my 3rd semester at Amherst, I yanked on a door handle and abandoned my dream of following the traditional college path. I'd chosen this school because the in-state tuition was cheap and, as my dad had advised me one day in his dining room, "Unless you go to Harvard or somewhere like that, no one's going to care what college you went to." And with over 18,000 other students swarming the campus, disappearing in a sea of people brought the comfort of anonymity.

My brother and a friend drove me to the campus and we ambled along the rolling hills while gawking at the coeds. My high school graduating class didn't have women that looked like *this*. After my brother and his friend left me in my dorm, I slouched on my swivel chair. The early fall day was hot and sticky. Part of me flinched whenever other students ran nearby or giggled. I looked around the room—the off-white cinderblock walls, the closed door to the dorm hallway, my small pile of clothes. None of my pants were long enough for my lanky body, and the shirts were growing holes. But I couldn't go to a store at the mall—I was sure they'd sniff me out as a loser and a gorgeous woman working there would laugh at the clothes I wanted to buy.

The gym still wasn't open. Classes didn't start for a couple of days.

Now what?

Anonymity was easy. Even though my acne was mostly gone, my ugly energy rippled outward like sonar. When I got my student ID photo taken, the photographer flinched when it uploaded onto her screen.

"Oh, did I frown? Sorry. I'll try again," I said.

She re-took the photo, flinched again, gave up, and handed me my angry-looking picture.

I felt invisible wandering the campus, but worried that everyone knew I was pretending I had somewhere to go. Whether walking to the library or a cafeteria or along one of the web-like paths between buildings, part of me found comfort being alone, but another part was ashamed.

Now what?

Within days, the whole college seemed like a giant party with crowds of people laughing. My roommate joined a fraternity and I hardly saw him. One Friday night, as he rushed down the dorm's four flights of stairs to a frat event, I raced down the stairs with him, so I'd look like I was going somewhere fun, too. After he was gone, I went back up the stairs.

All the cool kids had formed their social groups and fallen into the rhythm of college life. I joined the chess team and silently played with a few people who were as emotionally shut down as I. Once, at the cafeteria, I approached a table nearly full of football players and, as I balanced my tray of food, asked if I could sit at one of the empty seats.

"Uh, okay," one guy said, while staring at the athlete sitting across from him.

I ate my meal next to them in silence—my failed attempt at friendship via osmosis.

When I wasn't hibernating in my dorm room, as if it were my childhood home's den all over again, or staring into the distance during auditorium-style class lectures with over a hundred other students, or eating meals in the cafeteria alone, I was lifting weights in the gym. My misery, anxiety, and hostility had followed me from high school, but so did my passion for working out. I wanted to push myself and enjoy the pleasure chemicals all day every day. Maybe after college I'd own a gym, or work as a personal trainer, or create fitness products.

Two weeks into my 3rd semester, I trudged a mile across the campus for an exam in an unfamiliar building. I found the door—or thought I did—and gave the handle a yank. The door didn't budge.

Was I at the wrong place? Wrong time? Smartphones didn't exist and I didn't own a regular cell phone or have anyone to call, anyway.

Now what?

I badly wanted college to be fun, but the gulf of emotional maturity between me and the other students seemed to widen by the day. Maybe college wasn't for me. My crumbling grades agreed. Instead of feeling excited to master difficult subjects in the classrooms, I felt I was losing what little energy I had.

Instead of waiting until after college to start a business, why not do it now?

It's time. That's it. I'm done. No more college classes. To hell with them.

As I strolled back to my dorm, my eyes darted around the grass and trees. I felt naked yet invisible. I was still alone, but now I'd choose a different path; a secret path that would take me far from the students who trudged to classes and would eventually trudge into jobs they might hate. Until now, I'd always been stuck in some phase of school, either languishing in a classroom or counting down the hours until I'd have to return. For the first time, school didn't stalk me anymore. I'd forge my own way. Now it was 100% on my shoulders to figure out life. I felt unshackled. The split I'd felt earlier—wanting to hide yet wanting nobody to know I was hiding—was mended.

Because I'd already paid for room and board, I stayed on campus and got my wish to get lost in a sea of people. As a freshly minted adult, my thirst for knowledge roared back like a retreated ocean tide coiling into a tsunami. I studied business and marketing books in my dorm, staying up later and later until I slept at sunrise. I awoke, lifted weights at the gym and ate alone at the cafeteria, a ghost on the campus. I snuck food back to my dorm. The odor of tuna fish and mayo wafted as I spent the night reading.

The solitude comforted me, much like spending time at my dad's home on the weekends. Instead of digging into old emotional wounds, I put my head down and planned a new future.

One night in October 2014, I stepped into a shuttle van while carrying a backpack stuffed with clothes. I was leaving the UMASS college campus to catch a flight to Florida for a seminar on marketing, taught by a man named Mike. I'd admired how he'd built his own business selling health and fitness how-to products. After telling the driver my destination, he stared at me from the rearview mirror and said, "You're going the wrong way."

"Huh?" My pulse quickened.

"Hurricane Wilma!" he said.

"Oh! Yeah, I hope it doesn't hit Florida too bad."

I was already nervous about the trip and the driver deepened my worry. Four days later, Wilma turned out to be a bust, but I learned more about marketing and persuasion at the event than I ever did in school.

On the final day, Mike offered all the attendees a chance to join something called a Mastermind group where we'd meet four times per year and have monthly phone calls to get support as we started and grew our businesses. In 24 hours, I'd be schlepping back to my college dorm and returning to my old life. I signed up.

Back at my college, I continued to study marketing by myself. On the last day of the semester, my mother picked me up from my dorm room. I carried a couple of bags to the car. I said goodbye to no one. She figured she was giving me a ride home for the winter break. I told her I wasn't going back.

"Aaaah..." she said, eyes fixed straight ahead, choosing her words slowly. It takes time to phrase a suggestion while choking back a demand. She said something about it being a bad idea. But I inherited a genetic double-dose of my mom and dad's stubbornness, so nothing she said could change my mind.

Instead of college, I'd already turned to a slightly less traditional path, although one that permeates our culture: self-improvement.

I'd always believed I could change my life. I assumed it required only hard work, belief, and time. Lifting weights seemed like an example, even though I hadn't morphed into the muscular person I'd dreamed of being, and my shoulders, right knee, and lower back were hurting more and more. I didn't realize how much of the puzzle I was missing.

After leaving college, I still thought a change of scenery would help me. Colorado had bounced around my head ever since seeing the movie *Dumb & Dumber*. As the two main characters, Harry and Lloyd, journeyed to the snow-covered Aspen mountains I yearned for my own adventure. I began attending the quarterly meetings of the Mastermind group. For the next five years, I learned from them and from Mike about marketing, business, and self-improvement. At the first session, someone in the group suggested I move to Boulder.

I packed up all my possessions and drove west. I crossed the multi-day stretch between the East Coast and the Rocky Mountains and arrived in Boulder, with its expansive views and crisp Colorado air. I tossed my stuff in a condo I'd found on Craigslist and, pushing myself through the discomfort of spending money, I bought a couple of dishes, forks, and a cup at Target. My one splurge was a quality mattress.

At Mike's Mastermind, he lectured me and the other students on choosing income goals and visualizing what we wanted to achieve in vivid detail. We collectively stoked the fires of our desires and felt what it'd be like to satisfy them—or at least, we imagined what it'd feel like. At the end of meetings, some people had tears in their eyes.

I convinced myself that I could spend all my time on internet business ventures, make it rain money, date beautiful women, and finally feel good. Goal-setting, affirmations, visualization, and hard work could program my brain into an unstoppable self-help Terminator, the world complying with my ego's most primitive cravings.

For the next three years, my delusions disintegrated into more suffering. I started a business with my brother selling courses and DVDs on yoga. He was the talent and the star. I handled the business and marketing side. Sometimes, the venture brought in windfalls of income, but it was never consistent. I scrambled and sunk into debt. As goal after goal remained unachieved, I grew more baffled and weighed down by self-doubt, and sought escape through television. I stockpiled glass bottles of Smirnoff's triple-distilled, and drank from them every day.

At Mastermind meetings, Mike reminded his students, who clung to his teachings even while they stalled on starting any businesses, that all achievements begin in the imagination.

He took us through drills where we "practiced" activities like selling or writing by going through the motions. The room pulsed with odd silence as some of us tapped our fingers on invisible keyboards and others pretended to speak to imaginary prospects about our products or services. The exercise was based on athletes "shadow boxing" in their training. Mike said if it worked for winning fights, it'd work for winning in business.

Usually, we sat passively as Mike told stories.

Most students did the visualizations, slurped up their motivation fix, went home, promptly crashed, and did nothing, showing up at the next Mastermind meeting for their next dose. But I pushed myself to do exactly what Mike taught.

Yet, no matter how I tried to change mentally and physically, something deeper chained me in place.

Was everything I'd learned a lie? Was succeeding in life just chance? I didn't understand what was going on…yet.

Then a wake-up call sent me flying through the air.

One late morning in 2007, I stood on 28th street until the "walk" signal flashed and I marched forth, intending to lift weights at the YMCA, when I saw something like The Magic School Bus veering toward me. As it barreled closer, I jumped partially out of the way, which may have saved my life, but the yellow SUV smashed into my hip, blasting me through the air. I landed on the road's double yellow line and sat up in a daze. One of my feet had a shoe on. The other didn't.

The driver—a high school kid—pulled over and jumped out to grab my shoe, which was 20 feet away. He apologized over and over. He asked if I was okay, looking as if he were about to cry. I felt fine so I made a stupid choice. I accepted the kid's apology and walked home without writing down his license plate. As I limped back to my condo, the kid's girlfriend jumped out of the SUV and hugged him. *Lucky bastard.*

Some part of me thought, I've made so many mistakes in my life and was treated mercifully, so I'll pay it forward and not get the kid in trouble. I didn't consider the value of holding the teenager responsible, let alone how I deserved to be taken care of from the accident. Instead, I shuffled away, thinking all I had to do was nurse a few scrapes and bruises. For a few moments, I considered turning around and going to the gym after all.

That afternoon, my right ankle ached. As I surfed the web that evening, it hurt. While trying to distract myself with TV, it screamed. Then it started to twitch. Every half-second, my foot snapped from side to side. I crawled to my bathtub to douse it in freezing water, but the pain shouted right through the cold.

Should I go to the hospital? What would they even do? How much would it cost? Around one in the morning, I hopped down to the bottom floor garage, slipped into my car, and drove to the emergency room. Limping to the front desk, I said a car hit me and I needed something for the pain. The guy behind the counter flinched. *Now they think I'm a junkie.* They x-rayed me, confirmed I truly was hurt, and gave me a couple of Vicodin. After resting on the exam chair that resembled a La-Z-Boy recliner, I realized the pain was gone.

"Yeah, it's good stuff, isn't it?" the doctor said, hands resting in his white coat pockets. He sent me home with a mini bottle of ten Vicodin and a prescription for 40 more.

The next morning, I sat up from bed and eased my feet onto the floor to test my ankle. Nothing. Like it was normal. *Well, the Vicodin sure was great, but I don't need a month's worth.* I threw the prescription into my recycling bin, not realizing how bitterly I'd regret this. I kept the remaining ten pills, just in case.

That afternoon, I took two more. And two more the next day. Probably the day after as well. The details are fuzzy. But I still remember how the Vicodin washed over me. I felt empowered. Ready to live. Giddy. Grateful. Years later, a friend would describe the drug as *God massaging your temples.*

Confident, at peace, and vividly imagining a bright future. Why couldn't I always be like this?

A few days later, I flew to Los Angeles to attend a marketing seminar—led by someone other than Mike—and made sure to bring a couple of pills.

The hotel's check-in line was blood-pressure-raising slow. When I got to the front, I handed over my credit card and ID.

"Sir, there's a problem with your card."

Almost half a dozen people behind me shifted their weight from one leg to another, sighing. *Oh, no.*

The lady at the front desk picked up the phone and held my card to dial the number on the back.

I'd paid off the damn card—what could be wrong? My jacket and pants suddenly turned into a sauna. My forehead grew wet with sweat.

We waited. Waited. She handed the phone to me. I didn't care if

I smeared it with ear sweat. Turns out Capital One had lowered my credit limit. Hard to blame them when I was skipping so many monthly payments.

I counted bills from my wallet and said to the person at the front desk. "I'd like to pay for just one night—then I'll pay the rest tomorrow. Here's cash—please charge the rest on my card." My flight home wasn't for another three days.

I got my room key and called Capital One again. They said I needed to call their special customer service line for a chance to re-extend my credit limit. The line would open at 6AM East Coast Time. Okay, that's 3AM here.

In my room, I tossed back two Vicodin pills and flipped on the TV, landing on *The Sopranos*; the episode when the titular character is in a coma, dreaming he's a salesman stuck in a hotel because he's lost his wallet, but has someone else's. The Vicodin swept over me, like being wrapped in a blanket fresh out of the dryer.

Tony Soprano eased onto his hotel bed, dared to peek once at a beckoning light in the distance, and let his head shift down. The grieving strings of Moby's *When It's Cold I'd Like To Die* played. I slept until the alarm woke me at 2:55AM. I called Capitol One and begged. Got put on hold.

"Mr. Rifkin, please rest easy and enjoy your trip because I have successfully raised your limit back up."

"Thank you. Thank you so much." Another fresh, warm blanket.

After the seminar finished, I clutched my drink coupon, went outside to the bar, and stood in line. The sun was setting and I wanted to get back to my room before night fell. Businesspeople arranged themselves on the hotel's outdoor furniture and mingled. I tried to look as if I was supposed to not talk to anyone. I scuttled back to my room, locked the door, and watched more TV.

I lacked the street smarts and social connections to score any Vicodin. But I wanted more. I wanted the superpowers it tricked me into thinking I had, but I wanted them for real. *Why couldn't I feel good? Is there a way to feel confident, clear-headed, and energized without a crash? Is there a way to change not just how I feel, but how I move through life? And how life treats me?*

Those questions gnawed at me until I was introduced to the standing meditation and I began practicing it. Then, to my surprise, it gave me a taste of what Vicodin had. I'm not saying meditation is a way out of addiction or that it's somehow equivalent to an opioid high. But some people use addiction to fill the hole in their lives because humans are meant to have a spiritual discipline. Without it, we feel a constant emotional ache, which we bury under layers of numbness. I didn't know it then, but I had that longing, and part of me knew, somehow, that I was missing the energy I needed. Without it, my life had a hole I was trying to fill with drugs and alcohol. It took me a few years to figure this out. First, I had to keep trying to fill the hole with more self-help. In the next chapter, I'll show you the painful results.

CHAPTER FOUR

SUICIDAL

As the months passed in Boulder, I piled on every new self-help trick I learned, my brain like a dinner plate at a dollar-per-scoop buffet.

Although I felt uncomfortable spending money on anything else, self-help became the void into which I poured my savings. I pimped out my place with all the standard items a self-improvement junkie collects. My cheap steel wire bookshelf groaned with tomes about thinking your way to riches, changing your self-image or whatever gobbledygook was trendy at the time. I customized my computer's screensaver to flash images of secluded beaches, twinkling cityscapes, and luxury rooms—gathered mostly from hotel and vacation resort websites.

But I let my credit card bills remain unpaid, except when I needed available credit for Mike's Mastermind fees.

I wrote lists of goals, like a six-figure income by a certain date, or gaining a certain amount of muscle or being in a relationship, and taped these lists where I could see them, so I could propel myself toward them and bask in the eventual glory. This was supplemented with elaborate verbal affirmations I'd repeat while staring myself down in the mirror.

To top things off, I made a vision board composed of photos of stacks of cash and beautiful women, like a creepy, glue-stick picture ransom note I'd assembled and mailed to myself. On the rare occasion I had a visitor, I hid the poster.

If all this were a buffet, my desserts were visualization exercises. First, I remembered successes from my past; that was the hardest part. Once I immersed myself in the vivid memory, I'd switch to imagining what I wanted my life to be like. The idea was to gather the "vibe of success" from the past and somehow dump that feeling into the future. Every time I performed this ritual and dredged up successful memories, it rang hollow. But that's what I'd learned, so I did my best to shove the square peg of whatever previous success into the round void of my future.

Then came the fun part. As I sat in my chair, surrounded by a room barren of decoration or furniture beyond "I still think I'm in college," I imagined living in a dream home, feeling a tingle up my spine while checking my bank account, big numbers flashing up as if I'd spun the *Wheel Of Fortune* just right. Would I celebrate with an impromptu ski vacation? Purchase some foreign real estate? What would that even entail? I didn't know! And I wasn't supposed to dwell on logistics. The point was to feel as though everything were already there. Those miniature highs felt wonderful.

Ah, I nailed it. Everything is so lined up for me. This is going to be great. I mean, it already is great! Yep.

Then I worked on marketing campaigns at my computer. Slept. Consumed more self-help. Worked. Went to the post office. Gym. Grocery store. Surfed the web. Made spaghetti—my condo smelled like sauce and cheese. TV. Porn. Repeat. More working at my computer. Sauce and cheese. Sometimes, I'd turn my head and remember I could admire the Rocky Mountains, lounging in the west like craggy sumo wrestlers, holding space as clouds blanketed them. A whole world waited for me, but I kept saying no, faced forward, and marched on with my lonely routine.

As I worked and visualized more and more, receiving hit-or-miss success, with the misses gaining ground, my gnawing doubts grew sharper teeth. There are many wealthy, successful people. Do they all visualize and set goals? If not, then how effective could those practices truly be?

I told Mike that I got my best results from hard work.

"Before you take an action, do you see it in your mind?" he asked.

"Yeah."

"Then you are visualizing," he said.

True. Except that's different from taking time to sit in a chair and imagine what you want to achieve, as if playing screenwriter and director for your own private movie. Plus, seeing an action in my mind did not require paying a guru thousands of dollars per year.

Later, I found a study[4] out of New York University showing how visualization can *harm* more than it helps. From the study's conclusion: "Positive fantasizing alone, as pleasant and relaxing as it might be, does not help us prepare for solving challenging tasks. It leaves us happily enjoying the future laurels, just in our minds."

One of my teachers is more to the point: "It's mental masturbation."

Except, unlike actual masturbation, where you know it's a fantasy, visualization exercises set up the expectation that your fantasies will come true.

Everything I did was designed to program my brain to achieve my goals and, supposedly, broadcast a signal to the universe that attracted those goals to me. I didn't understand that the faulty wiring in my brain and body, built to maintain belief systems, coping mechanisms, and emotional numbness, was holding me back.

Every self-help idea I implemented assumes a person can disregard bad programming via massive action and positive mental chatter, like pouring flavorful sauces on a sandwich's rotten meat.

This process of massive action and positive mental chatter is rarely questioned for a couple of reasons. First, because some people need this sort of giddy determination as a kick in the butt. If your most self-destructive coping mechanism is to hide from life and sit on the couch, then a cocaine-fueled motivational pep talk might be the perfect medicine for you. If you've truly never bothered fantasizing about a better life, then visualization might be a revelation for you. Mostly however, these teachings aren't exposed as hollow, because people throw themselves deliriously into such practices, only to sober up and abandon them. They quit too early to discover how empty the practices are and how, even though massive action is a prerequisite for change, it can't be steeped in the avoiding of bad programming.

Sometimes, in moments of clarity, I knew if I got into a relationship with a woman it would almost certainly be dysfunctional, and I knew I needed to learn healthy financial habits, but I concluded that I'd wait until after I achieved my goals. So, I stuck to my self-help guns, even when they jammed. Then I blamed myself.

Why isn't this working? What am I screwing up? What's wrong with me?

My old classmates were probably enjoying seeing their careers blossom. Maybe they got married and were raising children...while I had a vision board.

Even with the fanciest self-help strategies, I was as much of a ghost in Boulder as I'd been in college. I could push away the pain, if I pretended I was the only human alive. But when I went outside, saw other people, and got to know them, I was reminded that some never seemed to worry, never had problems attracting what—or who—they wanted, and were no doubt rolling in bed in orgasmic pleasure.

More images twisted like a corkscrew lodging in my brain.

If I decided to kill myself, how would I do it? Pills? Maybe I'd buy a gun. How would it feel to square off with the barrel? What about jumping from a roof? Never. No matter how deep my desire to die, it always retreated like a sickness that finally gets beaten back during sleep. The next morning the worst had passed, and I was still alive.

My future wasn't what I'd envisioned, so I drank more. "Breakfast" was three fingers of vodka and an equal serving of an energy drink. Orange-flavored and close enough to the Orange Slice I drank as a child. Even though I neglected so much else in life, including basic food staples, I never missed this ritual. Even though my credit cards were nearly always maxed out, I found a way to buy more Smirnoff's. The fog of alcohol helped me swim through the day as I accelerated my financial train wreck toward bankruptcy. I watched eight hours of TV daily. Every morning, I hid under my covers longer and longer, my mind drowning in painful thoughts, until I was getting up when the sun set, my misery too naked in daylight. When I showed up at the quarterly business meetup, a couple of people commented on how pale and drained I looked. I was separated from myself at a fundamental level I couldn't begin to name.

Around this time, I co-founded the nutritional supplement company with two partners. I also gave up weight training. The aching in my lower back, right shoulder, and right knee went from an occasional faucet drip of flare-ups to a steady pour of pain. Plus, I couldn't afford the gym membership.

Questions pulled at my mind like horses tethered to someone's limbs, galloping in separate directions. Could my mind affect reality or not? If so, why did I sometimes make more money when my conscious thoughts were negative? Why did I feel on the verge of success instead of swimming in it? *What am I missing?*

Maybe I wasn't missing anything. Maybe it was all bullshit. And if I was going to be miserable either way, why should I take care of my health?

Where had my effort gotten me?

Sometimes, I wondered if I were missing something massive. Maybe there was more to excelling in life than visualization and goals.

In an email to Mike, I admitted I thought about killing myself. It was the first time I'd told anyone how I'd felt for over a year. He didn't reply.

At Mike's next Mastermind meeting, as he spoke to the group about challenges people face, he said, "You know, maybe you think about killing yourself."

He said that as if he were being hypothetical. He looked straight ahead, not making eye contact with anyone, but I knew he was speaking to me.

He shrugged. "So, do it."

The room was silent. He continued, "You think you won't come back in your next lifetime with the same problems?"

Perhaps he was right, and my back was to the wall.

If I was going to keep facing this nightmare anyway, I decided to overcome it, no matter what.

Then in 2008, Mike casually introduced me to Daoism.

Something about the teachings grabbed me. They were like nothing I'd learned before. Heck, maybe I was going to discover how to harness the *Force* from *Star Wars*. I didn't know, but I was going to find out.

CHAPTER FIVE

DISCOVERING DAOISM

My journey into Daoism started with the standing meditation.

I had to bend my knees and hold still, which made my thigh muscles burn and quiver. I had to hold my arms up, which made my shoulders twist and sway like stiff tree branches in a hurricane. Plus, I had to pay attention to all kinds of other details. At first, 60 seconds of standing in the awkward position was all I could handle. Still…something about the meditation felt right.

As I inched my way from standing for one minute…to two…to three…to five…I started to feel a tiny-yet-pleasant buzz. Every morning, I showered, did the practice…and then yanked open my freezer door to fish out my vodka bottle.

I continued this exciting experiment on myself, while wondering: did legendary spiritual figures throughout the centuries find their beginnings with a few minutes of weird meditation? Was I cracking some mystical code? I had no evidence of this yet, but I was clearly changing something. *What would happen if I kept doing this every day?* A short time later, I did my standing meditation practice for several minutes and then took a swig of my vodka/energy drink combo. The alcohol absorbed into my body and quickly dulled my senses. But the standing meditation had already given me the buzz I craved. The alcohol dampened it and left me woozy. *What if I began feeling so good that alcohol would make me feel worse?*

A day or two later, after my standing meditation practice, my body buzzed and my mind rested like a lake's peaceful surface. I took a drink and the buzz fizzled, my mind suddenly foggy.

I never touched that bottle of vodka again; I drained it down my sink when I moved out of Boulder. (Years later, I resumed drinking—but from a much healthier place. It's now easy for me to drink responsibly because I no longer need alcohol to feel good).

If that were the only change, I'd have been impressed, but it was just the beginning. My whole body began developing a strength that wasn't associated with any specific muscle—like getting rewired. Or upgraded.

But there was a price to pay. Because of the way I stood, it challenged my muscles. Some days, there was no buzz and I felt like I was wasting my time. My body felt uneven, like one foot was standing on a stack of books. My stiff shoulder ached. Some days, right before my meditation, I'd sit in my chair lamenting how unpleasant it was going to be. *Oh man, I'll be so bored. Why the heck can't I relax my shoulder? Ugh, I've got to get up and do it. Okay I will...in a moment.* But I noticed enough positive effects to keep going. My saving grace was, no matter how much time I spent silently complaining to myself and hesitating, I still got up and did it. Some days I felt amazing and others I ended my practice frustrated and confused. I learned why it's called "spiritual discipline" and not "spiritual vacation." Visualization and goal setting may have gotten my happy brain chemicals pumping, but they didn't transform me at a deeper level. This seemed to be doing it.

A few months later, I practiced one evening for around ten minutes. I forget the exact time because that night the exercise went beyond the physical. A warm golden glow permeated every fiber of my being, like an unseen force was washing all the emotional pain out of me and replacing it with new energy. Even though I could actually see the glow, it wasn't just a vision. It felt like coming home.

For so long, I'd tried to change my thoughts and habits while ignoring the energy controlling both. It was like trying to correct a laptop's low battery signal by rearranging the icons on the screen. I hadn't opened the most fundamental connection of all. That evening, when I staggered back to my futon to sit and contemplate what had happened, I didn't magically have all the dots connected, but I felt the power of finally *connecting.*

Like an archaeologist who'd spent over seven years gently sweeping away at the ground with a tiny brush and discovering little more than discarded candy wrappers and dilapidated beer cans until finding the artifact, I'd at last stumbled upon lost treasure. Except this wasn't an object, but what I'd been seeking: *a way forward.* The practice didn't just give me a temporary high; it reset how I felt about life and myself.

I'm going to dedicate my life to Daoist training, especially this standing meditation. Little did I realize how soon this simple practice was going to rip away some of my deepest roots. My ignorance was probably for the best.

In the meantime, more signs from the world showed me how real this change was. I wasn't merely getting stronger and feeling better. At the next meeting Mike facilitated, I strode through the meeting room's doors and Mike darted his head to look at me, surprise registering in his eyes. The other students remarked on how happy and confident I looked. I hadn't told them what I was up to. *What else could happen? How far can this go?*

Despite my excitement, my financial life had already derailed—no brake-slamming was going to stop that. The crash would be epic, but worth it. Next, let's break down what caused this inner transformation.

CHAPTER SIX

CHI

The night my life changed, I was a clueless guy who liked the idea of doing an ancient, secret meditative practice. Since then, I've learned more about Daoism and how the energetic practices work.

The Daoists harness energy to transform themselves, using meditations. Some of these meditations are done sitting. Some are done moving. And some, like the one I learned, are done standing still. But all of them utilize something called *chi.*

Chi has been translated in English as energy, breath, or even as "stuff." Its original meaning is "the organized power behind everything that is." In our time, it's been represented as *the Force* in the Star Wars saga.

So, is there any science behind this?

I can sense a collective *whoomp* as some people just snapped this book shut.

"Chi? This is woo-woo!"

Is it?

For years, I chuckled at people who claimed to feel energy. *Placebo effect! Group influence! A combination of hormones and body heat! Chi is a concept invented by those who'd yet to map out the Periodic Table of Elements.*

Or is it? Is the idea of chi still relevant today? Or should we regard chi as a quaint concept, long since replaced by the study of psychology, chemistry, etc.?

Some scientists hypothesize that chi is an organizational energy that powers our embryological development, metabolism, and runs through channels in our fascia.[5]

Our fascia is like saran wrap for our body. It encases our organs, muscles, and bones. Scientists have shown that a particular kind of fascia, individual fiber strands of type 1 collagen fibrils, produces piezoelectricity[6]. This form of electricity is produced by moving materials like bone and crystalline structures. They've also found that electricity governs how stem cells move[7].

The book *The Spark in the Machine* by Dr. Daniel Keown[8] goes deeper into the theory that biological electricity is part of chi.

Just as we can change our physiology with our intention (proven easily and enjoyably with a sexual fantasy), I believe we can direct our energy with our intention. It's possible that reports of miraculous healings are driven by mechanisms Western medicine hasn't yet identified. Antibiotics would be seen as miraculous if one didn't know the science behind them. As Dr. Dean Radin wrote in his book Supernormal, "...all scientific laws are just regularities that are true on average in limited contexts."[9]

I predict that within a few decades, scientists will investigate more thoroughly and discover what the Daoists call chi is indeed part of our existence and essential for health. Once it gets a more scientific-sounding name, it will be accepted as a self-evident fact.

Daoists believe that chi is the behind-the-scenes battery powering nature and human life. Trees have chi. Clouds have chi. Mountains have chi. Animals have chi. And people are born with chi. Ever gotten an acupuncture treatment? The practitioner was using needles to regulate your chi.

The ancient Daoists optimized their minds and bodies to regulate their chi, which helped relieve negative emotions. They also harnessed chi from outside their bodies to increase their energy, strength, intelligence, insight, longevity, and more. When I first heard these ideas, which were formed thousands of years ago, part of me thought "energy" or "chi" was a crock. After all, today we have germ theory, detailed knowledge of anatomy and physiology, an understanding of hormones, chemistry, etc. I figured Daoists used the concept of chi because around 3,000 B.C. that was the best they could do to explain phenomena invisible to the naked eye. Plus, when I tried to feel chi by breathing a certain way or visualizing something, I couldn't.

Even when the standing meditation started to transform me, my analytical mind kept pushing against my direct experiences. I began feeling chi, but tried to convince myself it was something else.

I eventually broke through my doubt and decided that chi is real, especially after my experiences were validated by others, including others feeling and seeing the same things I was, at the same time.

For instance, I've imagined projecting chi at my wife to help her relax and, without her knowing what I was doing, she fell asleep while working on her laptop. I've done the same to help her with a bout of nerve pain in her foot. Projecting chi actually made it worse, but when I used a different technique to regulate the chi, she felt relief. In another instance, a friend visited our house and remarked how she felt more Zen all of a sudden, while I meditated in my office. She didn't know where my office was in the house, but pointed toward it as the source of the vibes she was feeling. I could rattle off many other stories, some of which are far more bizarre. I'll share some of them in future chapters. Follow the instructions in this book and you may soon have some stories of your own.

I feel chi as heat and see it as light—and I've ruled out more conventional explanations like better blood flow, skin sensations or simply better health from exercise and mindfulness. Other people feel chi as cold or wind within the body. At a certain point, my inner skeptic threw up his hands and accepted what I was living through.

The idea of chi is crucial because it's the "X Factor" that almost all personal development paradigms ignore. In this book, I'll use the word *energy* to describe working with chi. Many people can succeed with conventional self-help because the mental, physical, and energetic levels are intertwined. You can't change one without the others being affected, and you can't change one without utilizing the others. For instance, when you exercise your body—a physical change—your brain chemicals change. When you change your thoughts, you change your body's chi. Have you ever felt someone's anger even when their back is turned to you and you can't read their body language? That was their subtle energy—chi. Even people who don't believe in chi are working with it all the time. For many people, focusing only on the physical and mental won't help them change nearly as much as also working directly with energy—like trying to construct a healthy diet out of fat and carbs, while ignoring protein.

Before I began working with energy, my personality was closed down by pain, and I self-sabotaged any business or relationship I tried to grow. I didn't know why I kept getting hit with bad luck; worst of all, I felt powerless to change. I was trapped in a loop of using thoughts to change thoughts and pushing myself into new habits to attempt to change old ones. I'd never gone deep enough to change my wiring. When I began working with energy, I finally did.

Next, more about how your coping mechanisms harm you and how Daoist meditation can help when other techniques fail.

CHAPTER SEVEN

HARNESSING ENERGY

Unlike many spiritual traditions, Daoism starts with the body. The ancient Daoists mapped out our body's energetic systems in as much detail as modern physical anatomy and physiology.[10]

However, just as an athlete can build a strong body without memorizing the Latin name of every muscle group, we don't need to know all the details—just what's useful.

The Daoists did more than map out meridians and their emotional connections. They knew how to remove the emotional blocks that exist beyond the mind's reach. They figured out the best ways to unblock, increase, harness, and utilize chi, discovering exercises and meditations for repairing and enhancing energetic health.

According to Daoism, your body contains rivers for energy to travel throughout it. For optimal health, we need them to be open and flow freely. These rivers are invisible to most people, yet they can be felt with the proper training. Today, in the West, acupuncturists call them meridians. If you've ever gotten an acupuncture treatment, you've had work done on your meridians.

These meridians are associated with your organs. If meridians are like rivers for energy then organs are like lakes. Certain organs can store energy, and this energy can be good or bad for your mental, physical, and emotional health. Each organ and each meridian are associated with negative emotions, like grief and anger, as well as virtues, like courage and compassion.

Some modern-day evidence for this comes from organ transplant recipients. Anecdotal evidence[11] shows they take on the food and music preferences of the donor, and even personality traits and memories. A study[12] from the University of Hawaii supports this: "Parallels included changes in food, music, art, sexual, recreational, and career preferences, as well as specific instances of perceptions of names and sensory experiences related to the donors (e.g., one donor was killed by a gunshot to the face; the recipient had dreams of seeing hot flashes of light in his face)." This is not an accepted idea in Western science, but worthy of exploring.

The energy that flows through your meridians and organs can, according to the ancient Daoists, become *stagnant*, or *stuck*.

Stagnation can cause:

- Pain—a common saying in Chinese medicine is, "Where there is stagnation, there is pain. Where there is pain, there is stagnation."
- Poor sleep
- Irritability
- Sadness
- Worry

- Anger
- Trouble focusing
- Fatigue
- Weakness
- Memory lapses
- Low sex drive and performance
- Lack of willpower
- Lack of creativity
- And more[13]

Why does this stagnation happen? Painful experiences. Stagnation starts as soon as you're born and comes from parents, culture, other people, accidents or your own thoughts.

Painful experiences don't disappear or merely take the form of bad memories. They affect your energy—your chi. According to *The Secret Teachings Of Chinese Energetic Medicine Volume 1* by Dr. Jerry Alan Johnson, "Throughout our lives, any time we repress the flow of feelings connected to an event (especially those that are painful or difficult), we instantly freeze the energy of that particular event and lock it within our cells and tissues."[14]

This allows you to limp through life without your emotions pummeling you into a blubbering mess—most of the time. But the stagnant energy builds up and festers, like cramming more garbage into a wastebasket without removing it from your house. This stagnation drains your energy, puts a ceiling on your development, leaves you vulnerable to the rise and fall of emotions, and even harms your health.

Say you get into a new relationship, and when the slightest conflict comes up you seethe with anger at your partner. You know it's wrong and something you've tried to work on, explain away, develop strategies around, and attempted to avoid. Yet here you are, angry again, and there's nothing you can do about it.

Or whenever you're put in a situation that conjures up past anger, fear, or abuse, a lightning bolt of panic shoots through your body. You've tried talking yourself out of the panic and attempted expressing your feelings to supportive people around you, but you still get triggered, again and again, as if everything's beyond your control. But the energy *is* in your control—you just need to learn how to work with it.

One of the most powerful exercises I have learned for working with energy is the standing meditation. By standing in a certain position and using your mind in a certain way, you open your meridians to more energy. This helps clear stagnation to improve your mental, emotional, and physical health.

When I started the standing meditation, I opened myself to more energy and connected to a nurturing force I'd never known. I cleared anger from the times my mother yelled at me, and grief from my father's emotional absence. I was accessing parts of my mind and body I'd previously been unable to reach. As a result, I began to feel a new and wonderful relief from being shut down.

As one of my former teachers said, "You can get more energy from the Earth than you can from other people." Even if your family let you down when you were a child, you can cultivate a better relationship with both yourself and the Earth, and repair what you believed was broken.

Once I began consciously connecting more to this greater power—the chi in my environment—I began processing the buried feelings within me: the stagnant energy. As that cleared, I finally had the power to unravel my twisted beliefs, emotions, and coping mechanisms. As I let go of my emotional armor, I stood up taller, smiled more, and people began to remark on my improved physical appearance. They picked up on the difference in my energy field. I had no idea how this was happening, but I knew the results. I felt happier and began making friends.

There's no limit to how much chi you can utilize. As you remove more layers of stagnant energy, you open your body to more healthy energy—like cleaning a dish before you put food on it. You can even harness chi to improve the health of others. It's the little-understood science behind miracles.

Back when I lived in Boulder and felt the standing meditation change my life, I was a long way from moving chi to help another person get healthier. I was still working out the kinks in my own life…and some of the biggest challenges were barreling toward me.

Next, I'll show exactly how to do the standing meditation.

CHAPTER EIGHT

THE IMMORTAL POST

When I first learned this meditation, I had no idea how it would transform my life. I also received only a small amount of instruction, but enough to begin changing my thoughts, emotions, and to spark my curiosity. After over twelve years and thousands of rounds of experiments, I figured out some deeper aspects and modified how I did it.

Two years before I wrote this, I took my Daoist studies deeper with a group of master teachers. Because of their trainings, I've modified my practice to get even better results: a more powerful flow of energy and a quieter mind. The name Immortal Post comes from their teachings.

Let's dive into how to practice the Immortal Post. When you see how many details there are, you might be tempted to skim the instructions, but every detail matters. They make the difference between a powerful meditation and "just standing there." To perform this meditation, you stand straight up. Position your feet wider than the edges of your shoulders. Bend your legs slightly and keep them bent, just enough to unlock your knees. Raise your arms as if you're hugging a giant bowl or a large tree trunk and rest your arms in that position. Here are drawings of what the Immortal Post looks like:

DETAILS OF THE IMMORTAL POST

Start with this checklist. As you begin your practice, go through each item on the list:

1. Choose an environment that's calming and distraction-free.
2. Position your feet wider than the outside of your shoulders.
3. Unlock your knees and lower yourself a couple of inches straight down as if you're about to sit on a high stool.
4. Tuck your pelvis forward, to flatten your lower back.
5. Imagine your spine is part of a vertical pole that extends above and below you.
6. Hold your arms in front of you with your elbows bent. Form a hoop-like shape with your arms, as if you're holding a beach ball or hugging a tree.
7. Hollow your chest.
8. Tuck your chin down slightly.
9. Close your anal sphincter.
10. Rest the tip of your tongue on the roof of your mouth, behind your front teeth. Say the word, "Love" to feel where this is.
11. Hold this position while relaxing your muscles. Rid yourself of as much tension as possible, while still remaining upright.

Here's what the Immortal Post looks like from multiple angles (Figures 1, 2, 3, 4, and 5).

Figure 1

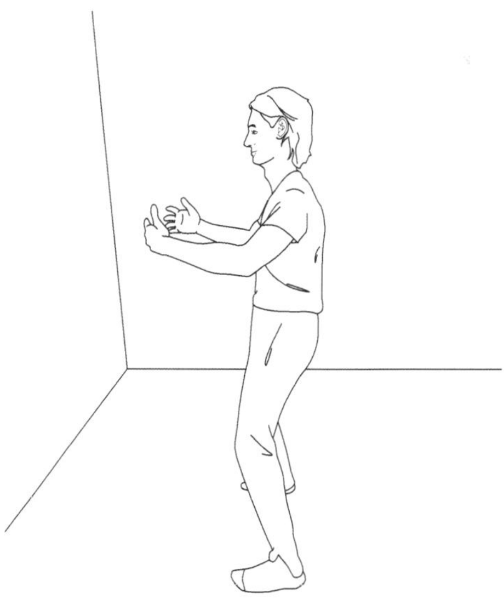

Figure 2

Figure 3

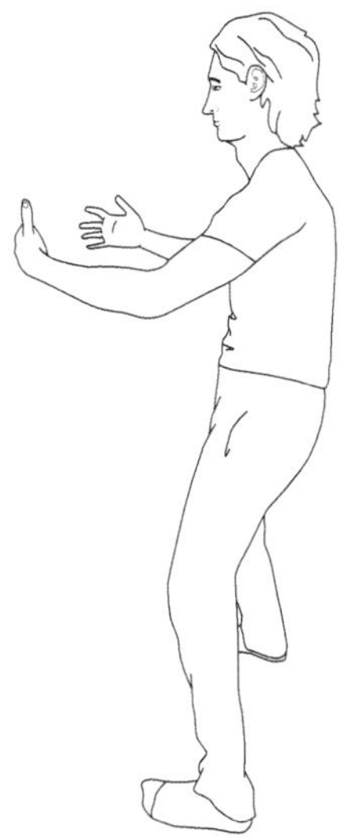

Figure 4

Figure 5

We'll dive deeper into each of these steps. For now, let's go over what you might notice the first time you try this practice.

You will feel tension. In this book, I'm going to talk about tension. A lot. Tension is when your muscles contract and remain contracted. This is often useful, like when you walk or lift a cup of coffee. Muscular tension powers your movement. The problem is when your muscles don't turn off—when they're chronically tense. Ever turned your head and felt how stiff your neck was? *Yeah, only about a billion times.* That's tension. Ever gotten a massage and the person grinding away at your neck and shoulders said you've got some knots there? Tension.

When you start practicing the Immortal Post, it'll be like looking at a Magic Eye picture just right; all your tension will jump out at you.

The stance will initially feel odd. By tucking your pelvis and chin, you're lengthening your spine in a way you're probably not used to. After taking a few breaths, you'll notice tension in your shoulders and upper and lower back. And, if you're anything like me when I started, you'll quickly feel your thighs burning as your muscles begin to protest.

All this is normal. As you keep practicing, you'll notice many kinds of chronic tension you never knew you had. This is a natural part of paying more attention to the sensations in your body. The tension will melt away and, as it does, you'll start to feel how you can settle into this stance naturally.

That's because the standing meditation perfectly positions your body to let your bone structure and tendons support your bodyweight. When you start feeling more grounded and more able to "rest" in this position, you're on the right track.

The standing meditation is designed to release muscular tension from your body and align it, so maximum chi can flow into you and through you.

Your muscles block the flow of chi when they're tense. Your body blocks the flow of chi when it's misaligned. Misalignment is almost always the result of tension—the two are usually mushed together like peanut butter and jelly in a sandwich that got stepped on. Alignment is when your body is positioned to enhance the flow of chi. More details to come. For now, let's explore each step.

Step 1: First, create an environment where you can relax and focus. This is part of setting your intention for this practice. The proper environment will also allow you to devote more attention to the sensations you'll feel. This practice is self-care time, and you won't benefit as much if you're fighting distractions. Eventually, you'll be able to practice even if your phone and doorbell are ringing, but first you need to build a foundation of focus.

When you're learning the meditation, it helps to practice in front of a mirror. Once you get a feel for how to stand, you can practice anywhere you find peaceful. I prefer to stand with my bare feet on carpet in a quiet room.

Step 2: Focus on your feet. Place them a bit wider than the outside of your shoulders and point them directly forward. The exact width will depend on your body proportions but, in general, the bigger and taller you are, the wider your feet should be. Check to make sure both feet are pointed forward. If one foot sticks out, adjust it.

Step 3: Bend your knees slightly. Emphasis on *slightly*. All you need to do is unlock them. We're not squatting or trying to give our thighs a workout. When you bend your knees just enough to unlock them, make sure your knees don't bow inward or stick outward too much, as this puts pressure on your joints.

When you stand correctly, you should be able to draw a line straight through your knees down to your feet. The line might go through the outer part of your knees and the inner part of your feet but it will still be a straight line (see Figure 6).

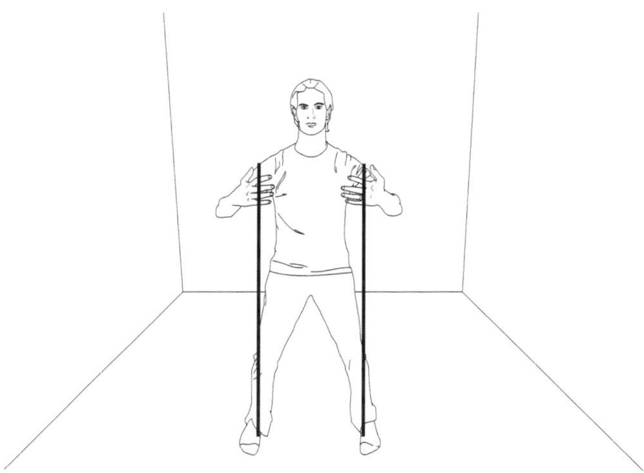

Figure 6

Step 4: Tuck your pelvis forward. This is the opposite of sticking your butt out backwards as if you're squatting down to lift something heavy. Imagine you sidled up to the bar to order a Guinness and you ease yourself onto a very high stool with a tiny seat just underneath you.

Picture a mama grizzly bear scratching her back against a giant tree. Even though she'll bend her knees to get into position, she'll stay upright so she can rub her entire back along the tree trunk. If she were to squat to get into position, she'd merely wipe her butt against the tree, keeping her back itchy, making a mess on the tree, and mocking her species' mascot role in the Charmin toilet paper commercials.

Be like the non-squatting mama grizzly bear: a back-scratcher, not a butt-wiper. Lower your body by relaxing straight down and not sticking your butt out. Keep your glutes relaxed. Check by grabbing your own butt. If it feels firm, relax your muscles.

Step 5: Imagine your spine is a pole anchoring your entire body. It extends through the middle of your spine upwards and downwards, as if there were a stripper pole behind you, and you backed into the pole until it melded with your spine. Just don't expect anyone to toss you dollar bills until you reach a super-advanced level in your practice.

Step 6: Hold your arms in front of you, like you're hugging a big tree. Ancient Daoists described the position as carrying a giant bowl of water or embracing a tree. Raise your arms, but keep your elbows slightly bent. Only slightly—don't make them limp to the point of being perpendicular to the ground. If someone looked down at you from above, they'd see your arms form a circle.

Step 7: Hollow your chest. Don't let it stick out. Imagine someone in front of you tapping on your chest, saying, "Hey. Stop sticking your chest out so much!" Let your chest melt back so they can't tap you.

When you do this, allow your upper back—the area of your shoulder blades—to flare outwards. This helps create the arm circle someone could see from above.

Step 8: Tuck your chin down. This is so your head can rest as high as possible. This might sound like a contradiction, but if you raise your chin you actually flex your spine and lower your head overall. Look in a mirror to see. If a mirror isn't handy, put this book down and grab your ears. Your ears are aligned on the same vertical plane as the highest point of your skull. By pulling your ears up, you get a visceral sensation of where your skull's highest point is. It might surprise you. When you raise your chin, you'll feel your ears pull down. When you tuck your chin down, you'll feel your ears rise up; that's the feeling of your spine lengthening. Once you've got a feel for the highest point of your skull, imagine that point is connected to the ceiling, and you can gently push the ceiling up.

When you tuck your chin down and tuck your pelvis forward, you'll gently stretch your spine (see Figure 7).

Figure 7

As you align your head to its maximum height, you allow your neck, shoulders, torso, and entire body to relax as much as possible. That may seem counterintuitive, but consider this: if your head isn't held as high as possible, it's off-kilter. That means muscles are tensing to keep your head from flopping sideways.

To get a feeling for this, stand and lean your upper body to the left by three inches. How much tougher is that to hold, and how much more tense do you feel, compared to standing straight? Your head is about the same weight as a bowling ball. Holding it upright via muscular force is no easy task.

Standing taller means less tension, provided you don't get more tense when you attempt to stand taller. This brings me to another point I'll hammer home as much as possible:

Do not *push* or otherwise *force* yourself into a more aligned position.

The last thing I want people to do is try the Immortal Post and, when they see their lower back isn't straight enough, *wrench* their pelvis forward and hurt themselves.

Don't force your body into any position, as if you're Gumby. You're not. You're a complex system of tissues that responds to force as if it's trauma, which stresses your nervous system, shuts down your sensitivity, and clogs your ability to generate energy.

Even if you don't immediately hurt yourself, you'll harm yourself in the long run. When you force yourself, you're fighting tension with tension and making a bad situation worse.

The answer is to *relax* your way into a proper position. Let's use the same example of your lower back being too curved. Instead of forcing your hips forward, imagine the back of your pelvis dropping straight down. Imagine your spine lengthening downward. Allow your buttocks to drop down and forward.

Step 9: The only exception to the relaxation rule is your anal sphincter—keep it gently contracted. This is unique because if your anal sphincter is relaxed, chi will escape from your body. This may sound silly, yet it's one of the closely-guarded energy secrets of Daoism.

Some misalignments are subtle. For instance, your arms might look uneven and you're not sure why. In these cases, figure out which tense muscle is the cause. Chances are, it'll be a group of muscles, like the back of your shoulders and your traps. When you relax them, your stance will align. Of course, relaxing isn't as easy as simply willing it to be so—at least when you begin—so we'll soon dive into specific techniques.

Step 10: Relax your jaw, but keep your mouth closed. Rest the tip of your tongue on the roof of your mouth, behind your front teeth. To get a feel for this position, say the word, "Love." Love, love, love, L-L-L...when you form the L-sound; that's how to position your tongue.

It's okay if you don't get everything perfect the first time you practice, or the second, third, fourth, fifth...or six hundredth time. Imagine you're a sculptor who takes years to finish a piece. In this case, the piece is your body. Even years after learning these steps, I'm still perfecting my practice of them and expect to continue for the rest of my life.

If you're an athlete and you do resistance training, you might find this posture especially awkward. That's normal. Many of the steps, like tucking your butt under you and hollowing your chest so it caves in slightly, are the opposite of traditional postures for lifting weights. It helps to acknowledge that this is a different kind of training and you will need to build another kind of muscle memory.

Here are some more tips for after you get comfortable with the basics of the posture:

BALANCE YOUR WEIGHT BETWEEN BOTH FEET EVENLY.

Chances are, whenever you stand, one of your feet supports more than 50% of your bodyweight and the other less than 50%.

Without two identical scales, you can't prove it with the precision of an engineer. But you can tune in and discover if one of your feet bears 51% of your weight or 52%...or more. Look straight down. Follow the line formed by the center of your body, down your chest...solar plexus...belly...and keep following that imaginary line as it descends between your knees and finally arrives at the floor. Look where that imaginary line touches the floor. Are your feet an equal distance from it or is one foot a little closer? If so, the closer foot bears more of your weight.

Any imbalance is the result of tension. Find the tension in your body causing you to lean to one side and relax that tension using techniques you learned in the previous chapter.

BALANCE ON YOUR FEET EVENLY, SIDE-TO-SIDE AND FRONT-TO-BACK.

Make sure you're balancing your bodyweight equally between the balls of your feet and your heels. Too much weight on either end of your foot is probably a sign of tension in a certain part of your body. Err on placing more weight on your heels, but make sure you tuck your pelvis. If you don't tuck your pelvis, you'll strain your lower back.

Here's how to get the proper footing when you're learning the standing meditation: Rock back onto your heels and relax as much as you can. Then slowly transfer the weight until you feel it press straight down through the arches of both your feet. When in doubt, keep more of the weight closer to your heels. It might seem unnatural, especially if you have an athletic background, because you're taking the stress off your muscles and transferring your bodyweight straight down, via your bone structure.

BEND YOUR KNEES EQUALLY.

For months, when I practiced the standing meditation, I'd look down and see that my left knee wasn't as bent as my right, because my hips twisted slightly counterclockwise.

When you begin your practice, glance down to make sure your knees stick forward an equal distance. If one knee sticks out too far that means it's too bent. Allow that leg to stand up a little straighter.

Remember that even if your form looks perfect when you begin your meditation, chances are it will disintegrate. Check every few minutes, until you don't need to.

RELAX YOUR KUA.

Kua (Pronounced KWAH) is a word from Mandarin that's little known in the West. If you're seated as you read this, look down to where your thighs meet your torso. Notice the folds made between them. That's your kua.

Your kua is probably chronically tense from a lifetime of sitting, like a book that can't lie flat and open without the tight binding closing the pages. A tense kua shuts off your flow of energy.

Within the kua are a pair of muscles called the psoas (pronounced SO-as). They are unique compared to every other muscle in your body, because the psoas are the only muscles that bridge the span between your legs and your torso. They connect your spine down to your femurs. When you examine the psoas in an anatomy chart, you can see how they're intimately related to the kua (see Figure 8).

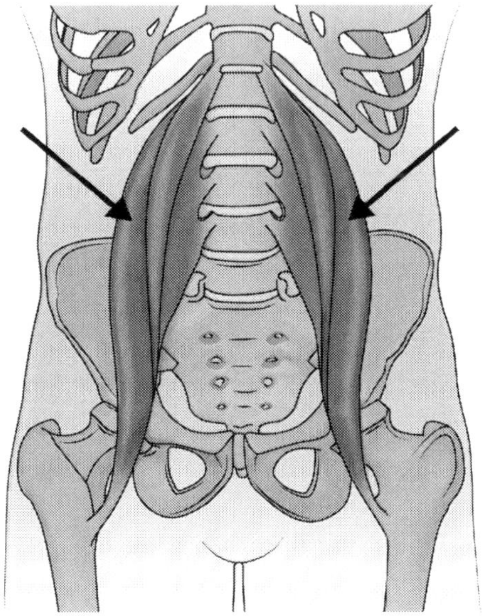

Figure 8

These muscles are tricky to relax because they're buried too deep within your body for massage, unless you're working with a practitioner who has received special training. The psoas are also sensitive to stress from vigorous stretching. The relaxation techniques from the previous section can be effective when you focus on your psoas. You might be surprised by how relaxing your psoas affects your hips and lower back. Another option is to search online for devices you can place on the floor and lie over so they press into your psoas.

When you start practicing, focus 100% on getting the mechanics right. Your focus might shift to how tough it is to hold this stance and how stiff you feel. But don't worry. As you practice, you'll feel more and more settled. Layers of tension—both physical and emotional—will bubble to the surface and evaporate. Once you master the basics of the standing meditation, start quieting your mind so you can experience the power of stillness. Then the real fun begins. While relaxed in this position, you'll mentally settle into the zero-point in your consciousness, allowing more chi to flow, resolving harmful programming in your brain and central nervous system, optimizing your body and brain for peak performance, and empowering yourself to enter the flow of life.

When I was taught the standing meditation, I didn't learn any fancy visualizations or ways of working with my mind. Instead, I learned how to properly position my legs, torso, and arms and how to make micro-adjustments to feel into what worked and what didn't. At times, it felt like groping around a dark room with my limbs randomly tied with ropes. But I was able to get my bearings and, eventually, thrive using the **four pillars of Daoist meditation**. These pillars are your tools for making a seemingly-ordinary practice—like just standing there—into something that transforms your life.

The Four Pillars Of Daoist Meditation: Intention, Attention, Sensation, and Imagination

First is **intention**. You want to meditate for a reason. It could be to reduce your stress, increase your sensitivity, rid yourself of hurtful emotions, increase your creativity and resourcefulness, build energy to heal yourself and other people, or attain enlightenment. Perhaps you do it simply because it feels like you are coming home. Whatever your reasons for beginning this journey, you set your direction and build momentum with your intention. As you meditate, you'll use your intention to make changes. Your intention guides you toward more helpful outcomes, not letting your subconscious biases run the show.

Next is your **attention**. This is where you choose to position your mental magnifying glass; your in-the-moment focus. You might have heard the saying, "What you focus on, grows." With your attention, you can grow your relaxation, your sensitivity, and the experiences you're trying to create.

Next are your **sensations**. These are the bits of feedback you get through your sight, smell, hearing, taste, touch, and proprioception—the perception or awareness of the position and movement of your body—along with your subtle psychic abilities. These senses provide feedback, like teachers and partners helping to guide your practice.

Here's a practical example: You settle into the Immortal Post and sense that your stance feels a bit off, which is using your proprioception. You look down to see one of your feet sticking out farther than the other, so you adjust it inward. You've used your sense of sight to help you make a correction. As you get deeper into your practice, your sensations will become more subtle and profound. You might feel a flare of warmth in your lower belly when you breathe a certain way. This is helpful feedback to guide and amplify your experience.

The most important sensations will be the subtle ones. You'll feel heat, but not because the room got warmer. Or you'll see light, but not because anyone shone a flashlight on your body. Instead, you're picking up inner sensations you might never have experienced (or noticed) before. These are a natural part of this practice and all you need to do is gently notice them.

Finally, there's **imagination**. This is your creative force for constructing a new reality. During your meditation, you can use your imagination to change your physiology, psychology, and your inner world, which plants powerful seeds for changing your outer world. As my teachers like to say, "The imagination leads the mind, and the mind leads the chi."

With the amount of detail we covered, you might feel as if it was your first day of learning a foreign language…via interpretive dance. But as you practice, you'll get a feel for how natural this is. Every detail matters because they're all designed to maximize the flow of energy through your body.

You tuck your chin so energy doesn't get cut off at the back of your neck. You hollow your chest so energy doesn't get stuck in your chest. You tuck your butt under you so energy isn't cut off at your pelvis. You unlock your knees so energy can flow up your legs.

Think of your body like a system of energetic rivers. If you cut off the flow somewhere, you disrupt the flow everywhere.

You don't need to pretzel yourself into some painful, cross-legged position. The Immortal Post is based on what makes you most stable and grounded, because when you're truly grounded, you can open yourself to energy, like an oil rig tapping into the Earth's reservoirs of chi. To an observer, you might look as if you're "just standing there" and it might feel that way at first, but you're doing so much more.

Here's the list of steps again. See how all the details we covered fit into the steps:

1. Choose an environment that's calming and distraction-free.
2. Position your feet slightly wider than the outside of your shoulders.

3. Unlock your knees and lower yourself a couple of inches straight down as if you're about to sit on a high stool.
4. Tuck your pelvis forward, to flatten your lower back.
5. Imagine your spine is part of a vertical pole that extends above and below you.
6. Hold your arms in front of you with your elbows bent. Form a hoop-like shape with your arms, like you're holding a big bag or hugging a tree.
7. Hollow your chest.
8. Tuck your chin down slightly.
9. Close your anal sphincter.
10. Rest the tip of your tongue on the roof of your mouth, behind your front teeth. Say the word, "Love" to feel where this is.
11. Hold this position while relaxing your muscles. Rid yourself of as much tension as possible, while still remaining upright.

As you go deeper into your practice, you might notice unusual sensations. For a list and explanations of these experiences, see **Appendix A**.

For a list of common mistakes when practicing the Immortal Post, see **Appendix B**.

To sign up for instructional videos of the Immortal Post, visit **www.naterifkin.com/ImmortalPost**.

A little over a month before writing this section, I stood beside a tree estimated to have sprung to life around the time Charlemagne ruled the Roman Empire. That's roughly 400 years before Genghis Khan conquered most of East Asia and about 1,000 years before the United States was founded.

The redwood stretched up 250 feet, almost the length of a football field. Considering the tree has a greater girth than a couple of SUVs parked side by side, it doesn't so much stretch as *muscle* its way skyward like a mini mountain.

My feet slipped a few times on the mossy slopes surrounding its base, and I had to take care not to fall. Then I realized something that sent shivers up my back. The hill I was perched on, with slopes falling all around me, was actually covering the tree's massive root system. The redwood engulfed me while hosting its own personal ecosystem.

Be the giant redwood as you practice your Immortal Post. Feel your legs and torso represent the solid, stable trunk of a tree.

As with a tree, your body doesn't stop with your feet. It forms roots underground, as stable and solid as your trunk, drawing nourishment from the Earth.

Your arms and head become the leaf-filled branches that absorb life-giving sunlight from Heaven.

Emulate the redwood tree's patience. While generations of humans were born, grew up, had children, and died, the tree stood and grew. Sometimes, your changes will be so subtle you might think you're not growing. But you're like the tree, which doesn't seem to be moving, but eventually reaches the sky.

My changes came slower than I wanted. First, I felt good enough to stop drinking as soon as I woke up. As the weeks went by, I felt stronger, more energized, and more in touch with my body. My hurtful thoughts quieted, like a TV station with a dying signal. After a few months, the standing meditation made me feel so amazing that there was no turning back.

I read that J. Robert Oppenheimer once said, "Any man whose errors take ten years to correct is quite a man." It was probably a tongue-in-cheek remark about how an important person can make an error so catastrophic that it takes a decade of cleanup. My first interpretation of the quote was different. I thought of it as meaning one's errors can last a lifetime, so resolving them in a mere decade is impressive. If it weren't for Daoist meditation, my errors would have kept me stuck for my whole life. If rerouting my ship took years, I accepted that, as long as it turned around.

Daoist practices—starting with the standing meditation—unraveled my self-sabotage and sadness when nothing else made a dent. They helped me rewire my mind when so many other things had failed. They've made me a better man, so I've dedicated myself to this more than anything else in life.

I'm not saying you need to dedicate your life to Daoism. Just try it and find out for yourself how it can transform your energy.

Let's move on to more specifics. These instructions are the base blueprint. But to make sure you're not just "standing there" you need to know how to use your intention, attention, and imagination during the practice, as well as what sensations to expect. Then this meditation will come alive for you.

First, I'll share more of my story. After learning the Immortal Post, my problems were not over. In fact, some were just beginning. Next, I'll share how I got sued, and how this helped me get the most out of the standing meditation.

CHAPTER NINE

ELIMINATE TENSION

"An inflexible army
seals its own fate.
When a tree branch grows brittle,
it easily snaps,
whether long or little."[15]

Knock knock knock

Adrenaline squirted into my belly. Knocks on my door were bad news. Like how nine out of ten calls I received began with, "This is an attempt to collect a debt..."

I'd been living in my Boulder condo for about two years and I hadn't yet learned the standing meditation. Instead, I was practicing a daily routine that was slowly killing me: roll out of bed, shower, and two shots of vodka. That quelled my misery enough for me to grind away at my business ventures as daytime television blared in the background. Whether closing my blinds to avoid the harsh Colorado summer sun, occasionally admiring a blizzard behind my window, or sometimes basking in the electric fall season from the comfort of my patio, my life was reduced to mostly staring at a screen, alone.

Even with sporadic windfalls of income, I spiraled further into debt. I paid as much attention to credit card bills as I did the gorgeous outdoors—ignoring even the monthly minimum payment of $25—and let the unopened envelopes stack beneath piles of junk mail.

One day, while talking with my dad on the phone, he said, "Someone, uh, called for you here. It sounded weird. When I asked what it was about, he said he couldn't say."

I felt a cold gnawing in my gut, knowing it was a debt collector.

So, I assumed the worst when loud knocks echoed from my condo door and I opened it. A sheriff stood on the other side of the threshold.

"Good afternoon!" He handed me an envelope. "This is for you. It's nothing bad."

I took the envelope, thanked him, and tore it open as he left, the thud of his boots echoing farther and farther away.

For the past couple of years, I hadn't paid my state taxes. Not because I felt like breaking the law, but because, as a self-employed person, I was responsible for saving money to eventually pay these taxes. At the end of 2006, I filled out the pages on TurboTax, typing in an income that barely covered my rent and food. When the software calculated I owed more than $7,000, I figured I made a typo. I didn't have seven grand, so I filed without paying. The IRS sent me letters demanding payment. One was signed by someone whose last name was—no joke—Slaughter. But even Mr. Slaughter didn't get a check from me.

I could have contacted the IRS to arrange a payment plan. I could have gotten a day job in addition to the business selling yoga products that I was trying to grow. I could have moved somewhere cheaper. I could have done a thousand things. But, as an emotionally shut down, rigid, ego-turbocharged 21-year-old, I ignored the problem. I treated the IRS and state taxes like an aggressive street merchant: don't make eye contact, and hope they move onto someone else. The IRS isn't a street merchant. It's more like a quiet, methodical mob enforcer.

In 2007, I checked my bank account to discover my balance was $0. Thinking it was an error, I called my bank and found out the IRS had withdrawn every penny. "Oh, okay," I said on the phone, trying to sound casual, as if having all my money ripped out from under me was my idea. It was especially fun to email one of my vendors and explain why they needed to delay cashing a big check I'd sent them.

When I ripped open the envelope, I found an official notice that a debt collector working with the State of Colorado had filed a lawsuit against me. And the sheriff said it was nothing bad? This *is* bad!

The state made me an offer I couldn't refuse: Either show up in court to defend myself—and pay the court's legal fees if I lost—or start a payment plan. I chose the payment plan and began scraping together $200 per month. As the months and years went by, I played a clever and shameful game of agreeing to payment plans with various creditors, paying regularly for a couple of months, and then stopping to see how quickly—or slowly—they'd fire threatening letters at me.*

That wasn't the most embarrassing part. At least with bills and collector calls, you can keep your struggle a secret. One evening I had

* I've found the IRS is the slowest to react to non-payment, but with the direst consequences. The quickest are medical bills; after I went to the ER and didn't immediately pay my bill in full, they did everything to get their money short of hitting my condo with a SWAT team.

dinner with my friend Jim, a successful consultant, at a restaurant facing Boulder's outdoor 16th Street Mall.

Years ago, Jim, his wife, and five young children visited Colorado from Iowa. When his children jumped from their car and careened around the hills and almost took flight in the crisp winds, he knew they'd move here. For over two decades, Jim had dressed up as Santa Claus. With his foundation-rattling belly laughter and white hair, he's the closest thing to a real Santa I've ever seen. Some people keep in touch with friends as they grow up. Jim keeps in touch with friends, their children, and grandchildren.

We got together every few months to catch up and for our last couple of meals, he'd covered the tab. This time, I was broke and hoped he'd pay again. The server placed the folio with the bill between us, and it stood like an eerie miniature monolith. I didn't grab it. Neither did Jim. We kept talking and I started to feel flushed. Jim eased out of the booth to go to the bathroom, leaving me alone to stare at the bill. I still hadn't touched it when he came back. We kept talking, ignoring the bill as if it were a lingering fart. I gave up on stalling and remarked, as casually as I could, "I'll get this!" as I slipped in my credit card.

The server left and a minute later returned, tapping my card against his other hand, saying, "This was, uh, declined..."

Jim reached for his wallet. "I'll get this!"

I thanked him and apologized, ashamed, a feeling that would haunt me for a very long time. Declining cards had become so regular for me that I often called the card issuer before any purchase to make sure I could cover it.

A couple of years later, when I moved from Boulder, I discovered all my old piles of unopened bills, hiding underneath other mail. I shook my head. How could I have been so blind? More accurately, how could I have *made myself* so blind?

The pain of my situation was too scary to face, so I'd cringed away from it. I was hell-bent to become a success in business, but no matter how I strained and trudged along, I couldn't overtake my self-sabotage. While rigidly committing myself to financial goals, I ignored the most basic, healthy financial practices. I tried to focus on achieving abundance, but my mind was tense, choking off my creativity and ability to self-observe. This made my life brittle to any disruption, like a sudden expense, as I blindly stumbled past opportunity after opportunity.

I was physically tense. My shoulders were so hunched up that I constantly looked like I was trying to squeeze through a tiny hallway. Each day, I wrenched my neck to crack it like a deranged chiropractic adjustment, which made my tension worse. Every muscle group around my spine was tightening like a boa constrictor, cutting off my energy flow. I excused the tension as a necessary byproduct of my weight training. I never fathomed that it was rooted in emotional stagnation or that it was connected to my self-sabotaging behavior.

My mother used to call me "pigheaded," and I pretended it was a compliment, but now I was terrified and the fear was making me stupid. Even a lawsuit and constantly declining credit cards couldn't wake me up.

That humiliating dinner with Jim didn't shake me out of my stupor. Walking home that night, I called my credit card company to find out how much I still had available—not enough to pay for the meal with my friend, but enough to swing by the liquor store and pick up another bottle of vodka.

Later, when I formed the business selling nutritional supplements with two partners, I figured I could drag the venture forward by sheer force of will, even if it meant ignoring one of the partner's unethical behavior. Then I woke up to discover the passwords had been changed for the business's online platforms. My partners' betrayal didn't wake me up, either. Blaming them, I kept trying to claw my way forward.

Nor did bankruptcy awaken me.

I'm grateful for everything I experienced, even if those experiences didn't melt away my rigidity. Life's wake-up calls work only if you're relaxed enough to slip out of ingrained patterns. Sometimes, shock slips you out. Many people get pulverized with a heart attack, and as soon as they get out of the hospital they change their habits. But others suffer a second heart attack.

Rigidity causes pain and can kill you. The way out is recognizing pain as a signal to change. You must relax enough to make the proper change.

"A reed before the wind lives on, while mighty oaks do fall."
— Chaucer Troilus & Criseyde[16]

Stiff trees get destroyed by hurricanes because they break before they bend. A blade of grass gives in the slightest breeze. The grass could seem weak, but it's rooted in the ground and dances in any wind force. Grass lives on by not being rigid.

It was only after I got sued, got into horrible debt, embarrassed myself with my friend, and started a business with back-stabbing partners that I finally learned the standing meditation. It began to loosen me, unraveling the deep tension that blocked my energy flow. As I relaxed and unraveled my emotional stagnation, I stopped trying to blindly force myself through life.

The Daoists understand that you harm yourself when you apply unnecessary force.

All tension is unnecessary force. Think about your stiff neck. Would your head fall off if your neck muscles relaxed a tad?

Ancient Daoists knew it was vital to release all unnecessary tension because muscular tension blocks the flow of energy. If you stay tense, you can hold a posture that looks like the Immortal Post...but it's a shell of the real meditation. The fanciest car is nothing but a showpiece if its engine seizes up due to lack of oil.

As I practiced and felt my tension slowly—*very slowly*—unravel, I was horrified at how tense I had been for all those years, but also relieved to finally let it go.

"The stiff and strong
Are Death's companions
The soft and weak
Are Life's companions."[17]

Where does this tension come from? It's a coping mechanism your body uses to get through life feeling safer. When you are hurt as a child, you might store the stagnant energy of fear in your body. You'll hunch your shoulders—a little bit—as a defensive stance. Or you might store anger and push your shoulders out for a more aggressive posture. Your nervous system constricts your muscles to "protect" you as a coping mechanism. But a couple of decades later, you might develop neck or back pain from all the stiff muscles. Plus, you're cut off from the flow of energy that could relieve your body's need for the coping mechanism.

True relaxation isn't easy for your body or mind. You became tense to brace yourself against feeling pain. Part of relaxing might be reliving that emotional pain so you can finally let it go. One of my teachers uses an example of plunging your arm into a bucket of ice water. At first, it will hurt and shock you, but soon your arm will go numb. You'll start to feel comfortable, even though the cold water is still sucking away your body heat and damaging your tissues. When you remove your arm, it will begin to wake up and you'll feel the pain again, before you're fully healed.

Many people can't face the emotional pain, so they stay tense and numb, until physical pain finally gets their attention. Tension, so goes the saying, is the difference between who you are and who you want to be. That tension is supported by your belief system. Letting your body languish like this sucks away your energy, keeps you trapped in emotional patterns, and relentlessly drags you toward more pain and loss. The answer is relaxation. It took years for me to face emotional pain and relax into it. As I mentioned before, the shock of getting sued and drowning in debt didn't wake me up. I stayed tense and numb, until I practiced mental stillness and allowed healing energy to overtake me. And it wasn't until I relaxed away my tension that I could practice mental stillness.

It's difficult to identify our chronic tension, at least at first, because it's subtle. Chances are, you don't scrunch your shoulders as high as anatomically possible and wrench your head down as if you're about to dive into a swimming pool. But tension still lurks in virtually all your muscles. This is where relaxation comes in.

I'm going to bring up the concept of relaxation so many times that you'll get sick of reading it. At one point in writing this book, I used the word "relax" 164 times...not nearly enough.

Relaxation has plenty of down-to-earth benefits, like:

1. Your nervous system stops sending signals for your muscles to flex. It becomes quiet. As a result, your mental chatter quiets down.
2. You are freed of distractions, both mental and physical, so you can place more attention on the sensations in your body and your environment.
3. You communicate with more clarity.
4. Other people will pick up on your relaxation and appreciate and respect you more.
5. If you don't relax, you constantly burn energy, which could otherwise be deployed in more beneficial ways.

Those reasons are good enough on their own, but the ancient Daoists understood something more. Relaxing your muscles helps chi flow, like turning on a faucet to unleash the water.

"The soft and pliable overcomes the hard and inflexible."[18]

Imagine your body as a bellows. When you're bound with tension, it's like someone gripping the bellows so it can't fully inflate or deflate. You can't force energy into it. Instead, the bellows must be allowed to expand. Like a bellows, you must yield. Relax, and the energy cannot help but fill you.

As you practice the standing meditation and relax more, you'll feel this sense of fullness for yourself. You'll realize why the hard work of strengthening your body and relaxing is so rewarding. When you let go of tension, you'll feel like you can hold the Immortal Post forever. And paradoxically, you'll be more stable and stronger than ever.

To release tension, slow down and deepen your breathing. Your lungs are passive, empty sacks waiting to be filled with air. When you breathe deep into your belly and gently allow your entire torso to expand from the bottom up, you fill your entire lungs with air. When you breathe fully, deeply, and slowly, you signal your nervous system to relax your mind and body.

On an unusually warm January afternoon, I sat in my therapist's* office, clipboard in one hand and pen in the other.

"What I want you to do," he said, "is notice when you get irritated. Treat it as a sign."

"Yeah, I understand," I said, feeling irritated. "I already *do* that. It's how I was able to tell you about the times it happened. I want to *get rid of it*."

He sighed and darted his hand to his whiteboard. Earlier, he'd written "irritation" in big, red letters. And then, hovering above and to the right, like a little thought cloud, was the word "sign."

He pointed to it and said, "It's a paradox. My clients frequently come in and tell me to *get rid of something*. Don't try to get rid of it. Notice what brings it up. Trying to stop it fuels it. But treating it like a sign puts the seemingly-negative behavior into a constructive box."

* It might seem odd that—at the time of this writing—I see a therapist when I'm creating a book on a meditative practice to improve one's mind and body. There are a couple of reasons. First, the Immortal Post is not a cure-all. Second, I've gotten the best results by simultaneously using different modalities. The journey of developing oneself isn't just a path; it's also a recipe. Combining different elements and letting them interact and spark will accelerate your progress.

He continued, “Living generates irritability and pain. Getting mad about it won’t do us much good.”

I scrambled to write everything down.

You can use this same approach with muscular tension—a physical manifestation of feeling irritated.

Yanking on your tense muscles or trying to wrench your body into a different position will make your tension worse, like trying to bully your tension into submission. If you get aggressive with tight muscles, they’ll get passive-aggressive in response.

Instead, find where you feel most tense and merely notice what brings it up. Treat it as a sign. Putting your focus on the tense part of your body might be enough to relax it.

Here are several techniques to help you let go of tension:

BREATHE INTO AND OUT OF YOUR TENSION.

Take a breath through your nose. Feel the air flowing through your nostrils. You can do the same with any tense muscle or joint area. Imagine breathing in and out of it, as if the skin directly on top of the muscle could absorb and release air. This technique can help your muscles relax.

Let’s say you’re doing the standing meditation and notice your left shoulder is tense. Put your attention on that shoulder to help it relax. Then, when you physically inhale through your nose, use your imagination to picture and feel fresh energy going into your shoulder. As you exhale through your nose, imagine your shoulder releasing stale, tense energy through the skin on top. After ten breaths, focus your attention on the sensations in your shoulder and determine if it’s more relaxed.

Here’s a more advanced version of this technique. When you inhale into the tense muscle, consciously tense it even more. Then, when you exhale, allow it to relax. By consciously controlling the rhythm of its tension and relaxation, you empower yourself to consciously relax your tension. The better you get at tuning into the exact location of the tense muscle and consciously tensing and relaxing it, the more effective this technique will be.

Here's a variation that can help if you're stuck. If you've got some stubborn tension, it might be caused by a misalignment closer to the core of your body. For example, I work on tension in my neck and my shoulder girdle. But I understand it's partially caused by misalignment in my pelvis. Because of this, I'll do the same breathing technique with muscles surrounding my hips, even if they don't feel tense. As a result, my shoulders relax.

MELT TENSION DOWN YOUR BODY.

This indirectly commands your muscles to stop contracting. For instance, if you feel tense in your neck, imagine the "weight" of that tension dropping into your chest. Once you feel the shift, imagine that weight drop from your chest into your solar plexus. You go down and down to your legs and eventually into the ground beneath you. Then start over. Seek new tension to melt lower and lower. The cycle ends when you feel the tension is gone.

There's a reason why I describe this process as imagining the *weight* of tension *dropping*, and *feeling* the shift. You'll get the best results when you make this a kinesiological practice. Engage your imagination in a visceral way to feel the sensations in your body. Avoid the temptation to merely "see" your muscles relaxing. Use as many senses as you can. *Feel* what it's like to transform.

ICE-WATER-STEAM

This is a potent Daoist technique for ridding yourself of tension.

Locate a tense part of your body and imagine it as a cluster of ice. Next, imagine heat radiating into that frozen part. Apply more and more heat until the ice begins to melt. Keep going. Radiate so much heat into the ice that it melts into trickles of cool water...becoming warm water...and then eventually boils into steam. Imagine the steam rising several feet away from your body and disappearing.

Whenever I grab some frozen beef from the freezer, I feel how it's harder than stone. But after soaking the slab in warm water for a couple of hours, it's softer. Your tense muscles are like frozen beef. Now you know how to thaw them.

FOCUS ON THE TENSE PART OF YOUR BODY WITH A FEELING OF LOVE.

Tell your tense neck muscle, "I love you." It may sound silly, but this self-care lessens your stress. If your lower back feels tense, send it loving thoughts. Wherever you feel tension, imagine it receiving love and melting as a result.

Never condemn any part of your body. Don't refer to your "damn knee" or anything hurtful. Remember, the tension was initiated for your good, even if the outcome doesn't serve you now. Your body wanted to protect you because of an injury or stress. Berating your body won't help it relax. Loving it will.

LET THE TENSION LIVE OUT ITS INTENTION.

Earlier, you learned how tension is the difference between who you are and who you want to be. As counterintuitive as it may seem, you can rid yourself of a tense muscle by letting it flex as much as it wants. When your muscle finally gets to contract to its full potential, your nervous system decides it's done and lets the muscle relax.

If your quad is tense, flex it more. Give yourself an intense leg workout. Let your quad be who it wants to be. Then let your legs rest and finally relax.

ADDRESS SOMETHING YOU'RE AVOIDING IN LIFE.

Does someone close to you cause you stress? Perhaps you're making choices that aren't true to what you really want? *Tension is the difference between who you are and who you want to be.* Your tension could represent the strain this relationship is causing you. Ending the relationship or confronting the stress might be your key to relief. Same with your choice of job or home.

BREAK THE HABITS THAT CREATE TENSION.

Which hand do you use to brush your teeth? Chances are, you have a dominant hand for tooth-brushing because you've already developed a neural pathway for performing the action without thinking about it. The next time you brush your teeth, use your opposite hand. You'll find you need to go through the learning process all over again. This is how you start breaking the habits that cause tension. Using your non-dominant hand will help release the tension caused by body imbalances.

It's not just your toothbrush. When you put your shoes on, which hand do you use to grasp the "tongue" of your shoe? Do you use the same hand for both shoes? Which hand holds your fork?

Mostly, you create imbalances with mindless habits. But sometimes they can intertwine with emotionally-charged settings, deepening the imbalance. How often do you frantically click through webpages, while scanning emails that irritate or worry you? Which hand moves your mouse? That might contribute to your shoulder pain.

Do you slouch a certain way in your car seat, while ruminating about something during your commute? What are the chances your emotional state and your posture will meld together? Could that be contributing to your lower back pain? A teacher of mine, Dr. Chris Holder, reported that many people have an imbalance in their hip structure that causes their right foot to stick out more, caused by using the right foot to work the gas and brake pedal while driving.

I challenge you to find all your daily habits that might lead to imbalances. Then, test out using your opposite hand or foot for the primary movement (maybe not while driving). See how it feels to switch the roles of your hands when you put on your shoes. If you're also donning a coat, test putting your arm through the sleeve that you'd usually put through after your other arm. You might be surprised by how you feel more centered and alive as you step out your door to greet the day.

UNRAVELING TENSION IS A LIFELONG PURSUIT.

When you begin practicing the Immortal Post, you'll progress simply by learning the posture, how your body feels, and growing stronger. Your thigh muscles will burn as you challenge yourself to keep your knees unlocked. Your shoulders will ache as you build strength. Your mind will urge you to give up.

As you get stronger, you'll notice more and more tension. It might feel as if this meditation is making you more tense! But, if you're practicing it correctly, you're simply becoming more aware of tension that was already lurking in your body.

It's unlikely you'll free yourself from chronic tension in a day or two.

Or a week. Or a month. Or a year. The length of time isn't important. The progression is; you'll reap rewards as you go along. I'm still working on deeply embedded tension in my body. But the work I've done has made me feel like a new person many times over.

You'll know you're progressing when you feel your weight fall straight into the Earth, as if you're light as a feather yet welded into the ground.

As you keep relaxing, you might start to feel as if you're cruising. Your body seems relaxed and the stance is easy. *But you must remain vigilant.* Don't be tempted to assume your form is perfect. You might feel that your body is perfectly aligned and relaxed because you're still existing in a comfort zone of unevenly tense muscles. The tension pulls your joints out of alignment and keeps them skewed long enough for your brain to register their configuration as the new normal. In this state, genuine alignment would feel odd.

This can be true even if your form looks great in the mirror or to an observer. You're probably supporting tight patches in your body that look aligned on the surface. Think of trying to locate a knot on a string. It's easy to find because you look for the bulge. But let's say someone pulls the string and tightens the knot. It becomes smaller and harder to spot, but it's no less real. In fact, the knot's even more difficult to unravel.

Your tension can be the same, especially around your hips and spine, where chronic tension can "hide" by being unfelt, unseen, and unnoticed.

I don't say this to discourage you, but to affirm that unraveling tension is a lifelong journey. Never assume you're done. Keep refining your form. Keep breathing relaxation into different parts of your body, even if you think they don't need it. Keep letting feelings bubble up and evaporate.

Use your intention to become more relaxed every time you train. Pay attention to the stubbornly tense parts of your body. Feel the sensations of where you hold your tension. Use your imagination to melt it away.

You'll know you're getting somewhere when, as you do the Immortal Post, you feel what Peter Ragnar, author and teacher of Daoism, describes this way: "Imagine that your whole body, your flesh, is like a suit of clothes on a hanger. No tension. No muscular exertion. You're being suspended by a sky hook, holding you in space. Oh yes, your feet are touching the ground. You didn't levitate."

Perhaps you won't levitate physically. But the more relaxed you get, the more rooted and uplifted you'll feel. It's the opposite of feeling weighed down and stuck in your head, and it's how you can feel more creative energy, focus, and in the flow of life.

Mike's Mastermind got stranger and stranger. The students who built successful businesses began to leave. Mike got upset if anyone asked about them, but he'd frequently, and publicly, badmouth the former students. Mike usually didn't give any names, but his stories contained enough detail to figure out who they were.

He gave long talks about how various people screwed him over in business. Some of us began to realize Mike didn't have any healthy, lasting business relationships.

He took an event's entire first afternoon to read us a book he'd just published, and filmed us lining up to get an autograph from him. I stayed in my seat.

As Mike taught more Daoist trainings, I heard that the very best secrets came from a teacher of Mike's. I heard his name only a couple of times: Dr. Jerry Alan Johnson. I memorized the name.

Mike brought in a guest speaker to teach us about working with spiritual energy. The guest speaker began his talk by showing us a ring he wore on his hand.

"It's a Tiger's Eye," he said, and told us to pass it around. Once everyone in the group looked at it and returned the ring to him, he began licking and sucking on it. Freaky.

After one of Mike's Mastermind meetings, he drank beers at the bar, surrounded by me and a few other people. He said, "You know, when I put everyone through a guided meditation and I talk about sexual energy, all the women in the group imagine having sex with me."

Today, I'm grateful for his teachings, but also grateful that my time as his student came to an end.

Next up, I'll share how, right when light glimmered at the end of my dark tunnel, I got hit with one of the most painful emotional sucker punches of my life. I learned how the standing meditation doesn't merely make you resilient to stress, but helps you become stronger from it.

CHAPTER TEN

ANTIFRAGILE

On the morning of March 22, 2011, I ambled out of bed, slumped down in front of my computer amid a sleepy daze, and called Mike. He'd begun offering 20-minute, one-on-one calls as part of his coaching.

After practicing the Immortal Post, my emotional life had shifted more in a few months than in the previous few years—in a healthier direction. A few weeks earlier, I'd celebrated my 24th birthday with some new friends; the first time I'd had a birthday with heartfelt, loving people. But I had no clue of the shock that was about to shriek through me like lightning. It wasn't the first I'd experienced in the last couple of months.

I'd recently moved into an apartment in Denver. After almost four years of languishing in my Boulder condo, thinking about moving but never doing it, the universe deftly applied a crowbar to launch me out.

My body was getting stronger, I was feeling happier, and I was even meeting new partners in business. Opportunities were piling up. Then things began to shatter.

My Boulder condo landlord left me a panicked message—was he going to force me to leave or something? Nah…

When I called him back, he blurted out, "Nate, I need you to move out."

His family's home had gotten smoke damage from forest fires and they needed a place to stay. Within three days, I signed the papers on a Denver apartment. The next morning, my landlord left another voicemail, saying I didn't have to move. Too late. *Looks like the universe wanted me to move.* My gut told me it was because of practicing the Immortal Post.

Many of my moving boxes from years earlier were still mostly full, lids open, revealing scattered books and papers, like innards exposed on an operating table or battlefield. I tossed the rest of my stuff into the boxes and delicately wrapped my mattress in layers of plastic.

My business partners and I, now one year into our startup, argued more and more.

One of the partners, Brad, was a retired surgeon. From his eyes down, he was in his sixties. But his crinkled gaze shining with a kid's curiosity made him look decades younger. So did his dyed jet-black hair. "My son," he'd tell me, which pissed me off, "an ego can be a useful thing. Just don't feed it your friends." In thirteen words, he prophesied how our friendship would die.

The other partner, Steve, was a former salesman with his first heart attack already under his belt. He used his baritone voice for two things: telling stories, and giving opinions even if he didn't know the facts, which he usually didn't.

In our email exchanges, Brad called us the Three Amigos, but when our startup hit challenges, I lashed out at my partners. Sometimes, I apologized. Sometimes, I didn't.

A couple of months after I moved, they emailed me and said we needed to talk. I wrote back that I wasn't interested.

Steve replied with one word:

"Interesting."

We'd had our problems but, like a hapless husband wandering home to an empty house, I had no idea what was coming. The next morning, I woke up to discover Brad and Steve had locked me out of our company and kept my share of the profits.

At the same time, the steady income from my business selling yoga products with my brother had evaporated.

So, the scheduled call with Mike was going to be heavy, as in "I'm going to be bankrupt soon so what should I do? And, oh yeah, two people I met in your group just screwed me over."

I dialed the conference line number and getting on I heard eerie silence. I wondered if I'd gotten the time wrong. I checked my email and discovered a message from Mike saying I was banned from getting any more of his coaching. Instead of explaining why, he used the email as an opportunity to deliver the threat of legal action.

What the hell? I stumbled back to my bed, no longer sleepy, but drained from the shock. This man had laid the foundation for all my business knowledge—even though I'd been too emotionally immature to benefit at first—and introduced me to the Daoist practices that would transform my life. I felt as if the floor had collapsed underneath me. How would I keep learning? Would I lose the new friends I'd met in the business group?

As I crawled back into bed, my hand hooked onto my string

necklace. For the past few weeks, it had been slowly fraying, and that morning it snapped. I didn't know whether or not to take it as a sign. If this was a sign, it was probably a bad one.

An hour later, I rolled back out of bed to do the only thing that felt helpful—the only true anchor in my life: the Immortal Post. It made me feel a bit more grounded, but some shocks in life are so strong that no amount of meditation will get rid of that first wave of fear. Was my only chance for learning more of this esoteric Daoist knowledge gone?

A few days later, I received an email explaining my banishment. For my birthday, my friends and I had met to talk shop—we were all in the Mastermind—and to help each other out. Mike cited this as why. I'm not a mind reader, so I can only speculate that he interpreted our meeting as going behind his back and stealing his customers.

I drove north to Fort Collins to meet my friend, Wally, who'd been at that birthday party. As I parked in front of his house, I wondered if he'd turn his back on me, too. He greeted me and let me inside.

Wally was an amalgamation of laidback Colorado native and fierce capitalist. He could drawl like a lifelong skier when pontificating on pale ale flavors, but if you started brainstorming business ideas, he fast-forwarded his drawl and gestured as if juggling steak knives.

We stepped into his garage and, as we stood amidst the racks of skis and bikes, I told him I'd been kicked out.

"You graduated!" he said, shrugging.

Huh. I liked it. In congratulating me, Wally gave me a lesson in choice. We talked more and I started to see the pettiness behind Mike's decision. Turns out, he had his personal assistant call the other people at my birthday party to interrogate them about what had happened. From what I understand, Wally and another person had responded by screaming, in essence, "Are you insane? Why are we having this conversation?"

After Wally helped me expand my vision, I drove back to Denver. As I admired the rolling foothills to my right, the cold knots in my gut melted into warmth. At home, a voicemail awaited me from Mike's assistant.

"...we don't want there to be any...uh...we want you to come back."

Before, I had no choice in the matter, but now I did. I could return to the group and be surrounded by business allies—whom I sorely needed—but I'd still be dependent. Instead of facing the unknown on my own, I'd be returning for more of the same. Even if it seemed like the safe move, and even though I craved more knowledge, I knew what I had to do.

I politely turned them down.

When faced with challenges in life, we often think we have only two choices. We can be weak and cave in, or we can be strong and push back. When I got thrown out of the group I cherished, I figured my choices were fear and despair, or I could resist and try to tough it out. In other words, I could give up my standing meditation practice and go back to drinking. Or inwardly resist by seething with resentment and badmouthing my former mentor, while souring on the inside from a feeling of injustice.

It would have been easy for me to justify either choice by affirming, "Well, I knew this wouldn't work out—nothing else has..." or "Well, of course I feel betrayed and I'm pissed—he deserves it!" But would those sad or pissed-off feelings serve me? Giving up would slip me back to where I started and, even if anger seemed healthier than despair, it would stall my growth.

Thanks to my friend, I realized I didn't have to choose between caving in and pushing back. I could accept what is and grow stronger from the shock, treating it as graduating to the next phase of my education. When I got the opportunity to come back, I still had more than two options. Coming back or leaving were just the physical parts of my choice.

The deeper issue was my mental and emotional response. Despair and anger were the only choices I'd had as a child, and growing angrier nearly destroyed me. But as an adult, I had a third option. I could choose to process the shock and use it to grow. On an energetic level, I didn't have to create more stagnant chi or reinforce coping mechanisms. I could break the cycle.

In many ancient Daoist stories, the student gets kicked out of the temple. Instead of an act of cruelty, it's graduation day, when the student's true tests begin. When I got kicked out, life was stress-testing me, shattering my foundation to see how I would respond.

Today, I'm grateful for that graduation day. It built my maturity and rocketed me toward where I am now: happily married, homeowner, financially comfortable, and journeying far deeper on my spiritual path. I've also realized how I played a part in getting kicked out. I wasn't always a respectful student and frequently resisted the teachings that could have helped me the most. Many times, Mike was extremely patient with me and went above and beyond his role as a teacher to help me. He was a very flawed teacher and human being, but I could have handled myself better as his student—and I'm 100% responsible for that.

For nearly a year after I left the group, I felt as if the floor never stopped caving underneath my feet. Like when I dropped out of college, I'd thrown away the structures that had supported me.

I tried to revive my business and recover from getting shoved out of the company I'd co-founded. My sporadic income and increasingly aggressive debt collectors were barreling toward a convergence point, and the debt was going to win.

Across the street from my apartment was the Van Cise-Simonet Detention Center. Sometimes, when I stood outside, I heard the inmates playing basketball. Would I go to jail for not paying my debt?

In the summer of 2011, I remembered someone from my past and searched for him online. During my last semester of college, I'd gone to another seminar about writing advertising copy. One of the speakers looked like he'd recently awakened from something between a hangover and a coma, but his teachings rang true. His name was Doberman Dan, for his love of the dog breed.

Half a decade later, after searching his name, I discovered Doberman Dan had just started publishing a monthly marketing newsletter, hosting monthly webinars, and had scheduled days where you could call him for advice. He'd been bankrupt too, and before that he'd worked as a cop in Barberton, Ohio, often facing death. I signed up.

Later that year, while practicing the standing meditation, the vertebrae in my pelvis made cracking sounds like popping one's knuckles. At first, I didn't think more than, "*Well, I guess the muscles around my spine are relaxing.*" As time went on, I noticed the cracks traveled up my spine an inch, as if the muscles' tie-ins below had aligned enough so that the vertebra above could start aligning. It certainly felt that way.

One crisp fall day, I practiced the Immortal Post in the quiet corner of my bedroom with the Rocky Mountains peeking through the blinds. I thought about how much debt I was in. I felt like my apartment floor was an illusion and, at any moment, I'd fall six stories into the pit I'd created. Then a thought jumped into my head: "*When this cracking reaches the top of your spine, your financial life is going to turn around.*"

I was spiraling toward bankruptcy and grasping for hope, but I knew how to think rationally. So, why did it feel so *right* to conclude my spine's alignment coincided with my wealth? Without any answer, I continued practicing. Later, I'll reveal what happened.

The standing meditation continued to change my emotional health. On Halloween night, I stepped onto my patio and sat on my futon, the one I'd fallen asleep on for so many nights as my TV had blared. As I relaxed, I listened to the cheers from partiers across the city, flowing up to me like the mist from crashing ocean waves. Something like this used to make me feel lonely. Instead, I smiled.

As December approached, I finally admitted two bitter truths. First, I needed a job and, second, I was just a guy with a high school diploma and no resume. The 2008 financial crisis was still reverberating around the world. What could I do?

All the stress had exhausted my creativity and I wanted guaranteed income. I hopped on Craigslist to look for jobs.

Where could I get one? Accounting? No. Healthcare? No…

Then I found a category with potential: General Labor. Maybe I could dig ditches or something.

I scanned the listings and found one for spinning a sign to advertise a local business. I could listen to audiobooks all day. It sounded perfect. I replied to the ad.

Later, I walked to a local supermarket and interviewed for a job bagging groceries and stocking shelves. After the woman asked a few questions, she opened a desk drawer and pulled out a plastic device.

"Put this in your mouth, against your cheek. It's a drug test."

I sat with the swab in my mouth. Well, I guess my answers were good.

A couple of days later, I got a voicemail about the sign-spinning job. I called back, heard a busy signal, but called over and over until a man finally answered.

"I'm glad I got through!" I said.

"Yeah, things have been crazy over here. We're growing so fast," he said. Turns out, it was a chain of stores that bought gold and silver.

"That's a good problem to have," I told him.

He invited me to interview the next day.

"You're okay wearing costumes, right?" he asked. He seemed more comfortable looking at his phone than me, but when he asked that question, he looked into my eyes and waited.

As I sat in the cramped back office, just a few feet away from the fancy lobby where people haggled for bigger payouts for their jewelry, I thought, *Huh, so this is what my life has come to.* I almost had to choke back a smile. Even though I remained stuck beneath a pile of rubble, the Immortal Post practice continued to unravel my sadness, frustration, and ruminating thoughts. I felt the happiest I'd ever been in my life.

After a few more minutes of my future manager telling me about the job—especially the importance of not spinning the sign too fast, lest potential customers were unable to read what it said—I skipped out the door, celebrating a gig that would humiliate most people, and called the supermarket to let them know I'd taken another job. I'd only see that manager a few more times before the owner fired him for embezzling the gold and having sex with a couple of the employees.

My outer world wasn't turning around as quickly as my inner one, but I could feel the gears clicking into place. The meditation helped me accept my situation and utilize the stress to grow.

I needed the extra inner power because debt collectors were getting more aggressive. I could afford food, but not rent, and couldn't hold off the collectors for long. But I had a plan. It would cost me a few thousand dollars, but I figured it was the only chance I had.

Even if it seems that life hands you only two bad options, or forces you into a single horrible situation, you can choose how to respond; it's not a simple two-option choice. When you were shocked and hurt as a child, your only survival mechanisms were to feel sad or angry, which could devolve into despair or depression. You built coping mechanisms and belief systems to withstand future shocks, even if it choked off your energy and limited your life. Today, you have a third option. You can process shocks and utilize the energy.

This third option is so little-known that we had no word for it until Nassim Nicholas Taleb wrote a book about it: *Antifragile*. The book mostly deals with economic systems, but the same insight applies to emotions.

Taleb describes how all things can be measured on a continuum of fragility, robustness, and antifragility. Fragile things break down in response to stress. On page 268 of his book, he says fragility is "... vulnerability to the volatility of the things that affect [the object]..."

One example is a ceramic dish. When it falls from a table and hits the floor, the stress destroys it. If you drop a metal dish from a table, the stress of hitting the floor won't break it. You could toss it from the top of a building with the same result. That metal dish is robust.

Robust means the object is not vulnerable to volatility. Robust things can withstand stress—but here's the key point. Robust is not the opposite of fragile. A metal dish is not the opposite of a ceramic one. It's stronger, but they're both dishes. Neither dish can grow stronger after it falls from a table or ever transform itself into something more.[*] Just as despair and anger are two different ways of processing shock and hurt, neither will help you grow unless you get beyond them.

The true opposite of fragile is *antifragile*. Something that's antifragile doesn't merely withstand stress. It grows stronger in response to stress.

Few inanimate objects are antifragile. I was reminded of this one day when I put on a pair of jeans, caught my toe in a hole, and ripped the hole wider.

Damn. For the briefest moment, I considered letting the jeans rest and recover for a few days, as if that would repair the hole. Then I remembered denim fabric wasn't like skin. The stressor of my clumsy toe wouldn't inspire the jeans to grow back stronger. They weren't antifragile.

Humans, on the other hand, have the potential to be antifragile. When we get a cut, we take it for granted that our bodies will repair

* Although, to become somewhat robust, the ceramic dish gets exposed to at least 1,800-degree heat. Goes to show the hidden ways in which things can grow stronger.

it. Not only that, but minor stressors trigger our skin to become more resilient in the form of calluses. Of course, if we're cut deeply in the wrong place, we can die. Antifragility only exists within a certain range.

Our body has wisdom deeper than our conscious mind. We don't need to cajole or guilt ourselves into healing a cut. Our body knows exactly how to grow stronger without getting sad or angry. Our mind is different. When we get hit with a mental and emotional shock as a child, we simply take it in. As an adult, when we face a mental or emotional shock, we can consciously choose how to respond, but it's easy to choose wrong. Our physical body is antifragile to physical shocks, but our energy requires conscious effort to be antifragile. We must choose, and choose wisely.

How do we choose to be antifragile?

First, by choosing not to be fragile. Don't give in to pitying yourself. When you choose fragility, you let the situation control you. Next, choose not to be merely strong. Don't get lost in anger or resentment. When you choose strength, you resist the situation. That may seem like the healthier option, but resisting a situation saps your energy, creativity, and can make things worse.

These choices can be difficult because there's always a logical case for being a victim or for being angry. Once, I attended a private intensive with author Dr. Robert Glover on a houseboat with eight other guys. Another attendee complained how he was bullied as a teenager. Dr. Glover called him out.

"Another victim story!"

The attendee responded, "But they really did make fun of me!"

"I'm sure they did," Dr. Glover said. He leaned closer. "I believe you were *victimized*." He went on to describe how, just because you were victimized doesn't mean you need to soak in victimhood. Said another way, just because you were emotionally shattered doesn't mean you need to perpetuate the identity of fragility through your choices.

Same with anger. Here's a small example of how I made this mistake recently. A group of friends and I decided to eat some ramen for dinner. We got on the waiting list, and our group of six meant the wait would be long.

Instead of getting to know my friends, I fixated on the tables in the small restaurant. It seemed as if nobody was budging. *What a waste of time.* Forty-five minutes later, we finally got our table. Later that evening, I realized that I'd promised to call another friend for an important conversation. I could have excused myself and done that while everyone waited for our table, but I was so fixated on resisting the situation and feeling upset that I didn't think about making the call. If I'd accepted what was happening, my mind would have been freer.

"Practicing this path
We do not struggle.
To struggle is to invite resistance.
To invite resistance is to create suffering
In our life,
And in the world."[19]

Accepting a situation seems like being fragile, but true acceptance doesn't necessarily mean throwing your hands in the air and giving up. Acceptance gets a bum rap because people equate it with defeat. Instead, acceptance means you cease devoting your energy to reacting emotionally. When you truly accept a situation or event, you stop torturing yourself with thoughts like, "I'm such an idiot, I can't believe I did that..." or "I can't believe *they* did that..."

When I got kicked out of that business group, I could have stayed in bed, curled into a ball and cried, or gritted my teeth and muttered insults. To be fair, I did that for an hour or so. Then I got up and did the Immortal Post, because running energy through my system for 20 minutes was healthier than 20 days of ruminating thoughts.

Acceptance, paradoxically, is a launching pad to change a situation. Once you accept someone's behavior, and your own, you can decide what to do without being controlled by your emotions. Acceptance means using the present moment to free yourself from the past, so you have more choices in your future. Acceptance is part of antifragility.

The *Dao De Jing* puts it more eloquently:

"By accepting all that seems humble and plain,
We become masters of every situation."[20]

Life may suck sometimes, but you can choose to utilize that suckiness. You can learn from it and find hidden opportunity in it, but that won't happen if you resist it through grief or anger. You can't be fragile or even strong—you must be antifragile.

Guess what else is antifragile? Your coping mechanisms. Fighting against them can make them stronger, and withstanding pain makes them stronger. If you want to dissolve your coping mechanisms, to quote Clint Eastwood's character from *Million Dollar Baby*, "Tough ain't enough." You need to be more antifragile than they are.

It's crucial for you to practice antifragility because, as you practice the Immortal Post, it will shift your energy. You might want to make external shifts in your life. Pay attention, because life might do it for you. I was thinking about leaving Boulder and then I got shoved out. I was growing in different directions from my business partners and mentor, so when I didn't deal with it maturely, I was forced out.

Your spiritual path won't free you from tough choices or situations; it'll throw more your way. As my teachers joke, "No, don't thank me now..." The upshot is you'll handle them better and your life will get better if you choose to be antifragile.

How does this apply to the standing meditation and how you can use it to be more antifragile?

When you practice the standing meditation, you choose how to use it. If you merely want to get strong, you can turn it into a leg and arm workout by mindlessly bending your knees, raising your arms in front of your chest, and letting your muscles hold you in the position. The muscles will get stronger, but you'll never get the emotional or spiritual growth, because the energy will be held back by your tension.

Choose to make the standing meditation more. Open your body to the flow of energy by relaxing your muscular tension—hence the tips in the previous chapter. Then you open your body's energy channels. Then you allow your body's energy to connect with the Earth and the Heavens.

What on Earth (or in Heaven!) does that mean?

Remember, the Daoists believe everything has chi. You, me, the planet, animals, trees, etc. The Daoists thought of our bodies as batteries. Each end of our body is like the end of a battery. One end connects to the Earth and the other connects to Heaven. When you stand correctly, it's like pushing an AA battery into a charger *just right* so it snaps in place and gets filled with more juice.*

In this chapter, we'll cover how to open your body's energy channels to accept the energy from Earth and Heaven. Then, I'll show you how to test this esoteric concept in a practical way.

"The reason that rivers and seas be the
lords of hundreds of valleys,
Is because they are adept at staying low..."[21]

The *Dao De Jing*, like Daoism itself, uses paradoxes and metaphors to deliver its wisdom. On the surface, it seems as if the above quote is about being receptive and occupying a lowly position in life, but it's actually revealing very practical knowledge.

When you practice the standing meditation, you direct the force of your bodyweight straight down. When you align yourself in this position and you relax, you become rooted in the Earth. As the Dao De Jing says, you're getting adept at staying low or, more specifically, your energy is. When you allow your energy to flow down unobstructed, you initiate an equal exchange. You absorb energy from the Earth. Think of it as the energetic equivalent of you breathing out carbon dioxide and nature breathing out oxygen. However, if you resist gravity through muscular tension, you won't receive the energy from the Earth.

Here's a powerful technique to help you become rooted from Dr.

* Note to younger readers: We used to have these things called disposable batteries before all electronics were made with plugs for power cords (and, of course, before wireless recharging was a thing). You could probably find a mountain of used disposable batteries at landfills around the world, possibly leaking and creating a species of mutant cockroaches.

Jerry Alan Johnson's *Yiquan Neigong Daoist Training*: "To feel the gravitational power of the Earth, imagine that your body is constantly falling. As you imagine yourself falling into the center of the Earth, simultaneously feel all of your bones stacking from the bottom of your feet to the top of your head."[22]

As you practice, you'll notice this more and more. The more you relax your muscles and let your bone structure and tendons support your weight, the more powerful this will be. It feels as if your body ceases to exist. You don't feel the strain in your shoulder girdle or your hips or legs because it flows straight down, as if you're relinquishing your bodyweight to the floor beneath you. The more you relax, the more you'll feel this. Paradoxically, you'll feel weightless and empty yet, as you'll discover in the coming pages, you'll feel formidably solid to anyone who tries to move you.

When the standing meditation gets tough, don't give up and don't flex harder. Use the stress as a cue to relax more and more. You'll be gifted with more energy as a result. Let's dive into some practical tips on how to open yourself up to more energy.

TUNE INTO YOUR FEET.

Your feet are directly beneath you. It might seem weird to remind yourself of that but, if you're a highly visual person like me, you might have this odd tendency: when I imagine things, like my own feet, I tend to construct mental images in the area in front of me. For an idea of what I mean, imagine a ticking clock right now.

Chances are, you visualized a clock face hovering about a foot and a half in front of your face. And because you're simultaneously reading this, the clock face probably appeared a few inches in front of this text.

After all, what's the use of imagining a clock floating behind you? Take a moment and try visualizing a clock behind you. You probably imagined yourself from the point of view of the proverbial "fly on the wall," so you could see yourself with a clock behind you.

Now try it another way. Keep staring at these words and use your imagination to feel as if there's a clock behind you. It's a tricky concept, but key for your development. When you practice the standing meditation, tune into your feet in the same way. Feel them directly beneath you. Unless you look down, it's impossible to see them without a mirror, so focus on feeling. Strengthen your kinesthetic awareness. Tune into the feeling of your feet supporting your weight. When you do, your body will align to transfer the force of your weight straight down.

IMAGINE A BEACH BALL BETWEEN YOUR KNEES.

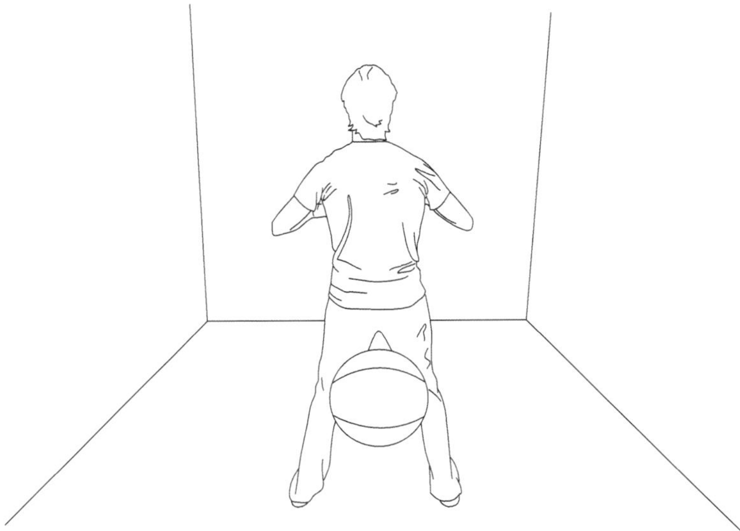

You can enhance how grounded you are, and how much energy you'll receive from the Earth, if you press your knees out slightly. When you do this, don't make your body more tense. Instead, use your imagination for this technique.

Imagine a large beach ball between your knees. Imagine it inflating enough to touch the insides of both your knees. Then imagine it getting a tad bigger. As a result, your knees will gently push outward by a centimeter or so. When you do this right, you might notice your body feels more stable and you might feel an uptick in your energy.

IMAGINE YOUR ARMS ARE SUPPORTED BY FLOATING BALLS.

When practicing, imagine you're standing in a calm lake with water up to your waist. Directly underneath your elbows are floating beach balls, big enough to support the weight of your arms. The balls allow you to rest your arms while keeping them raised.

Even though the balls are in your imagination, you'll notice that you can maintain the standing meditation with less muscular tension and you'll be more open to energy.

IMAGINE A BEACH BALL BEHIND YOUR SHOULDER BLADES.

Imagine a beach ball brushing against your spine between your shoulder blades. Gently push your upper back out slightly, so you meet the ball's subtle pressure. This tiny movement, combined with hollowing your chest, creates a bow-like effect in your upper body.

IMAGINE YOU'RE WEARING A CAPE.

When doing the standing meditation, leaning forward is a common mistake. Imagine wearing a cape and you will stand more regally—a good thing, because it keeps your torso aligned vertically.

IMAGINE YOU CAN PUSH THE CEILING UP WITH YOUR HEAD

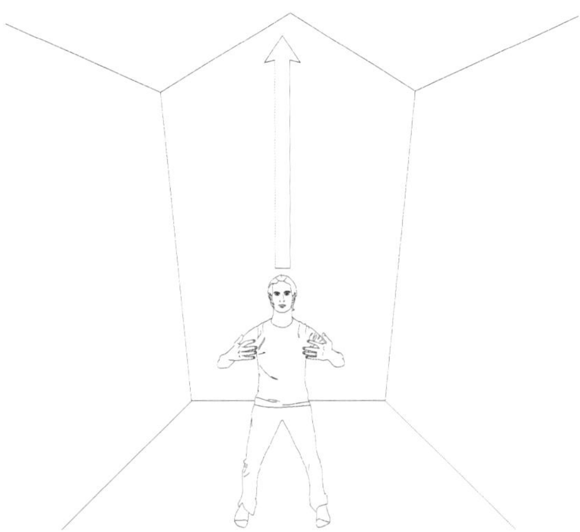

Pinch the top of your ears and pull them directly up. This gives you a visceral sensation of where your skull's highest point is. Next, imagine that highest point is attached to a pole that's attached to the ceiling. As you let your head rise, it pushes the ceiling straight up. Simultaneously, imagine you're standing in concrete up to your waistline, keeping you stuck. This paradoxical visualization will create the bellows-like effect in your body for energy. Your spine will lengthen and relax. Similar to how proper weight distribution and relaxation helps you connect to the Earth, properly lengthening and relaxing your upper body will connect you to Heaven.

"Following this path is like stringing a bow.
One end is pulled down
And the other is pulled up,
Creating a dynamic balance."[23]

IMAGINE YOUR FEET GROWING ROOTS INTO THE EARTH.

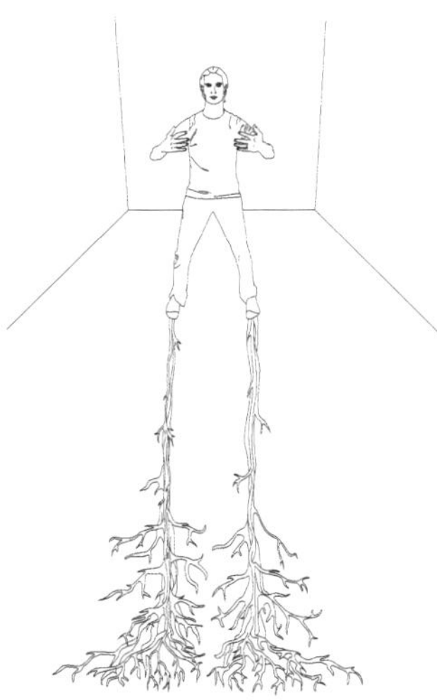

Use your intention and imagination to feel as if your feet are sprouting roots several feet into the Earth beneath you. Focus on making the sensations as vivid and real as you can.

This is a foundational practice to go from "just standing there" to working with energy in the Daoist journey. Not growing roots is like refusing to plug your power cord into the wall socket.

Everything you read might seem overwhelming or even like a ridiculous amount of detail. How can you possibly relax and meditate while keeping track of every square inch of your body and imagine you're pushing the ceiling up while supported by floating balls in a river that's apparently filled with concrete? Are the fish okay? You might start feeling paranoid that if you put a couple of extra pounds of pressure on your left pinky toe, you'll ruin your chances of enlightenment—or at least the power to levitate.

You don't have to focus on everything at once. Start with your physical form and, once you can do that without straining to remember where your arms and legs should be, add in the imagination practices. As you settle into your Immortal Post and align your body, switch your focus every few seconds. Make a quick check-in for all your body parts: "Okay, how's my weight on my feet? Am I imagining a beach ball between my knees? How about under my elbows? Am I imagining that my lower body is stuck in concrete? Is my cape on? Am I pushing the ceiling up with my head?"

It's a far cry from how many people think of meditation—as a way to unplug, tune out, relax, and retreat from the world. Daoists don't meditate to take a break from life, but to learn about life and themselves, and to grow their abilities. They use their *intention, attention, imagination*, and *sensation* to open themselves to the energy of Heaven and Earth. It's tougher, but the rewards are greater.

Using your imagination may seem like no big deal, but it's key to making the Immortal Post work. If someone watched you practice, they'd probably only notice tiny physical changes to your posture, yet you're opening your energetic channels for more chi.

Still, after reading this, you might be tempted to throw your hands in the air and forget it all. Don't let frustrations or feeling overwhelmed stop you—all of this will become second nature. When you first learned to drive, you probably struggled to remember to put on your seatbelt, adjust your mirrors, use your turning signal, put your car in the proper gear, and scan the road before you pulled into traffic. Now you do it without thinking. With enough practice, you'll be able to effortlessly scan through your body and feel and imagine everything you're learning about, as easily as driving a car.

HOW TO TEST IF YOU'RE CONNECTED TO THE EARTH:

As I wrote earlier, rooting in the Earth isn't just a mental concept. Here's how to test if you're actually doing it. Ask someone to gently push you from the side, while you do the standing meditation. They can push on your hip or on your shoulder and the side of your ribcage. Your goal is to remain still, relaxed, and to direct their force into the heel of your opposite foot. What will usually happen is you'll resist your partner's push with your muscular tension, which is practicing strength. Then it'll turn into a pointless pushing contest.

Your aim is to go beyond robustness and become antifragile—to allow stress to make you stronger. Relax your shoulders...let the force of your partner's push fall into your torso...down into your opposite hip...and let the force sink farther down, past your knee and straight into the heel of your foot. Transfer the force of your partner's push into the Earth. You're redirecting your partner's energy into the Earth, using your relaxed body as a conduit. This shows you're rooted in the Earth. As a result, your partner can push as hard as he or she wants—and help you supply the Earth with energy, which helps you receive more in return.

You'll know you're doing it right because it will feel effortless, yet your partner will be shocked by how immovable you are. If you feel strong, you're doing it wrong. The key is to relax more than you think possible.

Don't use your intention to fight back against your partner, but to match their force with relaxation. Pay attention to where your body holds tension. Sense the fear that comes up when you're pushed and relax it away. Use your imagination to melt and root yourself deeper into the Earth.

Because this energy flow is a two-way street, any force you receive makes you more empowered. That's the basis of all Daoist internal martial arts and an esoteric concept that's beyond the scope of this book. You use the same mechanism for your healing when you relax your bodyweight down. By relaxing and opening yourself up, you transfer more and more of your energy into the Earth and Heaven, which opens your body for an energy exchange.

A WARNING

This warning needs a preamble to set the stage. Before practicing the standing meditation, I used to be the type of person who'd receive an email, get upset, dash off a scathing reply, hit the "Send" button…and instantly regret it. Sometimes, I'd send a follow-up email to not sound like such a jerk, or I'd actually apologize…or I'd let the rude email simmer and possibly destroy any goodwill from the other person. Years later, email programs began offering a button to cancel the sending of an email, and I'm sure it was because of people like me. However, as I practiced the standing meditation, I became calmer. Emotional flare-ups had less control over me.

When I discovered my partners had cheated me out of a business, I didn't let rage consume me and I didn't remain in shock. Instead, I spent time pondering the situation. This might seem like a minor point, but it represented a complete shift in my personality during stress.

After thinking, I strategically reached out to Steve and we had a cordial conversation. I wanted to see if that cordialness would extend to giving me my share of the business's monthly profits. It did not. After that, I decided not to grovel or negotiate or file a lawsuit, but instead focus on my own growth. I never spoke to either partner again. At the time of this writing, it's eerily close to exactly ten years since that event and I'm grateful everything happened as it did. It was yet another opportunity for me to practice antifragility.

This is a warning because when you change your energy, you'll lose friends. They'll quietly exit stage left from your life or lash out at you and betray you. Only friends who work on themselves will be able to stick with you. Maybe many will. Probably most won't. The good news is you will gain new, healthier friends. In the meantime, the loneliness might discourage you away from your practice. Don't give up. This emotional pain is necessary for your growth.

This relates to another aspect of antifragility. Because we're designed to be antifragile, we suffer when there is too *little* volatility and stress. It's easy to forget we're constantly growing stronger in response to stress. When astronauts land back on Earth after a long jaunt in outer space, they have trouble walking. Not just because their leg muscles atrophied, but because their feet hurt. Floating in space, their feet calluses wither away.* When they walk on Earth and their more delicate skin gets exposed to the stress of the planet's gravitational pull, their feet can't take the pressure. When we avoid the stress and volatility of forcing our heart to pump blood faster and suddenly drain our muscle tissue of its chemical reserves—also known as exercise—our health deteriorates.

We also deteriorate when we coddle ourselves. When you cling to your current unhealthy relationships, you stall your growth. When I grew dependent on my mentor, I kept myself childlike and cocooned in an emotional bubble. I felt special while stuffing away feelings of vulnerability. By declining the offer to return, I was accepting a healthy dose of stress and volatility—the perfect nourishment for inner growth.

In the months and years that followed, I'd need all the nourishment I could get. In the next chapter, I'll give more details about how to integrate the Immortal Post into your life. Then I'll reveal whether my plan to revive my business succeeded or if I lost every penny of the thousands of dollars I'd invested.

---

* According to NASA (see citation #24), astronauts lose 1% to 2% of their bone mass per month. Turns out, bones stay strong when exposed to the stress of gravity, which triggers electric sparks. These electric sparks trigger the growth of bone cells, and are the same electric sparks that are potentially related to chi (see citation #25).

CHAPTER ELEVEN

BUILDING THE HABIT

On the fateful evening when I practiced the Immortal Post and felt my body light up like the sun, I basked on my futon for a while. Still marveling at what I'd experienced, I went to bed. The next morning, I awoke a different person, yet the same. I still lived alone in a Boulder condo and my most substantial decorations were my partially-unpacked boxes littering the living room. I still treated my finances as a two-year-old treats toys he's scattered and smashed on the floor. And I still couldn't get a date.

Inwardly, I was similar, with no permanent state of bliss pulsating through my veins, but something *was* different. I was discovering a way to help myself that actually worked. It was giving me clear, concrete benefits, like more energy, focus, and feeling better about my life. But I also got more esoteric benefits. People treated me differently and even said I looked different, even though my clothes and haircut were the same. Something had shifted, but I still had a thousand-mile journey to go. Because I slogged through the frustration and confusion, I can tell you what to expect when you go forward with this practice.

I started because I wanted to be cool. Devoting myself to a practice with a few thousand years of history behind it made me feel special. Engaging with a secret, mystical practice seduced me, and I'm glad it did. While I haven't achieved some of its more mythical benefits—yet—it's led me to harness and direct the flow of chi, which leads to some interesting abilities, which I'll mention in future chapters.

Embracing this practice felt like coming home to who I truly was. When you experience this, no motivational tricks are required. Habit-forming strategies become secondary, but I'll mention the ones I've found effective.

As I've said, when I started doing the standing meditation, I drank a vodka/energy drink combo every morning. Eventually, my Immortal Post practice felt so good that I lost the craving to start my day drunk. In a perverse way, I was practicing an effective routine for building ironclad habit patterns into my lifestyle.

Even if my drinking behavior was destructive, I was practicing commitment. Nothing got in the way of consuming my drink—not common sense, reasoning, or even a plummeting income and maxed-out credit cards.

Then I made a single change to my morning routine. Every morning—seven days per week—I woke up, got out of bed, showered, and did the Immortal Post. Then I fixed myself a drink.

The only difference was sneaking in the brief standing meditation, until one day I stopped the drinking. This isn't a cure-all for addiction. Everyone's situation is different, but slipping one habit into the midst of another, like a Trojan Horse, worked for me.

Practicing the Immortal Post before my drinking was easy; it just took a few minutes, and then I could imbibe. And, like a clever contract with a seemingly-innocuous clause, this routine bolstered my new habit. All I had to do was affirm *"Sure, I can have my usual drink, but I'll meditate for a few minutes first."*

Three important rules pushed me toward success:

1. I coupled a new habit with an old, established one.
2. I arranged my routine so the established habit demanded that I practice the new one first.
3. Accomplishing my new habit granted me the reward (feeling good!) that the established one—my drinking—provided.

Both habits—the old one and the new one—formed a symbiotic relationship until I ingrained my new habit further and further into my mental wiring and it eroded my established habit.

Paradoxically, you can use your bad habits to bolster good ones. Choose a daily habit you'd like to get rid of—perhaps drinking, eating a high-sugar food, repeatedly checking your social media feeds or watching online pornography.

Make a deal with yourself that your pleasure-seeking brain will agree to. Negotiate that you can have that doughnut or check your phone one more time... ***after*** you do five or ten minutes of the Immortal Post.

When your bad habit tempts you, remember your negotiation. Practice the Immortal Post for five minutes and then grab your phone or the doughnut—or both—and enjoy them guilt-free.

When you do this, you carve a place in your schedule for your Immortal Post practice and you give yourself a Pavlovian reward. A funny thing may happen: you'll start enjoying the feeling of your meditation more than the sugar high of a snack or the dopamine high of social media. Your bad habit will fade into the background.

This relies on *planning* your action steps rather than psyching yourself up or giving yourself a pep talk. Three different scientific studies in the UK found that we stick to new habits most when we outline specific plans.[26, 27, 28] One study compared three different groups of people who attempted to build the habit of exercising more. One group simply tried without any help; they were the control group. The second group got a motivational intervention. The third group got both a motivational intervention and outlined a specific plan for when they would exercise.

After a few weeks, the control group didn't succeed at building their habit. The second group wasn't helped by the motivational intervention and ditched their new habit. To be fair, according to James Clear's book *Atomic Habits*[29] where I read about these studies, the intervention was described as educating the participants in the health benefits of exercise. Thinking back to my days in school, I'm guessing the presentations were less than scintillating. The third group, which had the motivation intervention and outlined a plan, did the best. This suggests that you're not helped by emotionally revving yourself up. Instead, form a plan—*then* you can play *Hearts On Fire* from Rocky IV if you need the extra juice.

Your best times to practice the Immortal Post will change, because you will constantly change. Never feel that you have to do it at a certain time; explore when and where are best for you.

If you struggle to begin, start with one minute per day, every single day. Not because this will give you all the benefits you want, but because doing the stance every day, even for a minute, will change your identity. After several days, you can start saying, "I'm someone who does the Immortal Post," and you'll be right.

Don't underestimate the power of changing your identity with a one-minute habit. How long does it take to slam back a few shots of alcohol per day? A few seconds (especially if you have a slice of lime and some salt handy), yet you can call yourself an alcoholic if you do it every day. Do 60 seconds of an Immortal Post every day—the daily practice is the key—and you'll shift your identity. Once you've done that, amplifying your behavior is much easier.

Choose one spot in your home where you'll do your practice and face the same direction each time. This helps create a ritual that trains your mind to settle into a meditative state as soon as you begin. Because I've almost always done my practice barefoot on a carpet, I end up creating footprints in the fabric.

I used to use a timer on my computer that would beep once when the time was up. Now I use my phone and I keep it within arm's reach so when the timer goes off, I can slowly lean over to shut it off, return to the Immortal Post, and then slowly lower my arms. I always take at least a few seconds to relax before standing up. If I hold the Immortal Post for a longer time like half an hour, I'll relax for three minutes before standing fully.

YOUR FIRST 7 DAYS

Here's a sample schedule for someone who wants to begin with 60 seconds and add 5 seconds per day. Every day has a primary focus for your intention and imagination.

DAY	TIME IN IMMORTAL POST	FOCUS
1	60 seconds	Keep your pelvis tucked
2	65 seconds	Breathe into your belly
3	70 seconds	Relax your shoulders
4	75 seconds	Let thoughts come and go
5	80 seconds	Balance weight on your feet evenly
6	85 seconds	Melt any tension you feel
7	90 seconds	Imagine growing roots

Here's a sample schedule for someone more athletic:

DAY	TIME IN IMMORTAL POST	FOCUS
1	60 seconds	Keep your pelvis tucked
2	2 minutes	Breathe into your belly
3	3 minutes	Relax your shoulders
4	4 minutes	Let thoughts come and go
5	5 minutes	Balance weight on your feet evenly
6	5 minutes and 30 seconds	Melt any tension you feel
7	6 minutes	Imagine growing roots

After seven days, you'll get a feel for where you need to focus your intention, whether it's your posture, relaxing certain parts of your body, or something involving your imagination. As you progress, you'll cycle through your focuses, coming back to the same ones over and over, deepening your skill.

I could write more tricks and tactics to cajole you into standing still, but that's not what worked for me. *I wanted to plumb the same mysterious depths that Daoists have for thousands of years.* You couldn't have stopped me if you tried, whether through bribes or threats.

You're either ready to make this journey or this specific spiritual path isn't right for you. The Immortal Post—or Daoism for that matter—may not be what resonates with you. Try it and decide for yourself.

This doesn't mean you must experience some blow-out spiritual event. You don't need to feel like your body lights up like the sun; that just happened to be my experience. Everyone is different. What matters is that you feel better and your life gets better, over time.

Recently, I read that Amazon will pay up to $5,000 to full-time employees who quit and agree never to work there again. I won't give you five grand to walk away, but I'll give you hearty encouragement. If you don't have an intuition, no matter how meek and puzzling, declaring this is right for you, it might not be.

I can't count the number of times I ended an Immortal Post training session and thought it was a waste of time. Knowing this practice was right for me kept me going.

In this process, the biggest dangers are giving in to your discouragement and fear. The answer to both is to make your mind your ally—the subject of the next chapter.

CHAPTER TWELVE

MAKE YOUR MIND AN ALLY

Less than a month into my job as a sign-spinner, I staggered into the store to start my shift at 10AM, clutching my lunch bag, a one-gallon plastic jug of water, and barely holding onto my distracted mind.

I greeted another sign-spinner, who looked fresh out of high school and as if he'd already chugged three Monster energy drinks.

Our supervisor for the day was a petite woman who looked to be around my age, with equally dark hair and eyes.

When I stuck my hand out to greet her, I dropped the water jug and it smashed onto the reception area's carpet, instantly soaking it for several feet around. The other sign-spinner jumped back to save his shoes and pants, and laughed. The supervisor and I dove for the nearest paper towel rolls to mop up the worst of the mess before the store opened.

What a start to the day. I hope it isn't an omen of things to come.

After fifteen minutes of mushing half a dozen paper towel rolls, the carpet returned to its ugly green. I trudged outside to an unusually warm, sunny December morning.

Until 6PM, other than breaks, I stood on the street corner and waved a sign around, advertising the storefront. Between bouts of cringing at the memory of dropping my water jug, I fixated on something else, counting down the minutes until I could race home and check on something utterly critical. Or so I thought.

I was at the company's Iliff and Parker location, the intersection of two burly, six-lane roads. This place was all business—people rarely shouted from their cars. Big clouds of auto exhaust billowed against my body. Miles west, the Rockies peeked at me like a giant peering over our heads.

Breathing in the smell of burnt oil as thousands of cars droned by, I thought about the project I'd been obsessing over for the last three months. With the help of a consultant recommended to me and my webmaster, I'd created a new website to sell a short book on how to do the standing meditation. With all my other businesses and ideas grinding to a halt, I wondered if this was what I was meant to do.

The contractor had begun the work months earlier, telling me how awesome the website was going to be. He was referred by someone I trusted—his brother-in-law—but I still had something to learn about trust and brother-in-laws.

Then he asked for more money. I clicked the PayPal button to send him some. Later, he asked for more. I clicked the PayPal button again. He called me "bro" many times so he must have been legit. *It's worth it. You have to do it this way.*

Finally, it was time to test the website, so I spent two weeks' worth of pay to buy an advertisement. I needed that money, but needed this to succeed even more. It wasn't the first time I'd decided that I absolutely *needed* something to succeed. Throughout my life, whenever I'd tried to nurture an idea into fruition, I overwatered it by dwelling on how much it *had* to work. After pinning my happiness on things outside my control, I felt ripped apart every time this strategy crashed.

Since starting the job, I did a few minutes of the standing meditation each morning. After a full day of working on a street corner, I drove home and did a longer round of the practice. I didn't know if my knees could take the stress, but this was the most nourishing habit I'd ever developed and nothing was going to stop me from doing it daily. My previously pale skin was burning and tanning from so many hours exposed to the sun, but the Immortal Post seemed to have prepared me for standing outside and constantly moving—I rarely got tired.

I mentioned to my supervisor that I'd probably keep the job for only three or so months. The plan was to get some business income going and quit. It all comes down to this first advertisement. *If it works, I'm golden. If it doesn't, I'll be stuck here for a long time.*

The ad was scheduled to launch that morning. Maybe it'd make as much of a splash as I did with my water jug? I'd triumphantly come home, check my laptop, and see the screen overflow with all the big numbers I craved. Website visitors, book orders, and profits galore. Then Journey's song *Don't Stop Believing* would play as the credits rolled. Every time a vision popped up of the campaign failing, I shoved it aside, my brain still clinging to the law of attraction dogma I'd learned years earlier. *This advertisement had to work.* After everything I'd done for my growth, how could I possibly be stuck making $10 an hour?

Finally, as the sun set, my shift ended. I raced to my car and drove to my apartment, resisting the urge to blast through every red light. The elevator toyed with me, slowly lurching through the floors.

After busting through my door, I slid onto my chair like a runner stealing second base and turned my laptop on, pretending to be calm. The gnawing in my gut cranked up as I got closer to finally seeing the orders. I pictured the numbers: $600? $900? Maybe over $1000? I spent $900 on the ad, so I hoped I made more than that.

Even if it were $500, I could still recover. My fingers trembled as I typed.

Username. Password. The page loaded.

$0.

This has to be a mistake. After staring a few more moments, I slid off my rolling chair, flopped onto the gray carpet, and curled into the fetal position while emitting an "Aaauuughhh…"

My gut felt strangled—all the adrenaline turned sour. *How could this have happened? What am I going to do?* I'd be stuck in this job, flailing for an escape route. I shuffled to bed and drifted to sleep. When I woke up, the strangling in my gut resumed, as if an invisible stalker had been lurking in the corner, waiting for my alarm to go off. I did my standing meditation, packed my lunch, and marched to my car. Driving, I dwelled on the disaster and dreaded the months ahead. *This is terrible. What are you going to do?*

But then another voice spoke up, calmer, deeper, and commanding my attention.

"Nate, are you going to let this stop you?"

"No," I replied out loud.

"So, this is just a bump in the road, right?"

"Yes."

"One that you'll look back on years from now and remember fondly as the time you were in the thick of the struggle, working your way out to eventually succeed?"

"Yes."

"So, why not feel that way right now? Why not take pride in it and even enjoy yourself in a perverse way?"

Why not, indeed? As my car glided along on that sunny Colorado day, my mind zoomed to years in the future when I'd be more prosperous and tell the story of the time I almost broke down, until I rewired my mindset. Instead of my thoughts tearing into me, distracting me, draining my energy, confusing me, and making me feel like a loser, they re-focused, comforted, uplifted, and inspired me. I tuned to the bigger picture of who I truly was. Instead of my original wiring giving the marching orders, my true self stepped forward to guide the situation—a pivotal moment in my life.

For the challenges ahead, I'd need my mind to be my ally. The ad was still a failure and my $50,000 of IRS debt still hung over me like the sword of Damocles, getting heavier as it racked up interest.

When life hits you with pain, that's bad enough. It's worse if your mind turns on you when you need your compassion and comfort the most. If our mind isn't our ally, we convince ourselves that every setback is a permanent tragedy. We use our thoughts to make poison and then drink it.

"All of humanity's problems stem from man's inability to sit quietly in a room alone."
— Blaise Pascal

Some thoughts are so painful that we'll avoid them, even if it means hurting ourselves. Scientists made some alarming findings about people being alone with their thoughts, published in a review of 11 studies[30] by the Department of Psychology at the University of Virginia and Harvard University. The scientists conducted studies where college students sat in a room alone with no smartphones (cue the foreboding music). Most students struggled to concentrate for a mere fifteen minutes—even with no distractions—and almost all the students' minds wandered.

The scientists wondered if the unfamiliar environment was the problem. They did the same study, but students could participate from home. It didn't go well. Some students admitted cheating via checking their phones. Distraction levels failed to go down.

If you're thinking this is more proof that kids today can't focus, you're not alone. The scientists tested to see if age was the issue, and discovered participants up to 77 years old had just as much trouble sitting without distraction.

The scientists ran one more experiment. Participants had to occupy themselves with their thoughts for fifteen minutes, but with a twist. They had the option of giving themselves electric shocks. The scientists emphasized it was a mere option:

"We went to some length to explain that the primary goal was to entertain themselves with their thoughts and that the decision to receive a shock was entirely up to them."

Before the experiment began, the participants got to feel how painful the shock was. If anyone actually *enjoyed* the shock, those participants (apparently some) were not included in the results. When the time came to sit quietly, 67% of the men and 25% of the women shocked themselves at least once. Rather than simply be with their thoughts for fifteen minutes, they chose to shock themselves. The scientists quoted a fitting line from the epic poem *Paradise Lost* by John Milton in their published paper:

"The mind is its own place, and in itself/Can make a Heav'n of Hell, a Hell of Heav'n."

These results amused me until I remembered when I used alcohol to escape my inner pain; then the idea of using electric shocks didn't seem so strange. This gives perspective to why many people try regular meditation and toss the practice aside. Most meditation involves sitting quietly, relaxing, and letting your thoughts go. If you managed to do this until you successfully reached Nirvana, I tip my cap to you. However, your experience might have been closer to this:

You sit down to meditate. "Okay," you think, "I'm going to relax and silence my thoughts."

Within a second, you notice one of your butt cheeks is slightly askew. You adjust yourself and settle in again. "Okay, this time I'll start for real." Then you remember an email you need to reply to. "Whoops! Mental note. I'll get to that when I'm done. Shoot, I'm already thinking about stuff I have to do. Oh well, I'll reply to the email when I'm done here." Within moments, you think, "But wait, why is she emailing me with that anyway? It's not even my responsibility. Why don't people take me more seriously?" Then you remember some embarrassing moment from when you were a teenager and you realize you're daydreaming. "Focus!" "Just let it go!" "Why can't I just concentrate?"

You try again and remember an argument from a couple of days ago, imagining what it'd be like to tell the other person what you *really* wanted to say. The fantasy's visuals get sharper, the voices louder. Suddenly, your thoughts echo in your head like an ambulance siren. And, much like slipping into a dream, you don't register your mind stealing your focus away. You take a few breaths, which sound like sighs of defeat. After a few minutes, you feel more stuck in your head than ever. You check your phone in an attempt to settle down and feel better because the "meditation" made you feel *worse*.

I've found most spiritual traditions have few answers to this other than, "Just keep trying." The Daoists were more practical. But before diving into the nitty-gritty of making an ally of your thoughts and helping them quiet down, why should we care? Sitting quietly in a room isn't the sexiest concept in the world and doesn't make for a good party trick. So, what good does it do?

First, because an out-of-control mind can bully you, and unlike the lunk from junior high school, your mind is with you 24/7 and knows all your secrets. As I drove to work the day after my advertisement failed, my thoughts could have pushed me to feel more hopeless. They could have fed me every secret reason why I was a failure. I could have let the programming from my mom or dad take over.

Once we reach young adulthood, we don't need our parents to hurt our feelings or teach us to lash out at others because we already do it in our own heads. But when you quiet your mind, it's like turning on a self-cleaning oven. Your quiet mind rewires the nature of your thought patterns. When your mind's chatter returns, it's less of a condemning enemy and more of an encouraging ally. The more you quiet your mind, the greater this transformation. This is why quieting your mind provides an array of psychological and health benefits.

There's another more esoteric reason for quieting your mind. A loud mind *blocks the flow of chi and consumes it*. It also distracts your attention and imagination, blocking you from feeling subtle sensations. When you're stuck in your head, you can't connect to Heaven and Earth.

However, when you still your body, relax your tension, and quiet your mind, you'll open yourself to a tremendous amount of energy. This is hinted at in both Daoist and Christian traditions:

"Something formless, complete in itself
There before Heaven and Earth
Tranquil, vast, standing alone, unchanging
It provides for all things yet cannot be exhausted."[31]

"Be still, and know that I am God."
— Psalms 46:10

Now the tricky part begins...

HOW DO WE QUIET OUR MIND?

First, here's how *not* to do it. Think of a pink elephant. Now think to yourself, "There I go again...I'm so stupid for thinking about this pink elephant," and then, "It's all your fault, pink elephant, damn you!" I'm attempting to be funny, but this is a serious point that emotionally cripples many people. If you pick a fight with your thoughts, you're doomed.

Demanding your thoughts be silent is like trying to goad and guilt your partner into having an orgasm.

However, your thoughts have a weakness. They're like the Tyrannosaurus rex in the movie *Jurassic Park*. If you remain still and don't react, your thoughts won't eat you. Instead, they'll lose interest and disappear.

However, you have more tools at your disposal than remaining still and waiting. When you relax your muscles and align your body, this helps quiet your thoughts. Here's how that works: Earlier, you learned that muscular tension and a loud mind block the flow of chi. It's a two-way street. Relaxing muscular tension unlocks the flow of chi and unlocking the flow of chi helps to quiet your mind. Aligning your body and opening it to Heaven and Earth—which unlocks the flow of chi—also helps to quiet your mind.

I've found it's easier to quiet my mind in the Immortal Post than when sitting. It's counterintuitive but it works; **by focusing your mind on aligning your body and relaxing your tissues, you pave the way for it to become silent**.

It's a healthy cycle. You've already learned techniques for the first two thirds of the cycle. Now, let's cover the third piece.

LET THOUGHTS POP UP...AND LET THEM GO JUST AS EASILY

Let's return to the phrase, "Don't think of a pink elephant." It reveals how our brains cannot help but fixate on something, even if we want to avoid it. This is why we can't "push away" our thoughts. Even by wanting thoughts gone, we feed them attention and they stick in the forefront of our consciousness.

By now, you've probably forgotten about that pink elephant, right? That's because you let it go. By not feeding the idea attention, your mind moved on. Now the pink elephant has wandered back on your mental screen because it got fed new attention. You can see how trying to push thoughts away paradoxically gives them what they need to remain.

The Daoists cite how chi follows attention. When you pay attention to your thoughts, even by trying to silence them, you feed them chi. When you don't feed thoughts with your attention, they don't receive the chi they need and will disappear. Just as the pink elephant, once again, faded away...

...and now it's back. By now you know it's only a matter of time before it leaves again. It's the same with any other passing thought. If you let it pass of its own momentum, your mind will eventually become empty.

This technique is getting backed by science. Studies[32] show something called Acceptance and Commitment Therapy can reduce depression and anxiety. Here's an excerpt from one of the studies.

"The patient is taught that any action to prevent or control these unwanted mental experiences are ineffective or inversed, which exacerbates them. The experience should be completely accepted without any internal or external reaction to remove them."

One of the studies[33] found this mental acceptance can increase your lifespan, even when you're beaten down by grief.

It's easier to deny our unwanted thoughts attention when we focus our attention on something else. We do that with the next technique.

LISTEN TO YOUR BREATHING

"When the breath wanders the mind also is unsteady. But when

the breath is calmed, the mind too will be still..."
— Svatmarama, Hatha Yoga Pradipika

Your mind can listen to all kinds of things, like horns honking, television blaring, the wind blowing, another person speaking, or even information delivered silently, like a social media feed on your phone or a beautiful painting. When your mind listens, it also responds, as in a conversation. When you're surrounded by more peaceful things, like the wind or a painting, your mind usually responds with more peace.

You can't always control your environment, but you can redirect your mind's conversation. Instead of reacting to your outer environment, you can listen to your inner one, by paying attention to your breathing.

Think of your inhales and exhales as cresting, crashing, and retreating ocean waves. Listen to your breath's nuances and let your breath carry your attention. By giving your breathing attention, you give it chi and feed its power.

In Indian and Tibetan spiritual traditions, meditators pay extra attention to the turning points of the breath cycle between inhaling and exhaling. When you fully inhale, there's a pause before you exhale, which is one turning point. Then, when your lungs are nearly empty, there's a pause before you inhale, which is the other turning point. When you focus on these points of stillness, they will expand, and so will your mind's stillness.

ASK, "WHO ARE YOU?"

Recently, as part of a training for a doctorate in Chinese Energetic

Medicine, I did an exercise with a partner where we sat in chairs facing each other and took turns asking the other, "Who are you?"

If my partner answered with his name, I replied, "That's just your name. Who are you?" Same with job titles, family roles or esoteric concepts of our soul. Everything was answered with, "No. Who are you?"

The key is, we didn't relent. When my partner asked me, "Who are you?" and I answered, the answer was never deemed correct.

Eventually, the mind cannot help but silence, as it runs out of assumptions and identities. This exercise is best done with a partner who, like mine, shows no mercy.

Instead of fighting your thoughts, these techniques indirectly quiet your mind. You spiral your way toward mental stillness.

This doesn't mean you'll avoid pain. You'll face straining muscles, a screaming mind, and hurtful emotions. Sometimes, techniques won't make them go away. At this point, you must endure.

When I drove back to work after that failed ad, changing my thoughts didn't change how the advertisement lost me money. I remained at the same job with the same obligations and the same bills to pay. On top of that, the contractor who helped with the project disappeared after the ad ran. My situation was the same, but I regained my power to alter my trajectory. I reaffirmed that my **intention** was to eventually succeed. I placed my **attention** on the long term. I **imagined** the future where I'd look back on this and feel good about it. The **sensations** in my body changed. I made an ally of my mind, giving it the best chance at becoming quiet and giving me the best chance to succeed in the future.

You get no promises of instant or permanent results, but the good news is, this will be some of the most powerful work you ever do on yourself. It'd be nice if the work were easier. Slipping into a meditative state is tricky. Doing so when you're frustrated, worried, distracted, or greedy to get results is even trickier. You can't make your mind do it, but you can walk your mind toward it. When you keep your sense of humor and let time work its magic, it's one of the best things that can happen in your life—like falling in love.

One of my teachers, Dr. Diego Sanmiquel, told a story about an ancient Tibetan mystic:

One day, a man seeking enlightenment journeyed to a distant temple to ask for a master's advice. As the man entered the temple, the master looked at him and asked, "Who are you?"

"Oh, thank you, thank you!" the man replied and hurried away. He sat in a cave to practice and, each time a thought popped up that made him feel angry, sad, anxious, overexcited, or fearful, he asked, "Who are you?" When he did, the thoughts faded.

After seven years, the man returned to the temple. Some people around the temple noticed he was more radiant and at peace. The man approached the master and the master said, "Get out of here!"

"Oh, thank you, thank you!" the man replied, and hurried away. As he practiced in his cave, when unneeded thoughts popped up, he whispered, "Get out of here!" Because of his previous training in getting to know his true self, he made the command without extra strain. He wasn't fighting his thoughts, but choosing to align with his true self; the conflicting thoughts ran away.

After seven more years, the man returned to the temple. More people around the temple noticed his radiance. The man approached the master and the master turned to him and laughed.

"Oh, thank you, thank you!" the man replied, and hurried away.

For the next seven years in his cave, as he enjoyed his quiet mind, he laughed. He achieved enlightenment and was never seen again.*

The morning after my ad campaign failed, I had my "Who are you?" moment. Instead of making myself miserable, I tuned into my true path. My destructive thoughts lost their power and it was easy to let them go. I might have even chuckled a bit as I pulled into my workplace's parking lot, feeling at peace.

In the next chapter, I'll show how I used my bankruptcy as a launching pad to build wealth, while paring down my lifestyle to the bone to grow my spiritual life.

* According to my teacher, one of his friends visited this cave and he could hear laughter still echoing from the walls.

CHAPTER THIRTEEN

LIVE SIMPLY

"What? You don't like paying taxes?"

The judge glared at me as the room rustled with laughter.

I sat with about 30 other people in a small room on the 8th floor of 1999 Broadway Street in Denver. We were there for our 341 Meeting, named after schedule 341 in the bankruptcy code—more commonly known as a Bankruptcy Hearing.

The room was about the size of a high school classroom and stunk of the same pre-exam anxiety. I sat at a desk, facing the judge as he flipped through a binder of my financials. Each page turn echoed in the silent room—until everyone chuckled, of course.

What the f&%$? You're all going bankrupt, too.

I'd been working my sign-spinning job for a few months and my delusions of it being temporary work were shattered. Debt collectors were nipping chunks from my heels and even minimum payments were unaffordable. If I didn't take a sledgehammer to my situation, within weeks I'd be penniless and homeless.

There was no way I could rebuke the judge who stared at me with the tundra-cold gaze of a lifelong government worker. Even though he wasn't towering over me as in the courtrooms we see on TV, I still felt like a bug positioned under his raised shoe heel. He had the power to deny my bankruptcy and let my debt hang me like a noose.

I slowly muttered, "It's not like that."

"What happened?

"For a few years, after I paid rent and living expenses, there was nothing left over. Then the interest piled up."

My lawyer nodded as he sat next to me. I'd worked with his law firm, but only interacted with him for a couple of minutes, total. Months earlier, I'd searched the internet for bankruptcy attorneys and picked the cheapest one with good reviews. The lawyer's name was Jude. When I sat in his waiting room, I spotted an autographed photo of the actor Jude Law hanging on the wall.

His staff walked me through the bankruptcy process, which forced me to pop open the hood on my finances and organize everything—an odd way to finally get the lesson. Listing my assets was easy; I had almost nothing.

"Just a heads up," one of the legal assistants had told me. "Sometimes the judge will collect all the cash out of your bank account."

"Is there anything I can do?"

She held up her hand and, as I admired her tattoos, she said, "Hookers," ticking off one finger, "and blow," as she ticked off a second finger. "Spend the money."

"Gotcha." A few days later, I crammed a cart at Walmart with all my staples—flour, beans, salsa, cheese, and spent a bit over $200, a high amount for me.

Would they take all my money? Or maybe interrogate me about my list of assets? Would representatives of credit card companies show up to browbeat me? I had to swear under oath—what if I made a mistake? Would they believe me or would I go to prison? My obsessive internet searches, for once, put me at ease. In most cases, apparently, the meeting was a drama-free affair.

Still, after I explained why I'd neglected my tax bill, I wondered about that. The 341 Meeting room, teeming with laughter a moment before, grew silent, like the moment before an answer is revealed on a game show. But the judge didn't ask any more questions. I sensed I'd be granted my bankruptcy. As he led me through the swearing, relief swirled through me—six figures of debt would get wiped out with the stroke of a pen.

As I got up, my lawyer leaned and whispered to me in a Texas drawl, "Good job. Call me about those taxes."

He meant my $50,000 of more recent tax debt, ineligible for Chapter 7 bankruptcy and still hanging over my head. Considering my meager income and how the IRS racked up interest charges every month, it was mathematically impossible to pay the debt off unless something changed.

Bankruptcy can break a person's confidence. I chose to use it as a second chance and an opportunity to mature. Yes, I'd screwed up. A bunch of credit card companies got stiffed, but I could make sure it didn't happen again. In the meantime, I still owed over $50,000 and had to figure out how to pay it off—plus the avalanche of interest that would accrue—while making $10 an hour. I couldn't give up and I'd proved that beating my head against a wall for over half a decade didn't work, either.

I simplified my living and searched for a cheap home. Unfortunately, my credit score was floating around deadbeat status. I tried renting a month-to-month studio that resembled a storage unit, with online reviews so awful that even the bedbugs were complaining of cramped quarters and foul smells. My application got rejected. *Would everyone reject me?*

In a few weeks, my lease would expire, but I didn't panic or scramble harder to find a new place. Instead, a strange assurance came over me that things would work out perfectly. I didn't beg for divine intervention. Instead, I practiced my Immortal Post and embodied the centered, settled feeling when focusing on finding a new home.

On a day off from sign-spinning, I found a Craigslist listing for a condo in east Aurora with a patio and a fireplace for $525 a month. Within a couple of hours, I was standing in the condo with the owner. Someone knocked on the door and the owner answered, talked for a bit, and closed the door.

He said, "That's the second person coming to see this place." He sighed and shook his head. "A lot more are on their way." He spoke and moved with the nervous energy of someone who treated everyone better than family.

I wrote a check for the deposit and explained that I was going through a bankruptcy.

"It's fine. I've been through one too!" my future landlord said.

A year earlier, I'd vowed to stay in my Denver apartment, calling it my home. As I closed its front door for the last time, I cried. I'd thrown out my halfway-disintegrated particle board desk and abandoned my old futon where someone could take it. But I took along the comfy bed I bought in Boulder with me—my only item of value.

The new condo's AC window unit gurgled with whatever wet ecosystem grew inside—I turned it on only once until I couldn't take the stench anymore. The shower's wall had holes big enough that I peered out them every morning to check the weather, and I couldn't seem to escape wall-to-wall brown carpet. In the flat landscape of eastern Aurora, I had to squint to see the distant mountains. Sometimes, I felt like an astronaut hurtled from a space shuttle, momentum carrying me farther and farther away, too fast for any rescue attempt. I joked that east Aurora was like living a stone's throw from Kansas. Dorothy's tornado swept her away from Kansas. My life's tornado had dumped me closer.

I ran some calculations. If I paid $525 for rent and $30 per week on food (which I managed by buying beans, oatmeal, flour, and other staples in bulk at Sam's Club), I'd still had cash remaining. I decided to cut every unnecessary expense. No entertainment. No travel. I'd spend money for work, eating, and sleeping.

This is my chance to finally build wealth.

I devoted myself to an experiment. When my paycheck hit my bank account, I diverted 10% to a savings account and donated another 10% to charity. For someone bringing home less than $350 a week, it seemed crazy to earmark 20% and give away half of that.

Here was my reasoning. By saving and giving away money before paying bills, I was practicing the actions of a wealthy person, and *embodying the qualities* of a wealthy person. And I was doing it within reason—I crunched the numbers to make sure I could survive.

Everyone has experienced the phenomenon of *when it rains, it pours*. Have you ever been desperate for a job and gotten zero offers? Yet, when you finally landed a gig, floods of offers came your way. My experiment was to metaphorically make it rain to encourage a downpour; I was going to reverse-engineer the process. I wanted proof that when you build wealth and give it away—even a tiny amount—you create opportunity for more wealth. Similar to how, when you open yourself to more energy, you create opportunity for emotional, psychological, and mental transformation. The idea wasn't original to me, but I intended to see if it would work *for* me.

Instead of scrambling for wealth, which seemed as useless as fighting one's thoughts, I embodied wealthy practices in the present moment. Instead of hoping for wealth down the road, I proved I already had it, $30 at a time.

Once I crafted my weekly budget, I calculated that I had only an additional $40 per week—at most—to fund my entrepreneurial efforts, with no more room to jump from opportunity to opportunity. I had to face my emotional blocks to setting up a sound business: my impatience, overinflated ego, and a desire for a magic button.

But would it work? At least one former teacher of mine would laugh at what I was doing. "You're trying to scrimp and save your way to wealth!"

A common refrain in the self-help world is that millionaires have multiple streams of income. I misinterpreted this as running around like a beheaded chicken to start up multiple half-baked businesses. Later, I learned that most millionaires meticulously construct a single source of income, like creating a local business or practicing medicine or law, and then invest their profits to multiply their income streams. The result appears complicated, sexy, and exciting. The genesis is simple, boring, and often painful.

You need *simple, boring, and often painful* to push your project forward after the luster has worn off. If you bounce to something that looks easier or more exciting, you'll never cross the chasm between you and lasting success.

Simple, boring, and often painful, paradoxically, can feel like the opposite. When you devote yourself, the pain can galvanize your growth, the boredom can bring you a quiet joy, and the simplicity can fulfill you as no extravagance could. Wealthy people often cherish the memories of when they could barely afford a couch while they put themselves through school or funded their business. They may not have practiced Daoist meditation, but they were walking a different path up the same mountain and their energy supported their journey.

When I drove to work after that failed advertisement, I was staring down a path of drudgery. But my devotion to my eventual success and my belief in myself, as well as a more mature perspective and a dash of faith, transformed that moment for me. Simple, boring, and painful became joyful.

Before my bankruptcy, I craved looking strong, smart, and successful, even if it was an illusion. When I walked around in public, my lower back clenched with the question, *"What do people think of how I look?"*

When I became a smock-wearing, sunburned sign-spinner who looked like a bozo to everyone driving by, my illusions got sledgehammered. An average person can lose their mind if their possessions get destroyed, whereas monks give up their possessions and lose only mental shackles. Both end up with nothing, but the monk feels free. I chose to feel free.

That's why simplifying my existence was easy. It cleared my mind to focus on creating the life I wanted. I also had the physical, energetic, and spiritual capacity to devote myself to what I needed to do.

"Our harmony and focus allow us
To work all day at a single task
And not grow tired."[34]

When you simplify, you create space to devote yourself to the tasks you need to accomplish. There's no devotion without sacrifice. Devotion is more than a drive or a strong habit. When you devote yourself, you give your energy to something greater than yourself and cut off other possibilities. Devotion is like marriage, as you say "Yes!" to one person and "No!" to everyone else.

The construction of the word devotion is based on cutting out other possibilities. The "de" in devote is Latin for "down to the bottom, totally." The rest of the word refers to the vow you're making, and connotes sacrifice. It sounds grim. It can *feel* grim when you begin. And, if you devote yourself to something wrong for you, it can be grim.

Devotion means giving up more than you could imagine because you're saying no to the benefits of doing something else. This is called the opportunity cost. Your devotion can cost money, time, and effort put toward other things. For example, if you watch a half hour of the news, it will take up half an hour of your time, which is the cost. But the opportunity cost is how you could have enjoyed greater health by using that half-hour for exercise or greater fulfillment in life by catching up with a friend or meditating or building greater wealth by studying how to invest. You could have done any of those things, but you chose television. This isn't a guilt trip—it's a way of consciously deciding if something is worthwhile.

When I said devotion can seem grim, I wasn't kidding. If you want to change your life, you need to be this blunt with yourself. But here's the paradox. When you practice devotion and give up so much, you receive more than you ever imagined. I felt the happiest I'd ever been after moving to east Aurora and working as a sign-spinner.

When you partner with one lover who's right for you, you receive more joy and love than you thought you could handle. When you devote yourself to studying and apprenticing for one career that's right for you, you receive more wealth than you'll ever need. When you devote yourself to the foods and exercises that are right for you and sacrifice the ones that aren't, you receive all the health you want. Your returns aren't balanced. They come back *multiplied*. Nothing's guaranteed. Careers can end. But the practice of devotion will always help you because devotion can help you recover quicker.

Muhammed Ali said to himself, "Suffer now and live the rest of your life as a champion." The good news is, suffering is in your head, even when the pain is real. The financial handcuffs that followed me after my bankruptcy were very real, but that didn't stop me from feeling good. When you devote yourself to something greater than your immediate gratification, you escape suffering, even if you don't escape pain. I don't know for sure, but I think Muhammed Ali would agree. He might even approve of my edit:

"Devote yourself now to live your life as a champion."

Here's how to put this into practice. Make a list of everything you do in your day. Write down the benefits of each activity. Write down the opportunity costs. You're not just listing the drawbacks of an activity, but *the benefits of something you'll miss out on*. That's the difference between cost and opportunity cost—and it's a more intelligent way to make decisions.

Warren Buffet is a billionaire, in part, because of thinking like this. Instead of regarding a can of soda as costing a dollar or two, he considers the opportunity cost of *how he could have invested those one or two dollars and let the seed capital compound itself over decades*. With that kind of opportunity cost, each can of soda might cost a couple hundred dollars—or more—of future wealth. How would your spending habits change if you added a zero or two to the price sticker of every potential purchase? Cup of coffee? $30. Run-of-the-mill new car? $300,000.

Every time you buy something, mentally add a zero to the price and kiss that future wealth goodbye—and make it a loving kiss where you truly accept the tradeoff. This isn't a push to be miserly, but to show how unnecessary additions to your life destroy your more profound wishes and dreams.

Opportunity cost applies to time, as well. Just as spent money could have been invested elsewhere to produce wealth, spent time could have been used elsewhere to improve your life. An hour spent watching *Game of Thrones* could have been used to read a book about financial planning. Again, this isn't to guilt you out of watching a good show, but to make your choices with eyes wide open. When I watch The Hound verbally joust with Arya and then lose a duel with Brienne of Tarth, I know I could do many other things, but I choose to enjoy the show. When you include opportunity cost in your life choices, your life will get better and you'll paradoxically end up with more choice. Warren Buffet purportedly still drinks at least five cans of soda per day—he probably feels the financial sacrifice is worth it and he can certainly afford the splurge.

Put the Immortal Post on your activity list, too. You've read the potential benefits and some of the costs. It takes time. Your legs and shoulders might feel sore. You might need to wake up earlier to practice. Time spent in the Immortal Post means less time socializing or reading. You might miss out on some benefits of sleep. You'll have opportunity costs.

Once you've made your list, you'll have a bird's eye view of which activities enrich your life and which make it more complex. Look it over, and see how you could build your health or wealth or strengthen your bond with your family. Think about the joy that could bring you. Now whittle away at your lifestyle. What can you simplify? What can you sacrifice? Where can you create space for more devotion to that which fulfills you?

Find what you could live without. If an item on your list costs you something you cherish, get rid of it. You could give up a favorite television show so you can exercise for 30 minutes. When you write down the benefits and opportunity costs and stare them in the face, it's simpler to make the choice—but still not easy, because you're sacrificing. Many habit-building techniques try to tip-toe around sacrifice. Instead, we're going to sprint straight toward it, warmly embrace it in our arms, and cherish sacrifice like a lover.

When you simplify your life, you get a clearer head, along with more mental discipline and confidence. Many people drown themselves in chaos, addicted to the cheap brain stimulation that's little different from the way artificial sugar plays with your neurons. If someone's electronic devices aren't buzzing and they aren't rushing from one obligation to the next, they'll face silence and the emotional suffering that brings (remember the experiment with electric shocks?).

When I settled in that east Aurora condo, I had time to reflect on how my life had gone wrong. It was clear that, when I didn't devote myself and when I didn't simplify, I suffered.

Simplicity nourishes your spiritual discipline. Many people dive into a spiritual practice and their emotional gunk starts to bubble up. They think something's wrong, quit the practice, and jump to something else. They're not practicing spiritual discipline—they're playing as spiritual tourists. It's a trap because when you hop from practice to practice, idea to idea, book to book, guru to guru, you can claim you're walking a spiritual path—or some sort of path. The reality is, you're staggering between paths at a crossroad.

We all have excuses. "I don't have time! I've got too many responsibilities!" or "I can't do this every single day!" or "I'm not strong enough for this!" or even the sneaky, "This isn't working!" when you don't get instant results. That last excuse was the ace up my sleeve. Before learning the Immortal Post, I dabbled in other spiritual practices, like deep breathing and guided meditations. I believe the Immortal Post works better because it combines the mental and physical to open yourself to healing energy, but my lack of discipline prevented me from success with other practices. I clawed for results from whatever shiny spiritual bauble I grabbed before throwing it aside.

When I stood there and embraced something simple, painful, and effective, results came. I had to give up my projection of what the results would be. You noticed that I got a low-paying job and went bankrupt *after* I learned the Immortal Post. My life did turn around, but not as fast as I wanted and the standing meditation didn't help me avoid pain.

By simplifying my life and my spiritual practice, I stopped thinking "I'll try X now and see if it benefits me instantly," and I stopped asking, "Okay, what's next?" in favor of, "How can I take this deeper?" I stopped running toward an imaginary pot of gold and started digging for real, but hidden, riches.

Keep your Immortal Post practice simple. Then you'll have the mental, physical, energetic, and spiritual capacity to devote yourself to it and get the most out of it. **As relaxation is a foundation for going deeper with the Immortal Post, devotion is a foundation for journeying forward with it.**

Simplifying your practice and devoting yourself will help you face the pain—both physical and emotional—that will come up.

"When most people
Hear about the Great Integrity,
They waver between belief and disbelief.
When wise people
Hear about the Great Integrity,
They diligently follow its path.
When ignorant people hear about it
They laugh out loud!
By this very laughter,
We know its authenticity."[35]

The day after I learned the Immortal Post, I practiced in my hotel room for 60 seconds, using a timer on my computer. I tried doing another couple of rounds and my thighs burned from the struggle…but I felt good. Something felt *right*.

60 seconds was a good start. The next morning, I flew back to my condo and did another 60 seconds. The next day, I increased the time to 65 seconds. My muscles could handle the small increase and even five seconds was progress.

It hurt. Still, I added five seconds. Standing for 65 seconds was as painful as a minute, but I made it. 70 seconds was just as painful, too. As one minute turned into two, it still hurt, but I didn't quit. My mind flashed to stories of ancient Daoists achieving enlightenment. An inner knowingness spurred me to keep my practice simple.

My legs got strong enough that I could add more than five seconds at a time. *Huh*. I did the rough math in my head. *If I add ten seconds per day, I'll add about a minute per week to my practice. In less than a couple of months, I'll be doing ten minutes. In a couple more, 20 minutes*. It was fun to ponder my progress. But the important part was that I never skipped a day. If I'd decided to practice three days per week, it would have become twice per week, and then once per week, and then I would have quit.

Some days, I'd sit, knowing it was time to practice, but feeling like my butt was welded to my seat. I'd think about how, as soon as I started, my shoulders would burn, my thighs would ache, and my mind would start screaming like a two-year-old having a meltdown. So, I'd sit and dwell on it, decide to get up and do it, then decide to think about how much it's going to hurt, then berate myself for not doing it, and repeat this cycle for another few minutes—sometimes almost half an hour—and then, finally, do it.

My practice was so simple that discipline became a byproduct, as naturally as a tree grows fruit. A decade later, I can count the number of days I've skipped on one hand—usually days I was sick with the flu.

I kept my intention simple: do the Immortal Post with the best form I could, for five seconds longer. I kept my attention on perfecting my practice little by little. My sensations were simple—the meditation hurt! But as long as it wasn't sharp pain, I persevered. I used my imagination to help my muscles relax and, when I wasn't practicing, to remind myself I was continuing a tradition that goes back thousands of years.

Let's break down my training routine:

1. Do the Immortal Post in the morning for 60 seconds.
2. Add five seconds per day.
3. Repeat.
4. Make bigger increases in time when I was strong enough.
5. When I got to 25 minutes, I maintained that.

Simple, but not easy. When your thighs feel like scrambled eggs starting to sizzle on the skillet and you sneak a peek at your timer, thinking *of course this must almost be over* and your timer hasn't even ticked halfway down, you'll know how "not easy" this is. It'll be your make-or-break moment when devotion goes beyond a concept to something you embody.

I created a miniature ritual to prepare for the Immortal Post. I shut down my electronics to simplify my environment and my sensory input. I deepened and slowed my breathing, used the bathroom, maybe took a drink of water, and primed my body and mind for what I was about to do. Sometimes, I sat and dreaded what was coming but, either way, these rituals helped make the difference between new levels of alignment and stillness...or just standing there.

By creating the atmosphere of a sacred ritual, I helped my mind slow down, recognized that everything was safe, and prepared for inner work. I signaled my body to relax. I didn't psych myself up, but struck a balance between excitement and equanimity. This calm intensity focused and relaxed me, which was essential for my progress.

Meditation is as sacred as you make it. **When you devote yourself to your practice, you're proving that you and your growth matter.** Then your growth is unstoppable.

Here's how to harness simplicity during your Immortal Post practice. Pick one focus for every training session. You've already learned how to relax and align your body and quiet your mind. Choose a focus from those three. Then pick one of the techniques from this book and focus on that for your day's training. You could use the practice session to focus on your breathing, or imagine pushing the ceiling with the top of your head, or breathe into your tense muscles. You don't need to stick with one thing. There's value in switching focuses during your practice. But few people simplify and go deep on one.

Even the spiritual path contains a thousand and one distractions. They'll tempt you most when you're bored, hurting, and wondering if you're missing something. They'll also tempt you most when you're nearing a breakthrough because all breakthroughs involve a reshuffling of your ingrained emotional patterns.

Lao Tzu said, "The journey of a thousand miles begins with one step." Many people forget the thousand-mile journey continues with another step, and another, and another, frequently in the same direction with little change of scenery. *Simple, boring, and often painful.* Sometimes, my life seemed as if I was trudging toward a worse hell, but

I remembered other times when I felt strength and inner peace from the standing meditation, so I never quit.

What about my experiment saving $30 a week? By testing the idea, I discovered that it worked better than all the visualization and goal-setting I'd done. Even though it was only $30 at a time, my wealth-building was a fact. Every time I saved another 10% of my income, I proved my wealth was growing. If I could do it over, I'd be more careful about giving to charity. Judging by the volumes of direct mail I got after making a donation—and still receive to this day—I think I merely contributed to the charities' marketing budgets.

It seems too obvious to be profound. $30 a week seems insignificant because it is. But the experiment's power wasn't in the numbers. I switched from wanting and scrambling for success to embodying it. I wondered if I could afford it, but uncanny happenings supported me, like my car breaking down fewer times.

Plus, I slept better and felt more secure during the day, which clued me into how stressed I was before. I wished I could go back to my younger self and say, "I know you want to get wealthy. I know you want to achieve your goals. But I'm begging you, make your life simple. It will look boring on the outside, but you'll feel so good on the inside that you won't care. Plus, by simplifying your life, you'll develop the spiritual swagger you need to attract the opportunities you want."

In a negotiation, the person facing you from across the table can smell if you're desperate. I was discovering the energetic realm was no different. And you can't just say, "Yeah, yeah, I feel wealthy." You need to put your money where your mouth is—a fitting cliché here.

But $50,000 of debt was still stalking me and growing. I needed to simplify my business efforts. During my downward spiral, my list of former business partners rivaled a dysfunctional single's little black book. There were many reasons for my string of failures, but a root problem was my lack of focus. Instead of zeroing in on a single business idea like a laser, I flitted my focus around like a flashlight.

As the weeks turned into months, my savings turned from tens of dollars to hundreds. No matter what kind of financial chaos hit me, I always saved a little more. While my co-workers—even the ones who made more money than I did—complained of money problems, my situation and my inner peace kept improving.

The company's owner opened more and more stores, expanding as fast as he could. It seemed like, as gold's price kept rising, there was no limit to how big his business could get.

The simpler life gave me the time and energy to ask and answer, "How do I climb out?"

In the next chapter, I'll reveal the surprising way people burn up their chi and sabotage their lives.

CHAPTER FOURTEEN

TEMPER YOUR EMOTIONS

I might as well have snorted a line of cocaine.

I floated down the aisle of a King Soopers grocery store, off Speer Boulevard in Denver. My eyes darted around the shelves, drinking in the brighter blues, greens, and reds of the product labels, but I didn't want to buy anything. The scent of semi-fresh croissants wafted from the bakery, mixing with the distinct supermarket air conditioning and the fresh coating of disinfectant, like grocery store cologne. My senses were in overdrive yet everything felt 1,000 miles away. It was late January 2012, a few months before I went bankrupt and moved to east Aurora. Two weeks earlier, my advertising campaign had crashed and burned, leading to my *Who are you?* mental breakthrough when I drove to my job the next morning.

I'd paid for two ads to run two weeks apart, and it would be a disaster to reuse the same ad and webpage, unless I felt like languishing on the floor and groaning in the fetal position all over again. I decided to throw out all the contractor's work and rewrite everything. Two weeks was enough time to get the website redone before the second advertisement launched.

As the second ad's deployment day approached, I thought about how it would perform, but I wasn't nearly as fixated as the first time. On launch morning, I checked the stats before going to work. Three orders. *Okay, good. At least something's happening.*

At work, I enjoyed the unusually warm January day. I mostly forgot the advertisement was running—until it was time to clock out. Driving home, I wondered if I'd come close to making my money back on the $900 cost of the advertisement. *Hmmm.* We'll see.

Déjà vu kicked in as I parked, rode the too-slow elevator, entered my apartment, and turned on my computer. Last time, I'd been gut-punched with $0. But this time I already knew there would be at least three orders, maybe more.

I typed my password into the order-tracking software.

The screen loaded: Over $1,100.

A profit! A f&%$ing profit!

I read the stats over and over, then looked around my living room to confirm I wasn't dreaming. Instead of slinking onto the floor, I sat, stared, and my mind revved from second to fourth gear. These were the results I'd craved and they seemed to prove the money floodgates *could* get cranked open—I just had to place more ads. I counted up my future earnings and imagined living the good life in Denver, traveling, enjoying beaches and hot tubs. Hot tubs on beaches? It didn't matter; my brain was flooded with pleasure chemicals, as if a dam had broken and unleashed a dopamine tsunami, or I'd done a line of cocaine. I threw on my shoes, floated out the door, and power walked up and down the aisles at King Soopers. Everything looked beautiful, even the drug addicts standing around the stained asphalt out front. After I returned home that night, it took a couple of hours to fall asleep.

The next morning, my alarm blared. My memory of the ad campaign's results felt hollow and distant, even though it was just the night before. A hangover hit me as if I'd thrown back several whiskey shots, even though I hadn't drank anything.

My supervisor for the day buzzed me through the front door. I marched across the lobby to the break room, threw on the smock, and grabbed the sign. The clock showed 10:18AM. *Ugh.* The weather had veered from unusually warm to a blizzard, and the winds stung my face like wasps. As I stood on the street corner, I clenched my teeth, almost crouching while clutching my sign. *Why do I feel bad? What's wrong with me?* My confusion and guilt made me angrier. None of this made sense. *Why wasn't I still elated?*

Ever gotten promoted, graduated, or taken a dream vacation, ended up miserable, and wondered why? Whenever you desire something in life, your brain floods with dopamine—the reward hormone. It gives you a taste of pleasure and motivation, to get you going. As you race toward a goal, your dopamine rises, like zooming toward an orgasm (you do get waves of dopamine during sex).

The closer you get to achieving what you want, the more you might say to yourself, "Ah, yes! I'm on my way!" Life is grand, nothing can touch me now, and joy will last forever...but all highs lead to a crash.[36,37] It's like attending a too-long party when the alcohol gets cut off and you're stuck in a room of rapidly-sobering, hungover strangers who are no longer as interesting or attractive as when the night began.

When you buckle up for the dopamine roller coaster and relish the first climb, you might assume your new circumstances made you feel so good. But on a biological level, it's the temporary rush of the hormones. When the rush fades, so will your pleasure. You might feel sad, anxious or irritated. You'll probably think you *should* be feeling wonderful, but you don't. Then you feel *guilty* and the cycle worsens, which is what happened to me.

Ancient Daoists understood that emotions, if they become stagnant, harm your health. One such emotion is overexcitement. Many people will pay good money—or take drugs—to feel overexcited, but there's an additional price to pay because your brain has a devious trick up its sleeve. As you clamber toward a goal, dopamine will rise and rise until you achieve it, but the dopamine will vanish just as quickly. Dopamine is a hormonal fair-weather friend. When I awoke that morning with a hormone hangover, my dopamine had already gathered its things and snuck out in the middle of the night.

Then you feel confused and guilty with what you've achieved. Your circumstances are the same: you still have your promotion or you're still on your dream vacation, but you don't feel good. You might push yourself to achieve something else, chasing the high.

Some people push themselves to get an education they hate, to get a job they can't stand, to receive a paycheck to buy things they hope will perpetuate the dopamine drip. When I was in high school, someone told me he was going to attend an engineering college that was 90% male and he kept complaining how miserable he was going to be.

"Then why are you going to that school?"

"My dad said that if I don't go there and get an engineering degree, he won't pay for college," he said.

As my friend predicted, he was miserable in school. I'm guessing he's now making good money as an engineer, chasing little hits of dopamine wherever he can, and will never know how else he might have lived.

The night when I practically drooled at my advertisement's results, I failed the test of managing my emotions and self-talk. I scheduled more advertising campaigns and, like many activities that light up the brain's pleasure centers, the rewards were short-lived. The next campaign profited less. Then it didn't profit at all. And then I started to lose money. I confirmed I'd be a sign-spinner for a long time.

Emotional roller coasters have an energetic danger, best described by one of my teachers, Dr. William Welch, Jr.

Doing daily energetic practices like the Immortal Post is like stacking pages of rice paper. Rice paper is so thin that it's almost translucent. But as thin as it is, if you keep adding another page every day, you'll build a thick stack. But what if you lit a match and set the stack ablaze? All the pages you took so long to stack would burn in a minute. When you let your emotions rage out of control, that's what happens to your chi. It could be fear or anger or grief or even overexcitement—the result is the same. You burn the energy you've cultivated.

Emotions require fuel to build and sustain themselves, and they get this fuel from chi. When your emotions overpower you, you burn chi like crazy, even if you feel good. You'll pay for it later, both with a hormone hangover and a life that doesn't seem to progress and grow.

That's why Daoists are adamant about tempering your emotions.

Don't chase emotional highs and don't run scared from emotional lows. Cultivate devotion and embrace fulfillment.

This doesn't mean "become an emotionless robot." Stuffing your emotions isn't enlightenment. Even emotions like fear and anger are useful. Fear alerts you to danger and anger compels you to set boundaries. Emotions are warning messages that blip on your radar screen and bloop off just as quickly. Trouble comes when these emotions grip you for more than a few seconds, as they burn chi for fuel. Then they become stagnant in your body and you develop coping mechanisms—which also burn chi.

You can't dismantle the roller coaster of your emotions, but you can make the drops less precarious, the rises less nosebleed-inducing, and the twists and turns less nauseating. One of the biggest keys is knowing the roller coaster exists. When you remind yourself how fleeting emotions can be, you can let them slip away.

When you relax your body, you allow the energy to flow and process your emotions faster. When you quiet your mind, you become less identified with your emotions.

Here's what this difference can look like. Someone identified with his or her emotions and allowing them to become stagnant might say something like:

"I'm so pissed off."

"I'm so worried. I feel sick to my stomach."

But someone less identified with his or her emotions who's allowing them to process might say something like:

"Ah, there's anger popping up. I feel the blood rushing to my face and neck."

"That's worry I'm feeling right now. My solar plexus is flexing."

Whenever I feel an emotion bubble up, I call it by name: "Ah, that's anger." Then I focus on the sensations. By paying attention to them as an observer, I reduce their power. Sometimes, it works like a charm. Other times, not so much. An hour ago, anger burst through my body while doing the Immortal Post, and I wanted to roar and tear my office's door off its hinges, but I knew how to respond. I relaxed my body, kept my stance aligned, and treated the anger as a guest. It grabbed its hat, tied its shoes, and exited the door—which remained intact.

I also employ another method to take the reins on emotions.

USING THE BREATH

"We return to our breathing.
It knows exactly what to do."[38]

Here's a test to make sure you're breathing properly for tempering emotions. Place your left hand on your belly and your right hand on your chest. Breathe in and out a few times. How did your hands move? If the hand on your belly moved up first and was followed by the hand on your chest, you breathed to stay relaxed. If the hand on your chest moved up and down, but the hand on your belly remained still, your breathing was tense and agitated.

When you breathe into your belly first, you're not literally inhaling air into there, but it helps to imagine that you are. When you belly-breathe, you activate the diaphragmatic muscle in your solar plexus. This allows your lungs—empty sacks—to fully inflate and deflate, while massaging your internal organs such as your large and small intestine, liver, spleen, stomach, and gall bladder. Your digestion will improve, your stress levels will drop, and your mood will be better.[39] When you practice the Immortal Post and your mind races, deep breathing helps draw your energy downward, which helps quiet your mind.

When do you know you're finished processing your emotions? As one of my teachers, Dr. Diego Sanmiquel, likes to say, "Find the nearest pool and step onto it. If you can walk on water, you're done. If you sink to the bottom…"

Deepening and slowing your breathing and consciously observing your emotions are keys to feel at peace, no matter your circumstances.

HERE'S WHAT TO DO WHEN YOU MANAGE YOUR EMOTIONS UNTIL YOU'RE BLUE IN THE FACE AND YOUR DAYS ARE STILL CRAPPY.

Think of the last time you visited the beach. When the tide rushed in, did you panic and think the ocean would swallow you? Or did you understand that it would soon retreat?

As I worked as a sign-spinner and faced the same, simple days, I got better at spotting patterns. I began to think of my days, weeks, and months in terms of *ebb* and *flow*—like an ocean tide.

When I felt tired during my shift for no good reason and people flipped me off more than usual, and when even my meditations weren't going well, I sometimes called it an ebb day. It wasn't a coping mechanism to subtly point to myself as a victim, but to acknowledge the ups and downs of life. If I felt amazing the next day, buzzed with energy during my mediations and got cheers from traffic, I felt grateful—while reminding myself that flows come with ebbs. Relaxing on my ebb days and remaining calm during my flow days led to a smoother life.

Some of my closest friends know exactly what I mean when I say, "I'm having an ebb day." It's not a good or bad day, nor cause for despair or celebration. It means that things appear to be receding, but life is gearing up to flow again.

Value investors get rich in one of the most boring ways one could picture. They study companies, invest in them, and do nothing else for a couple of decades. Sometimes, the companies' stock prices plummet and it looks as if the investor lost a fortune. Other times, the price spikes and the investor appears to have gained a fortune. Mostly, it bounces up and down and, mostly, the value investor doesn't care. If it's a good company and they bought the stock at a fair price, they're happy because they know the real fortune builds long-term.[*]

Same with your life. Some days may be awful and others exemplary, but you'll keep yourself stuck if you judge your life by a single day's results. Instead, track the value of your habits and devotions over time. That sounds like a truism, but when you're in the middle of a massive failure or riding the drug-like high of a success, it's the first thing you forget.

Here's how to apply this to the Immortal Post. As you practice, emotions will bubble up. They'll smack against your mind like bugs on your windshield. Observe the emotions without taking them seriously, name them, and relax as you breathe into your belly.

Then you can release these negative emotions from the deep recesses of your body, like cleaning gunk from a refrigerator shelf. It

* And for the investors reading this whose blood pressure I can already feel rising, please understand this is a simplified example.

will look and smell nasty, but it's evidence you're clearing out emotional stagnation.

If you feel bad after doing the standing meditation, it doesn't mean you failed or that the meditation isn't working. Clean-up jobs and construction projects don't look pretty until they're done. This isn't a gentle meditation for relieving stress—it's serious medicine that Daoists have used for thousands of years for deep inner work.

Just as you can call out days as ebb or flow, you can do so for your standing meditations. Some will suck, no matter how much deep breathing you do. This is often true in the first couple of months, when it's most crucial to call an ebb an ebb and know the tide will come back in.

When you get in the flow during your Immortal Post practice, acknowledge it and feel good about it. Just don't hold yourself to the same standard every time. When I felt like a glowing sun, I didn't assume I'd always feel that way. I didn't think I had "made it," either. I took it as a good sign—a life-changing sign—and redoubled my commitment to the practice.

Measure your progress over months and years. On any given day, your thoughts will be loud or quiet, you'll feel tired or energized, hot or cold, tense or relaxed, and you can drive yourself nuts trying to make sense of day-to-day progress. If I'd given myself only a few days to judge whether the Immortal Post would change my life, I'd have quit. But because I was inspired and knew the benefits would come slowly, I stuck with it.

In the next chapter, I'll reveal how this practice helped me break another addiction—and warn you about a surprising enemy you'll face if you want to change your life.

CHAPTER FIFTEEN

SOLITUDE

During a sign-spinning shift, a car creeped to a stop in the middle of the road. Two men in the front seats pummeled each other with their fists.

The driver bailed out and the passenger hopped into his seat, wrenched the door shut and drove away. As he did, I dropped my sign, fished into my pocket for my phone, and called 911.

"What's your address?"

I told the operator.

"What's your emergency?"

I described the fight and carjacking. The operator thanked me and hung up.

Wow, that was efficient.

I grabbed my sign, hoping the driver hadn't seen me call. I glanced behind me as casually as I could. The driver, half-naked and chest spattered with blood, marched up the sidewalk toward me.

What was he going to do?

Since starting the job several months earlier, I felt like someone who had stopped struggling against a river's current and allowed the ripples to lift them where they needed to go. I practiced the Immortal Post daily.

Because I stood outside almost all day, I hardly spoke to anyone. People honked their horns, sometimes to cheer me on and other times to make rude gestures. People threw stuff at me—they missed—catcalled me, and someone even made a goat noise. None of the insults came close to the monstrous ways I'd talked to myself, three years prior.

After that drug-fueled woman I mentioned earlier grabbed me during a shift and then raced away, I wondered why it had happened. Wasn't all my meditation supposed to prevent stuff like that? But instead of asking *what's wrong with me* I switched to *what's the lesson in this*, and the next time the woman walked by, I stood with more confidence. She said hi while skirting a perimeter around me. *Good.*

On the outside, I appeared as some burnout who needed to make a buck. On the inside, I was beaming.

"You look like a hundred bucks!" people would sometimes joke, referencing my $100 bill costume. I'd respond, "And I feel like a million!"

One warm and quiet spring day on that street corner, I stood with my jaw dropped open. Cars lazily drifted by. But the weather and the traffic weren't why I basked in a state of awe. Instead, it was the warm breeze carrying seeds toward me—millions of them. They permeated the parking lots on both sides of the road and the road itself, like a gentle blizzard. Clouds of seeds drifted through the air.

What were they? Where did they come from? I didn't know they were cottonwood seeds and I glanced around to check if anyone was seeing what I was, but the drivers kept driving. How could they not be amazed by this display of nature? I peeled my headphones from my ears and stood, not crying, but *almost.*

I don't know how long this is going to last, so I'm going to savor it.

As the seeds rode the waves of the wind, the sun lit their wispy edges, making them glow. Their white bodies perfectly complemented the blue sky, with the occasional streak of clouds.

Some cartwheeled close enough to bounce against my sign, zooming around it, driven away as if the seeds were the ocean's water and my sign was the hull of a speeding ship.

The seed storm lasted many minutes. I'm not sure how many. I lost track of time.

My job helped relax my torso and let my body loosen. After all, I was moving all day. Waving the sign caused my spine to crack, sometimes hundreds of times per day, as if getting a constant chiropractic adjustment. I kept mental and written notes of where I felt them. The cracks hovered around my pelvis and began inching upwards. Maybe an inch per month. Occasionally, they'd leap up my back a few inches.

Soon, the space between my traps cracked. Would my financial situation change, once the cracks reached the top of my spine, as I'd wondered months earlier?

Standing outside all day, I got paid by the hour for a front row seat (without the actual seat), for life's dramas and miracles, while selecting the soundtrack of my choice on my headphones. Mostly, I listened to audiobooks.

A year earlier, my friend Jim—who'd generously paid our dinner tab in Boulder—had recommended a book called *The Awesome Science of Luck* by someone named Peter Ragnar, and I'd been learning from him since. Peter had spent a few decades as a hermit in the Tennessee mountains. I was drawn to him because, even though he was born in the generation before baby boomers, he was stronger and healthier than just about anyone I knew. He also went from working construction jobs to becoming a self-made millionaire and, best of all, he had many experience-based insights into Daoism.

For several months, I started every shift by shimmying into my costume, pouring coffee into my Styrofoam cup, grabbing a big, orange sign, and striding outside. I set the coffee on the sidewalk to my left, pulled on my headphones, and clicked the MP3 button to start a 90-minute interview that Peter gave on making money. As the intro music started, I took my first coffee sip and waved around my sign. *Best job in the world.* As I worked, his wisdom echoed from my headphones into my brain.

I had time to sit with my own mind, take in the train wreck of the past few years, and map out where to go. As a child and a teenager, I was emotionally shut down, angry, and disassociated from reality. I stumbled through life drunk on coping mechanisms and later, on alcohol.

Solitude and time allowed me to see how I'd been the architect of my failures. By being quiet, I could listen to my mind's workings and pick up on cause and effect. I acknowledged one of my ways to self-sabotage was getting perverse pleasure when someone's advice failed me. There was a twisted elitism in looking someone in the eye and declaring, "*Nothing* has worked for me." My failure felt better if I could drag down the person trying to help me, so I could dump the pain of responsibility on them. It was relieving to think I was cursed—if I had no hope, then it was pointless to put in effort.* I learned my words had had no power

* Oddly, as I studied Daoism deeper and learned how curses work, I discovered they don't absolve anyone from self-responsibility because you have the choice to unravel a curse.

behind them because I was trying to manifest fantasies rather than be real about my growth.

After almost two years of practicing the Immortal Post and shredding my old life, I started over. With my meager pay and a job so monotonous that some new hires quit after one hour, I could have felt imprisoned. But it was more like the universe dropped me into a new training ground to learn about the world, handing me soft, simple toys so I wouldn't hurt myself. I had a cheap condo. I had a job that paid my rent and car. I spent $30 a week on food and lost so much weight that my hundred-dollar-bill costume hung off me—at least in the summer. In the winter, when I wore three pairs of pants, a t-shirt, sweatshirt, fleece, hoodie, and jacket, shimmying into the costume and pulling it off felt like putting on and peeling off a full-body condom.

I was supervised by people in the store, usually an attractive woman in her mid-20s. I got to know them as real people and hear about their lives and their struggles—even taking one supervisor to the emergency room after she got gold-testing acid in her eye ("Well, now we know you're not made of gold," I tried to joke). Some of my co-workers looked and sounded like people from my high school. I don't mean that as a judgment of maturity—I mean they physically looked and sounded like them. One woman could have been a twin of someone who used to make fun of me, right down to her eerily similar name. Was I getting a do-over for all those years?

The women hardly learned a thing about me because I practiced listening. Here and there, I gave advice, cautious to say only what had worked for me and only when someone wanted to hear it.

That's how Daoists help others. By taking care of your own gunk, you help others with theirs. Our energy interacts—we swim in an ocean of it—so when we do something to raise ourselves energetically, we help our community.

There's an old saying. "Before enlightenment, chop wood and carry water. After enlightenment, chop wood and carry water." I wasn't enlightened, but I recognized how much I'd screwed up my wood-chopping and water-carrying before I began the standing meditation. This time, I'd be different, and if I had to prove myself with tasks that seemed menial, so be it.

I've heard some businessmen joke that they were "unemployable" and that's why they became entrepreneurs. I tried to adopt that badge of honor, but it was a clever line to cover up how lazy, disorganized, unfocused, and childish I was. Now was my time to chop wood, carry water, and prove I was employable.

I scrubbed toilets, cleaned windows, tolerated people shouting at me from their cars, worked every shift without cutting corners on time, sunburned in 100-degree summer heat, bundled layers against bitter and windy winter cold, and did my best to bask in every miracle along the way.

I picked up pennies, nickels, dimes, and the occasional quarter, writing about my good luck in a journal. When my work shift put me in view of the Rocky Mountains, I gazed at them, thinking about the day I'd live closer to their peaks. I lusted after them, as if my staring would propel me closer. Or maybe the opposite—if I lost sight of them, they'd drift away forever. I got used to smelling car exhaust and, when I was lucky, the wind engulfed me with the sweet scent of grass and trees.

At every lunch break, I sat on a plastic folding chair in the silent backroom and did an Inner Smile meditation. For around ten minutes,

I imagined a happy, smiling, golden energy drip down and through my body, bathing every organ and cell in smiling energy.

My mind was so relaxed during my work shifts that, in the evenings and on weekends, it was easy to focus on my business. While eating lunch, I phoned vendors. Every time I had enough spare cash, I spent it to test out my marketing ideas. I still learned from Doberman Dan.

One of his call-in days fell on my work shift. While standing on the street corner and waving my sign with one hand, I dialed his number with my other. When he picked up, I took my break.

I found myself regarding people with profound love. When I realized that I felt this while looking at smiling women in passing cars, and then their pissed-off-looking boyfriends, and felt the same love for them, I knew my heart was opening.

Every few months, a letter would arrive from the IRS, reminding me that I was still on "Status: Non-Collectible"—their term for "you're too broke for us to squeeze you" and that I had the option to make some voluntary payments, perhaps their way of saying, "You do realize we're charging so much interest on this debt that your bill will eventually require a forklift to deliver, right?"

I began to relish my challenges in a strangely peaceful way. The more hopeless my life looked, the more excited I got for my comeback. My Nissan Altima—getting long in the tooth—failed its emissions testing. I couldn't afford to replace the catalytic converter and my plates expired. Because police patrolled the parking lot of my condo complex, I couldn't park there. A sign-spinning co-worker gave me an idea—park at a supermarket open 24/7.

"They'll just think you're an employee there!" he said.

I began parking at the supermarket. I walked half a mile home, almost always in temperatures below freezing. I still did my Immortal Post practice after I shuffled into my condo. The next morning, I got up earlier to walk half a mile back to the parking lot, wondering if my car got towed or stolen (my key couldn't open the lock from the outside so I always kept one door unlocked). But it was waiting for me, seemingly amused at being left so conspicuously in a near-empty lot. For a couple of years, my battery regularly died; every time it didn't was a victory. When I keyed the ignition and the engine turned over and revved, I felt a little thrill rev through my body.

The more ridiculous it got, the more I refused to grumble—mostly. With my mind as my ally and my energy building, I recognized every goofy challenge as another funny side effect of my life getting stripped down to the bare bones.

For almost three years, I kept in touch with two or three friends, but saw them less than a half-dozen times. Some might call that isolation. In my teenage years and early 20s, I hurt myself with isolation. Now I was getting nourished with solitude. The difference was my standing meditation practice. Through this discipline, I supplied my mind and body with energy from Heaven and Earth to clear emotional stagnation. I rose out of emotional survival mode and had the spiritual bandwidth to feel universal love. If you had approached me twelve years ago and said I'd someday use the phrase "feel universal love," I'd have laughed. It was never something I strived for but, instead, something that happened to me.

On most work shifts, the big excitement was when an attractive woman waved from her car or when an ugly dude shouted at me.

Then came the day when I witnessed the carjacking and the bloodied, shirtless man marching toward me.

He got closer. As he passed by, he looked at me and said, "How's it going?"

"What's up?" I replied. He kept going until, two blocks north, police cars converged around him. He chatted with the cops for a while and then he hopped into one of the patrol cars, I figured, to get a ride home. My solitude returned.

I'm glad I took advantage of solitude while I could because my job and relaxing lifestyle would eventually get ripped from me.

The ancient Daoists knew solitude was needed for becoming enlightened. They didn't embrace solitude because of arrogance or disliking people, but understood that whenever people form a group, they create an *egregore.*

"Egregore" is the collective group mind generated, for example, when people gather in a church for prayer or meditation. Egregores aren't limited to places of communication with God and spiritual cultivation. When you were born, you entered your family's egregore. Your schools and classrooms had egregores. You create one with your friends, your job, your town, your state, and your country.

Some believe egregores are autonomous psychic entities that form a two-way relationship—groups influence egregores and the egregores, in turn, influence the groups. According to Dr. Jerry Alan Johnson in his book *The Hidden Teachings of Christian Mysticism (Vol. 2)* an egregore "...continuously interacts with its members, influencing them and also being influenced by them. This type of interaction works positively by stimulating and assisting its members, but only as long as they behave and act in line with its original purpose and aim."[40] That last bit is important. At its best, an egregore supports you and raises you higher, as when a group of workers builds a successful start-up. At its worst, an egregore tears you down or even kills you, as when a mob mentality sweeps through a group of panicking people.

Negative egregores use shared biases, emotional wounding, and common enemies as the bone, muscle, and sinew that keep them together. They need people stuck in their midst, including you. In the cliché of crabs that are trying to escape, but pulling each other back into the bucket, the egregore is the collective entity driving that behavior. With humans, it can take the form of family disapproval when you want to start a business, or friends making fun of you and tempting you with junk food when you try to get in better shape. These aren't rational behaviors; they're people maintaining the status quo of the egregore that dictates their lives.

This is why Daoists saw the need for solitude. When you spend time away from other people, you're less influenced by the egregores. When you practice the Immortal Post, you reject plugging into people for sustenance and, instead, plug into the energy of Heaven and Earth.

Sometimes, making time for your practice and putting in effort isn't the toughest part of your journey. It's saying "No" to other people's company. This goes beyond hurt feelings—you're pulling away from the egregore, which means cutting off part of its energy. Egregores don't like this.

Let's rewind back to when I lived in Boulder in my drinking days, before I learned the Immortal Post. Two powerful egregores sucked the life from me, without any face-to-face contact with another human. Every day, I woke up, started drinking, plopped in front of my computer, and turned it on. To my left was a television set. As my computer whirred to life, I leaned over and pushed the Power button for my TV. It emitted a faint ringing, like external tinnitus. I checked email and worked on whatever half-baked business idea held my attention as the sounds of daytime television echoed through my condo. Sometimes, I took a break from my computer and flopped sideways on my futon to watch TV. Often, I remained flopped for hours.

The day dissolved into this routine. I searched for shows to watch, memorized airtimes, and built my life around them. The commercial schedule kept me obedient. If I had to race to the bathroom, I returned before the show resumed. Plugging myself into my favorite shows numbed me, which I mistook for soothing. Nighttime was reserved for the news—I marinated in the news for hours. I don't remember learning anything important. It's like an ice slick on my mind, as if my brain were so embarrassed at how I'd wasted its potential, it hid the evidence.

As this routine continued to mutate, I stayed on my futon later and later into the night, struggling to keep my eyes open. The television's blare settled into seductive white noise as I let my eyelids rest. For months, I never slept in my bed, but on my futon, often waking up to my television screaming commercials at me. It was as if I couldn't bring myself to enjoy my bed, my only piece of quality furniture.

No wonder suicidal feelings snaked into my brain, struck at me, pinned me down for hours. The television programming's egregore left me vulnerable by stripping my mind down to a fraction of its potential.

The egregores created by television programming are—slowly—dying. But, much like the heads of a hydra, they're replacing themselves in more insidious ways. Shows on demand have birthed binge-watching. Commercial breaks are disappearing, but product placement is growing. This is nothing compared to the egregore's next evolution.

When I lived in Boulder, television programming was just one egregore that ensnared me. The other seeped into my mind from my computer screen. Every day, I read the message forums of a popular website about weight training. The site's audience psychographics ranged from teenagers with raging testosterone levels, to 20-somethings with raging testosterone levels, to older men who did everything they could to make their testosterone levels rage—including using anabolic steroids.

The site's message forum burst with new posts and 95% of them had nothing to do with lifting weights. The anonymous posters did what anonymous posters have done since the invention of anonymity and posting: argued about politics, bragged about sex and dating, and jockeyed for higher social status. It was an online egregore-feeding machine.

Because it was the internet equivalent of the Bronze Age, I had to refresh my screen to see if anyone had made a new post. Guess what I did, over and over, for hours throughout the day? I hit that refresh icon like a caged, opiate-addicted rat in an experiment.

The egregore helped warp my social interaction. One of the site's authors—a decent guy willing to write publicly about his learning, growth, and experimentation—became hated by the more prolific, and anonymous, message forum posters. Sometimes, I'd post a jab toward the author and relish the kudos I received.

When I wasn't feeling the thrill of being liked by total strangers who wouldn't have blinked if I'd dropped off the face of the Earth, I was fueling my self-hate. I scrolled through posts where guys described their success and the breathtaking sexual encounters they accumulated with an efficiency seen only in porno scripts. Without considering how much of these were lies, I weighed these supermen against myself and slouched lower in my seat, as I scrolled and scrolled. As I suffered, the online community's egregore grew stronger.

It sounds pathetic. Throughout history, humans hunted for food with spears, faced death while crossing oceans, and fought each other in pistol duels, but I was getting debilitated by internet boneheads. This problem is more dangerous than you might imagine. Some research[41] shows that social media use amplifies our envy of others.

Then I had a pair of epiphanies. One evening, while I spasmodically hit the refresh icon on the webpage, I recognized what it had reduced me to. There were an infinite number of things I could have been doing with my life. But here I sat, craving another forum post so I could react to it.

I closed the page and never returned.

Around that time, I pondered how television programming dictated my life's schedule. *How much time do you spend every day watching TV?* I could measure my daily tally in **hours.** *If you spent all that time meditating, what are the chances you could become enlightened in this lifetime?*

I'd heard stories of people who meditated for a couple of hours per day for decades and transformed themselves, leaving behind ill thoughts and ill health, living a dream life, and achieving spiritual insight.

Beats watching Seinfeld reruns.*

Could I do this by ditching television? Would missing my favor-

* And I'm picking on Seinfeld because I love that show.

ite shows be that bad? I was weighing the opportunity costs of an activity. I wasn't merely comparing hours of television-watching with hours of something else—I was thinking about the benefit of devoting hours per day to something more profound. My heart thumped faster. *Why not? Why not do it?*

And so, I did. It helped that I was so broke that I could barely pay my cable bill. I called my cable company and slogged through the process of cutting off my service. Egregores don't like having their food removed. I decided not to squander the momentum of my escape. Even before the cable company shut off my service, I hauled my television set to Goodwill and gave it away.

For the first couple of days, I felt television's addictive pull. At certain times, as if Pavlov was ringing his bell, my eyes darted to the empty table with lines of dust showing where the TV used to sit. But the addicted feelings vanished after three days or so, and I grew calm. Escaping TV's false reality also raised my self-esteem.

These days, the egregore of a mob doesn't require people rioting in the streets. Instead, it gets mainlined straight into our eyeballs and brain, via the tiny computers we've grafted to our palms—our smartphones. We can click on social media apps programmed to beep and bloop and flash and hijack our brains. They'll broadcast endless feeds for you to drink in, full of arguments and attention-seeking avatars. Because social media's interactions are devoid of body language, mutual eye contact, and pheromones, you won't get feelings of bonding or humanity. Everyone seems like a stranger and potentially an enemy. Even worse, the algorithm running these programs feeds you more of what you engage in, which is usually something that triggers you. It also feeds you the news, information, and friends you've already indicated you match with, therefore acting as an algorithmic crab in the bucket, keeping you stuck where you are. When you don't read news or information or interact with people who challenge you, your growth stalls.

Social media is a hydra-like egregore with a global reach, and it owns more data on your habits, cravings, secret biases, and weaknesses than you could imagine. The smartest programmers on the planet work day and night to get you to do one thing: engage with the online egregore that you're helping to create, whatever the cost to your fulfillment and health.

Sound overdramatic? Consider what science is now showing. One study[42] reveals that reducing Facebook activity by 20 minutes per day produced, within two weeks, "...a substantial positive effect on subjective well-being and (un)healthy lifestyle..." They concluded this after measuring smoking and exercise habits, life satisfaction, and depressive symptoms. Another study[43] from Stanford University showed that deactivating Facebook for 28 days increased wellbeing and the participants spent more time with friends and other offline activities. Tellingly, they used Facebook less, even after the experiment ended. These results aren't isolated to a couple of small experiments. A meta-analysis[44] (a study that examines other studies) of 124 studies showed that passively consuming social media is harmful to your wellbeing.* For something that's supposed to connect the world, why do people feel happier when they get rid of it?

Facebook even experimented[45] on 689,003 users. They reduced the number of positive stories in some newsfeeds and reduced the number

* To be fair, this meta-analysis showed that more *non*-passive forms of social media can be beneficial to wellbeing. Hence #3 and #4 of my 6 tips below, for managing your relationship with social media.

of negative stories in others to see if that would affect the emotional content of the users' posts. It did. The experimenters noted that, when the negative stories were reduced, so was the negativity of the users' posts. When the positive stories were reduced, so did the users' positive posts.

This was done without the knowledge or consent of the users.

Here are six tips on managing your relationship with social media and electronic communication so it's healthy and you're in control.

1. Remove your social media apps from your phone.
2. Keep your phone on Airplane Mode, as a default.
3. Use social media only for staying in touch with people who uplift and inspire you.
4. Communicate only with people you've already met in real life.
5. Designate some rooms in your home for social media and some to be free from it.
6. Eliminate all electronic distractions for several hours per day.

In my free time, I meditated using the Immortal Post. I wrote. I worked on my business. I took walks and, as silly as it feels to write, I heard the birds chirping more. Although my life was still a struggle, I became more awake to it and how to transform it.

When I got my job spinning a sign on a street corner, I found more opportunity to cultivate solitude. Each eight-hour shift became a training ground where I chose, every moment, whether to embrace solitude or distraction. I could hate every moment, curse the drivers who gave me the finger or yelled at me, and feel sorry for myself. Or

I could educate myself with audiobooks, enjoy the people-watching, make someone's day brighter, and relish the tranquility.

I'm not suggesting you abandon your career, friends, and family, unless they're hurting you. It was my path to work on a street corner for a couple of years. But if you want to change your energy, mind the egregores you're plugged into.

Solitude is essential for enhancing your chi because negative egregores block and drain your energy when you're caught in them. This can come from a group of friends or co-workers who are a bad influence on you, or from your in-laws or your neighbors.

Think back to last year's Thanksgiving. How healthy and energized did you feel the day after? It's not just stuffing yourself with your in-law's dessert that saps your vitality. You swim in the currents of your extended family's anger, worry, and grief. Solitude helps you shower that off.

As you transform yourself, you will shift the way energy flows through you. When you hang out with the same crowd with the same egregore, you expose yourself to the same energy and it will pull you back toward the old configuration.

If you take two steps forward in your development during an Immortal Post practice session, you'll take one step backward if you hang out with negative people. Eventually, you'll stop hanging out with them or they'll stop you from taking steps at all.

Ancient Daoists saw solitude as freedom from harmful people and the egregores created by groups of people. Negative egregores bind you with petty distractions, arguments, fear-mongering, propaganda, gossip, limiting beliefs, and emotional fixations. Solitude is the antidote.

Sometimes, the strongest pull we feel to avoid solitude is thinking we'll miss out on life and become ignorant and lost. The *Dao De Jing* was eerily prescient about how misguided this is:

"Without going outside
one can know the whole world.
Without looking out the window
one can see the ways of Heaven.
The farther one goes
the less one knows.
Thus, the Sage does not go, yet he knows.
He does not look, yet he sees.
He does not do, yet all is done."[46]

Easing back on your online relationships can be a cakewalk compared to real life. The people keeping you stuck and miserable might be closest to you—even the person you share a bed with.

When you begin practicing the Immortal Post, tell as few distant associates as possible. Your co-workers don't need to know, and your friends don't either. If you're in a serious relationship, your partner is probably going to wonder why you're standing motionless in your underwear, looking like you hoisted an invisible bucket.

If your partner doesn't support you, make the following statement and question. Adjust the wording to suit your personality, but make sure you understand the logic.

"I hear you that I seem more distant and I'm doing something that looks odd. Please understand that I'm spending more time alone to strengthen myself so that I can be a better friend/lover/parent/family member for you. And when I *am* present, I'm going to make more effort to be fully present with you."

Here's the question: "I understand you think this standing meditation is unusual and maybe even a waste of my time. But let me ask you, even if you are skeptical of me benefiting from this practice, do you support me taking time and effort to work on myself and develop myself spiritually? And do you support me discovering for myself if this standing meditation is worth my time and effort?"

Listen to the answers. If someone doesn't believe your first statement, then solitude isn't the real issue—they have a bigger problem with you and what your relationship should look like. If someone supports you as a person, they will respond to your questions in the affirmative. If there's a morsel of hesitation, mockery, debate or attempt to lecture you, that's a blood red flag. You might or might not be able to work through this problem with communication. You might need to make peace with being stuck in the bucket with a fellow crab pulling you down. You might need to escape the bucket alone.

No matter what, those close to you will sense that you're transforming and they will either grow to keep up, fall out of your life, or turn on you. Chances are, they'll fall away or turn on you. Think of it as more opportunity to practice solitude. This may sound harsh and this chapter's references to crabs in buckets may seem elitist, but the truth is this training—and any training that transforms you—will cause you to lose friends.

When it comes to your Immortal Post practice, choose a time of day for you to focus 100% on you. Ideally, it's the same time every day. Block out at least an hour. If you can't do that, you need to reevaluate your life. During this hour, keep distractions away. No TV, computer or phone. Create an environment of solitude so you can focus on your Immortal Post and, when you're finished, accomplish a project or do other things that are part of your spiritual walk. This is the most important time block that you will ever schedule.

In the next chapter, you'll find out how I almost died and the Daoist lesson I learned.

CHAPTER SIXTEEN

PATIENCE

I drove north on I-25, trying to slow my breathing. After working as a sign-spinner for over two years, I was about to get promoted. At least, that's what I thought.

Cars bunched together as I drove closer to downtown Denver. On the right side of the road, two had pulled over and billowed smoke. Bits of metal and glass shimmered on the road, like a fresh dusting of snow.

I turned to look at the mess and when I turned back, the wall of cars ahead rushed at me too fast.

I hit the brakes. The nose of my car dove and lurched to the right as the tires screamed against the pavement.

The front bumper hit a car ahead of me, bouncing it up as my hood crumpled with a soft crunch. The hood bent up like a giant piece of origami.

"Shit!"

As I pulled off the highway, joining the cars I'd just been staring at,

I tried to think that this wasn't real—just a scratch, our cars were fine, and we'd just keep driving.

Antifreeze dripped and spread on the pavement like alien blood. The lights on my dashboard faded. I tried the ignition. *Click.*

The car I hit pulled over. The driver got out. He was calm about the accident. "Yeah, when I saw you coming up behind me that fast, I knew you were going to hit me."

"I'm so sorry," I said, forgetting all advice about not admitting fault.

He looked at his rear bumper. "Yeah, this is totaled. The frame is all bent."

Am I cursed? I wondered if this was my self-sabotage roaring back to life or something worse: Maybe I wasn't meant to escape sign-spinning.

I'd been driving north to a meeting with the company's owner. His name was Don.

I'd been working as a sign-spinner for about two years and had gotten to know the company and most of the people, as we expanded from three stores to ten. I kept wondering about the company's marketing. *What if I could help them?* I grabbed my chance at Dave & Buster's, where the company hosted its annual party. Don leaned against a table, beer in hand, watching a pool game. He'd already gotten a few rounds of drinks in, including shots. Good.

I stepped beside him. "Thank you so much for putting this party on! It's been great."

"Oh, no problem, no problem," Don said.

"I was wondering about something..." and then I launched into my job pitch. A strange inner knowingness, like a rising tide, told me it'd work out perfectly.

"Send me a proposal," he said.

The next day, without any idea how, I wrote and emailed a proposal, but didn't get a reply. The days turned into a week and then two. I considered following up, but decided the best action was to wait.

Two weeks later, as I walked back into one of the stores for a break, I ran into Don. He was on the phone, but I had to ask.

"Hey Don."

He took his phone from his ear and pressed it to his shoulder. "Hey, what's up?"

"Did you get my email?"

"Yeah. Yeah. I'll get back to you."

I nodded and scampered away.

Another week went by...and then another. Again, I decided the best action was to wait. Roughly six weeks later, when I'd forgotten about the whole thing, he replied to my email.

The best part of his reply read: *I don't think you'll be spinning signs anymore!*

He asked me to drive to his office during my next shift. I did, and on I-25N I crashed my car.

The other driver and I waited for the policeman, who was already dealing with the wrecked cars behind us. Then the other driver's friend arrived.

The friend gave the guy's car a once-over. "Oh, it's fine!"

"Really?" the other guy said.

"Oh yeah! It's completely fine. You just need a new bumper and some paint work."

"I like him!" I said.

I called my mechanic, who rarely answered his phone. But this time, when I needed him most, he did.

"Hey buddy, what's going on?"

"I totaled my car. I rear-ended someone on the highway and destroyed it."

"Oh, shit," he said.

"Oh, yeah. Can I bring it over to you?"

As I waited for a tow truck, I called my supervisor at the store and asked her to tell Don that I wouldn't make it to the meeting because I crashed my car.

A tow truck hauled my car, plus me, to my mechanic's place. By the time I got a ride back to one of the stores, the workday was almost over.

My supervisor told me Don would reschedule. Maybe I wasn't cursed.

A week later, my mechanic said my car would be fixed by Tuesday. I emailed Don and said I could do a meeting Tuesday.

A voice rose from deep in my gut. *Are you sure? Why not schedule it for Wednesday? That way, you won't risk not having your car in time. You won't risk not keeping your word. It's just one day.*

I ignored the voice.

On Tuesday afternoon, my mechanic said he could drop off my car at 1PM.

I waved around my sign on the street until 12:45PM and then raced inside, tore off my costume, put on a dress shirt, and marched back outside.

At 1PM, I started darting my head back and forth, scanning the parking lot and the road. Where was my car?

1:05PM. Nothing.

1:10PM. I called my mechanic. No answer. *Oh, no.*

1:15PM. I called again. He said he'd be there soon.

I paced, watching every car that drifted by. With each step, I got more agitated. *How could I have been so stupid to schedule the meeting for the same afternoon I got my car back? Now I'd be breaking my promise twice. Maybe Don would be too disgusted to bother with me. And why couldn't my mechanic just answer his phone and get my car back on time? If he couldn't do it by that time, why did he say he could?*

The questions raced faster as I marched up and down the sidewalk.

Then I stopped. Wasn't I learning that a key to living a better life is to feel grateful? And that feeling frustrated and angry blocks you from receiving what you want?

I looked down to the grass and gritted my teeth. *Thank you. Thank you. Thank you. Thank you.*

I looked up. My gaze locked on my mechanic's face as he waved from inside my car, pulling into the parking lot.

I dove in. "Thank you so much."

He pulled back out of the lot. Maybe I still had time.

My phone rang. "Hey, Don just called. He's too busy and can't meet today. Maybe in a couple of days."

Ugh. All that anger, the stress, driving myself nuts—for what? Would I ever get that meeting?

A couple of days later, I did—when the meeting had already "cried wolf" enough times that I was too jaded to feel excited. Once again, I drove north on I-25, determined to glide by where I'd crashed my car without looking to the side of the road. It felt as if I'd entered another dimension when I passed by the spot, continuing the drive and parking in front of the company's headquarters. It was dreamlike. I'd made it.

I sat in front of Don at his massive, wraparound desk. Twin computer monitors displayed live security camera footage from all his stores.

"So, basically, what I'm thinking," he said. Then his phone buzzed. "Hold on."

He grabbed a pen and scribbled on a Post-It. "Tell him we're willing to pay $135. Okay, bye." He hung up, sighed, and looked back at me. "I want to try out some new..." His phone buzzed again. "Hold on."

He jumped from his desk and left. Ten minutes later, he returned holding a hefty metal bar that was either almost $200 worth of silver or a hunk of scrap. "Pretty cool, huh? I have no idea if it's real or not."

Over the next few months, I got to know Don better. He loved picking fights in bars, had slept with more exotic dancers than he could remember, and once got so inebriated that his grandmother found him in the living room—all 300 pounds of him—dancing buck naked. Yet, he was surprisingly shy. When I had first met him, Don looked to the side and his handshake felt like palming a short stack of pancakes, as if strong touch and eye contact were too intense to do simultaneously. He was also a shrewd businessman. Don could do math in his head that I could barely do with a calculator and, even though I doubt he'd ever read a business book, if he ever wrote one I'd pay hundreds of dollars for a copy.

In between more calls, he outlined the marketing help he wanted from me. "Start tomorrow. We'll get you a desk here."

I thanked him, stood up, shook his hand, and floated out. There was no curse.

Impatience spits forth a nasty attitude like a stench from a skunk. It causes stress, anger, ruins creative ability, and chases away fun. It infects the rest of your day.

Some people don't see impatience as a problem. It's like feeling anger—they think everyone else has a problem. They think their time's getting wasted. In reality, when you're impatient, you affirm that whatever is dangled out of reach has more value and more power over you than your happiness. Did the miracle and wonder of life disappear because your Starbucks order took too long?

Daoists understand that impatience blocks your emotional, mental, and energetic development. Its opposite—patience—is the bedrock for transformation.

Let's go over why impatience is more harmful than you might think.

Impatience has nothing to do with objective reality. You can be impatient in an airplane as you soar through the sky at hundreds of miles per hour. Imagine you're on a flight home that's scheduled to land at 2:40PM. The airplane makes its descent, bumps against the runway, and bears down as it slows.

Ah, you're almost home. The airplane pulls into the gate and sits there. A few minutes go by. Nothing happens. The heads of fellow passengers twist and turn in the seats in front of you. What's going on?

Normally, you'd check for texts and emails on your phone, but the battery died. You've got nothing to do but wait.

The intercom croaks to life. "We're, uh, experiencing a delay, but we should be getting you out of here in approximately 15 minutes. We apologize for the inconvenience."

You sigh and shake your head, joining the chorus of frustration from your fellow passengers. More minutes go by. Your body radiates heat. A trickle of sweat itches your back. *What's wrong with these idiots? They can't figure out how to open a door?*

Finally, there's a commotion ahead—passengers get up to leave. As you stomp up the jetway and enter the terminal, you glance at the first clock you can find.

2:38PM.

Wait, what? You can't be early. Everyone waited for so long at the gate.

It turns out, the flight arrived almost half an hour early and you didn't hear about it. You couldn't check the time on your phone.

Your impatience had nothing to do with reality. You were early, but felt late. You drove yourself nuts as you sat in a motionless airplane at the gate yet the plane felt just as motionless in the sky.

Boiling with impatience is an emotional reaction. No set of facts can justify it.

When my flights idle at gates, I read a book. Heck, I'd read a book later in the day anyway so I might as well take advantage of the situation.

But let's say you have a connecting flight and you do miss it because of the gate delay. What if you are delayed by someone's incompetence and that causes you harm? We could take it further. What if someone, out of spite, sabotages you?

When is impatience justified?

I recently wrestled with that question.

A couple of days before I wrote this chapter, my therapist and I were discussing how I can continue having healthy conversations with my mom. He dove into a story about a comedian.

I said, "Great. Whatever. I'll think about maybe looking him up. What does he have to do with my mom?"

My therapist chuckled. "Aren't you writing a chapter on patience?"

"Yeah, yeah, yeah. Sometimes it's right to be patient and sometimes it's not."

Something about my answer felt wrong.

Later, during my mental wrestling, I posed a question. "We have impatience for a reason. How is impatience useful?" Then I got the answer.

Emotions—especially negative emotions like impatience—are useful…for a couple of seconds. They alert you to danger, tell you something is wrong, and help you identify what needs to change.

Impatience can alert you to when someone doesn't fulfill their word, or to when a person might try to fulfill their word, but does so with a speed that mismatches yours. That's a useful alarm bell to feel… for roughly two seconds.

That brief alert of impatience can compel you to confront a person or situation and navigate how best to deal with it. However, once you switch from getting the alert to navigating the situation, it's time to drop the emotion, just like a rocket drops external fuel tanks as it takes off. Otherwise, the fuel tanks will weigh the rocket down.

Your impatience, which can alert you to a problem, can paradoxically prevent you from resolving the problem. The emotion muddies your rational thinking. Remember my story of waiting at the ramen restaurant for 45 minutes? My impatience clouded my mind and I forgot I could have used the time to call my friend.

So, when is impatience justified? It's not situation specific but *time* specific—it's justified for a couple of seconds. After that, the emotion is as useless and destructive as chronic worry or anger.

Instead of letting impatience control you, practice patience. It frees you to respond in a healthy way.

This brings up another crucial point. I believe some people scoff at patience for the same reason they scoff at acceptance: it seems passive. But patience doesn't mean blindly accepting the status quo.

The *Dao De Jing* states:

> *"Those with great courage,*
> *but little patience,*
> *tend to kill or be killed.*
> *Those with great courage*
> *as well as great patience*
> *will tend to survive."*[47]

I'll add that those with great patience, but little courage, will tend to get steamrolled by life. If you're concerned that losing your impatience will make you vulnerable to timewasters, remember that you still get to practice courage. You can be patient while removing a timewaster from your life.

Patience also does not necessitate plodding like a turtle and racing like a hare doesn't necessitate impatience. Remember, you can sit in an airplane traveling 600MPH and get annoyed at how you're running late. Or, the same day, you can power walk at 6MPH and be thrilled with your speed. The circumstances are irrelevant.

A driven entrepreneur can work 14-hour days, rushing to launch a product by a seemingly impossible deadline, yet practice patience.

Someone else can spend those same 14 hours watching TV and feel impatient when they think the commercial breaks take too long. Circumstances are irrelevant to impatience. It's not about objective reality; it's an emotional reaction.

When impatience starts to boil, you need to let it go. Easier said than done. I can attest to this, and my wife can confirm it as a witness. But I've found a few good methods.

First: when you feel that your time is being wasted and your impatience is justified, remember that the emotion is a mere signal. You're not meant to stew in the signal—you're meant to make a decision.

Decide what to do. It's helpful to ask, "What's best for me to do right now?"

Maybe the answer is to confront someone. Maybe the answer is to read a book. Maybe the answer is to just chill out. Whatever it is, switch from reacting emotionally to making a choice.

Remember that patience has nothing to do with objective reality. You can read stories of people who worked at the Twin Towers or had a meeting at the skyscrapers on the morning of 9/11. These people were running late and some probably felt impatient. A couple of hours later, they probably felt differently.

When I'm running late, I say to myself, "The timing must be perfect."

Peter Ragnar once told a story of driving home with his wife and taking a route he'd driven for many years—then making a wrong turn.

"Peter, what are you doing? Are you lost?" his wife asked.

"I don't know." He got back on the route and, when he reached the turn he'd meant to take, they saw it: a van had collided with a car. The ambulance had just arrived and firemen were dousing the flames with water.

If Peter hadn't missed the turn, it could have been their car.

Ever had a delay that turned out to be a blessing or even saved your life? The next time another delay frustrates you, remember that.

If you can't simply enjoy the moment, give yourself something useful to do. I grab a book or brainstorm writing ideas. But I don't mean that you should do anything to pass the time. When people stand in line or sit in a waiting room, most will automatically pull out their smartphones and get lost in scrolling through some feed. Resist that urge. Don't jump from feeling impatient to gratifying yourself. Let yourself be still. You might feel uncomfortable or think you're wasting time but, if you let it, a feeling of peace might settle over you.

As with other emotions, one of the most powerful ways to soothe impatience is knowing how it can grip you. Observe your impatience, acknowledge it's there, let the feeling boil to the surface, and ask yourself what is best for you to do.

If someone's causing your delay, don't make it personal. They aren't out to get you. But let's say they are. If you get impatient, then they *did* get you, didn't they?

Part of my marriage vows to my wife reads, "I vow to be patient because you're worth the wait." Even if my wife is sometimes on a different timeline than I am, that doesn't determine the value of the moment. The real value is the privilege I have of simply being with my wife.

If you remember the moment itself is a privilege to experience, circumstances won't control your emotions.

The Immortal Post is like stepping into the boxer's ring with impatience. No pads, no gloves, and you're blindfolded. You stand alone with no entertainment or distraction, confronting every speck of your body's tension and your mind's ruminations.

When you practice the Immortal Post, you'll face two kinds of impatience. The first will be when you beg for your practice round to end—for the timer to go off. Your eyes will dart around. Your mind will race. You can't rush through it. There's no cosmic fast forward button. If anything, when your legs burn or your mind howls like an animal, time will seem to slow down. *Has it been fifteen minutes yet?* You glance at the timer. Eight minutes are still left. *What? It's not even halfway through yet? The timer must be wrong.* Your chest heaves with a deep breath and the burning in your muscles amplifies.

In this moment, you are staring down the barrel of impatience. You can give up and feel the hollow relief of letting life's distractions wash back over you. Or you can press on; you can win the stare-down. You can marinate in the mental anguish and let it make you stronger. In the movie *Gladiator*, the character Maximus quotes the movie's version of Roman emperor Marcus Aurelius, "I knew a man once who said, 'Death smiles at us all. All a man can do is smile back.'"

Smile back until the timer rings. Then you'll get to smile for the rest of the day.

The second kind of impatience is when you demand results from your practice. You want your body to glow like the sun within a week. You want to feel blissed out within a couple of days. And if a month goes by and you're not levitating, then the Immortal Post can go jump in a lake.

But you can't demand a certain result by a certain time, as if holding the Immortal Post at gunpoint. As the ancient text *Bhagavad Gita* says, "You have the right to work, but for the work's sake only. You have no right to the fruits of work."

You can devote yourself to your practice. You can focus on relaxing and aligning your body and quieting your mind, but demanding a specific result by a specific time will bring you suffering. I speak from experience.

One of my teachers, Dr. Diego Sanmiquel, says, "Have unconditional love for your training."

There is no finish line. Sure, your timer will go off, but this is a lifelong practice. The timer will start tomorrow and the next day and the day after. A deep craving for results, or even a passionate love for your practice, won't get you through the tough days or weeks, especially if you hit a bunch in a row. I've had rough patches where I wondered if anything was changing at all, or if I should quit and do something else. Only *unconditional* love got me through.

When you feel unconditional love for the moment, you'll never be impatient.

When the company's owner, Don, wrote to tell me I'd never spin a sign again, a morsel of an opportunity got dangled in front of my face. I felt scared that I'd never get another chance and I chomped at it like an animal. Then I crashed my car.

Instead of giving myself one extra day to make sure I had my car back, I tried to speed things up, and that blew up in my face.

Only after I felt grateful and literally thought *"Thank you, thank you, thank you,"* did I get my car back. Only after life squeezed the impatience out of me like I was an orange that got shoved and twisted against a juicer, did I calm down enough to make it to my meeting and get my promotion.

Over the next few months, instead of standing outside and staring down a perpetual parade of traffic, I sat inside and stared down a computer screen from a comfy chair. Instead of the sun burning my body or the wind ripping my heat away, I got the buzz of fluorescent lights and the hums of ventilation.

The staleness ate at my energy.

Hey, you wanted this.

Sort of. I had craved the idea of what my promotion was—not the reality. It was springtime and, as trees flourished outside, I sat surrounded by cinder block walls in a room with no seasons.

Still, over the next few months, I revamped the company's website and online marketing. I doubled the number of customers the company got from the internet. Everything seemed to be going well...but life has a way of throwing a plot-twist.

Before I got the promotion, the company's owner had written that I'd never spin signs again. That turned out to be wrong. In the next chapter, I'll show how I lost my job for a surprising reason. But I learned the ingredient for success that's missing from every self-help book I've seen.

CHAPTER SEVENTEEN

SELF-EXPLORATION

In early spring 2014, Don called me into his office—the same room in which, three years earlier, I'd interviewed for the job. "I don't know how to say this, so I'm just going to say it..." the owner of the gold-buying store—and my boss—began.

Since I'd begun working for the gold buying company, I'd enjoyed a steady paycheck, the solitude of a simple outer world to rebuild my inner world, and had even risen in the company's ranks to handle all the marketing. I hoped it would last, but the previous few weeks had strangled those hopes.

When I'd started working for the company, the price of gold rocketed to over $1,900 per ounce and people piled through the doors with fistfuls of gold to sell. We hired and trained so many buyers that the company built a makeshift classroom for them. But as the company expanded, gold's value began to drop.

A few months after I improved the company's marketing, gold's price plummeted and so did everyone's desire to sell. The classroom became dark and empty. One morning, after gold cratered, Don sauntered through the back door and said, "I just lost over $12,000." He chuckled. In the office, the air began to feel stale with an undercurrent of panic.

The marketing world has a saying: "You can't multiply zeros" and sometimes that was the number of customers who walked into our stores. Standing outside waving a sign seemed more fun than withering in the office. Don switched my role to spending half the time standing outside and half working on marketing inside.

But something was now clicking in my own business, as my advertisements started to show positive results. If I poured more money into the campaigns, I could finally grow my business. But I had no money to pour. I reached out to Wally, my friend who'd given me some perspective after Mike kicked me out of his Mastermind. He had some extra cash and was interested in deals like this. For half a day, I mapped my business's customer-acquisition strategy and my plan for making a net profit, detailing the best and worst-case scenarios. I mapped my own strengths and weaknesses, including my federal and state tax debt. After lunch, we negotiated his investment, shook hands, and I drove back to Aurora. We ironed out the process with a written contract, which we edited a couple of times. Then we both signed and Wally mailed me a check for $3,000.

A couple of weeks later, I sat in the back room of the gold buying store and checked the ad campaign's stats. It did okay, but not good enough to reinvest.

Now I owed Wally $3,000. Every month, I mailed him $500. Then I received a bill from the State of Colorado for old taxes, saying I needed to pay the full amount—over $2,000—in 30 days or they would drain my bank account.

The debt was more than I could afford, but I couldn't cry uncle with a bankruptcy—you can only file for Chapter 7 bankruptcy once every six years. But maybe I could do a Chapter 13, where your debt gets renegotiated.

I visited the same lawyer, who'd changed locations. Instead of a quiet office with an autographed Jude Law photo, he squeezed his operation into an auto shop. His assistants typed at their desks and clients lounged on couches next to running cars coughing up exhaust fumes. When I sat with the attorney, he explained the biggest scam people face after a bankruptcy is predatory car loans—so he decided to add auto sales to his law firm.

"Need a car?" he asked, cocking his head and sticking a thumb at one of the sedans, its engine purring.

"Uh, no thanks," I said.

I discovered Chapter 13 would cost at least $1,300. No way. As I drove back to work, I gazed at pretty apartment buildings and somehow knew everything would be fine. There was no logical reason why, but I had the feeling just the same.

The State of Colorado phoned Don and they negotiated a $50 draft from my weekly paycheck.

As the gold-buying company shrank, Don called me into his office. "We're closing down the store on Broadway." I rented a U-Haul, parked it in front of the store, and packed away the furniture, supplies, and decorations I'd walked past for years, dismantling my comfortable world.

I began the stages of grief. *Maybe gold will go back up. Damnit, why does this all have to go away? Maybe one store can stay open.*

But every couple of weeks, Don called me in again. "We're closing down the store on..." More U-Hauls. Then more chopping away at my bubble.

At one store location, he couldn't negotiate a break in the lease. We moved out anyway and the landlord sued the company and got a judge to greenlight vacuuming $30,000 of past rent from Don's bank account. That night, alone in his office, Don wondered if he'd padlock the doors and disappear. "I was crying," he said.

That spring he called me into his office, where I'd interviewed years before.

"I don't know how to say this, so I'm just going to say it. We're closing." Don gave me a little nod. "Like, *closing*, closing."

Even though I'd physically emptied most of the old stores and said, "Goodbye" to them before stepping into the stuffed moving truck, I wanted to believe the end would never arrive.

"Okay. Okay," I said. "Well, nobody could say you didn't do everything you could to keep things going."

I sat at my desk and hunted through Craigslist ads for jobs. I found a want ad for marijuana trimmers. The company was looking to hire ten to twenty of them. Those odds seemed pretty good.

The line of applicants snaked outside the building and around the corner. As we waited for a couple of hours, someone muttered that over 120 people had shown up.

When I got to the front, I empathized with the interviewer about the crowd he had to deal with.

"Tell me a little about yourself," he said.

I talked about my sign-spinning job and made sure he knew I always showed up on time.

He switched to his wrap-up questions. "Any criminal record?"

"No."

"And you're current on your federal and state taxes?"

"I still owe some, but I'm on a payment plan," I said.

"I'm sorry. We can't legally hire anyone if they're not paying their taxes."

"Oh, I'm paying them—I'm on a payment plan." Hey, a weekly draft from my paycheck was technically a payment plan.

"Oh, okay, gotcha. Well, this is just a meet and greet before we do our next round of interviews. Thank you for coming in and we'll be in touch!"

For a few minutes, as I strolled past forty other people in line, I believed him.

A couple of weeks later, I walked outside for my final shift at the gold-buying store, at the southeast corner of Wadsworth and Mississippi, in Lakewood. It didn't feel right to listen to music or some audiobook, so I pulled down my headphones and listened to the traffic. It seemed muffled. God had splashed this painting into existence, but now the colors were dripping off the canvas.

For over three years, morning after morning, I'd marched outside while juggling a steaming coffee cup, a sign, and an MP3 player. I remembered how, on winter days, I'd yanked off two layers of gloves to press the MP3's buttons. In the summer, I'd slathered greasy sunscreen against my neck and cranked up U2's song *Red Hill Mining Town* when my shifts were almost over. Sometimes, I'd listened only to silence when blizzards gently massaged layers of fluffy snow onto the world, traffic rolling by quietly as if the cars didn't want to wake the sleeping trees.

In moments, that'd all be over.

I faced the traffic signal across the street. The big, orange sign thudded against my palms as I flipped it. The walk signal counted down in red numbers.

5…

How many days did I stand outside, a single street corner becoming my whole world?

4…3…

How many co-workers did I get to know? I'd probably never see them again.

2…

1.

Huh. I guess that's it.

I still had a few minutes left in my shift. Every noise outside was dead. The sidewalk felt like someone else's room that I'd wandered into. I went back inside.

An hour later, like a chain gang getting corralled back to prison, Don, a couple of remaining co-workers, and I shuffled out the back door for the final time. We went to our cars. I burst into tears and hid them.

The next morning, the springtime light pierced through the blinds and woke me. My condo was too quiet. Even though the same thick, brown carpet mushed between my toes when I eased out of bed, the floor felt torn from under me. Was I really broke and looking for a job *again?*

I did my standing meditation practice, reminding me that the floor did indeed exist. After many minutes of deep breathing and relaxing my muscles, I scanned more job postings. Lately, I'd noticed something odd. Even though some posts looked decent—good pay and a good chance they'd hire me—my intuition stopped me from responding. My solar plexus would tighten or I'd immediately feel a drain of energy. I literally couldn't bring my fingers to tap out an email.

Three days after getting laid off, I found a want ad that sparked a different answer from my gut. It advertised an open interview for a job loading trucks at a commercial laundry facility.

I drove to the interview site at a local library and parked my car in the eerily empty lot. Did I get the address wrong? As the cloudy day turned into a blizzard of sleet and snow, I waited. Other cars began to show up, which gave me both relief and a new fear—were they competition for the job?

Three minutes before the open interview time began, I marched inside and ran into a crowd of people. I waded through the bustling crowd to plop in front of an interviewer. I forget most of what we said except for the end.

"Can you get your hair cut?" the interviewer said.

"Yeah." While working as a sign-spinner, I'd let my hair grow almost down to the top of my neck.

"Can you get your hair cut right now?"

"Yeah."

She wrote down directions to the warehouse for my final interview and someone else jumped in with directions to a nearby barbershop.

Half an hour later, I lurched and plunged my car down the steep hills of the potholed street to the warehouse, trying not to scratch my fresh near-buzzcut.

I passed a chicken warehouse, rows of truck bays, and a stack of crushed cars piled so high and wide, they looked like a building of twisted steel. Finally, behind a metal fence was a blue building.

I got the job and, a week later, on March 25th, 2014, I entered the warehouse.

Machines whisked giant bags across the ceiling on metal railings. Workers sorted through racks of clothes, fingers working like those of a pianist flying up and down the keys. Trucks beeped as they lurched into the bay doors. Workers chucked the trucks' innards into bags. Footfalls beat against the metal walkways above like banging war drums. Metal cages thundered against the concrete floor, wheeling by. The trucks' running engines, the growling laundry machines, and hissing conveyor belts mixed their sounds into a howling chorus.

It was like being trapped in someone's mouth as they got a root canal. After a shift, it felt like the mouth chewed up my muscles.

Shifts usually lasted twelve hours with one break for a meal. Every time that break began, I dashed to my car, locked myself inside, and did the same Inner Smile meditation I'd done as a sign-spinner when I sat in the back room for lunch. It helped relax away the panic swirling in me.

I hauled tens of thousands of pounds of dirty clothes and grimy floor mats out of trucks. Then I threw clean ones back in. Some trucks had dirty laundry from a dog food factory. My shift partner puked as we unloaded. Another truck came from a spice factory. Unloading the baskets of chef's uniforms was like whiffing leftover pizza. Because we handled thousands of worn clothes, loose change constantly spilled around the warehouse. I got pickier about what I bothered to pick up.

Sometimes, we unloaded clothes soaked in cadmium, sealed in special bags that occasionally arrived torn.

"If we get the cadmium on us, will we get superpowers?" I asked my boss.

"No," he said. "Just cancer."

In the distance, an employee pretended to lick the open bag.

As the weeks went by, my body hurt more and more. Rogue waves of panic blindsided me. I wondered about my aligning spine. The cracks had reached the base of my skull. An inner awareness declared this was it. Part of me hoped my meditation would provide some unexpected money as a reward for spiritual development or high vibrations or some such gobbledygook. It was the same greedy madness that had gotten me into the "Law of Attraction" years ago. What a pathetic mess *that* had turned into.

This time I didn't hold my spiritual practice hostage and demand a cash ransom for my efforts. Maybe my practice orchestrated things behind the scenes to assist me, or maybe not, but I wasn't going to wait. I doubled down on taking action, the stress of the job pushing me to escape faster.

When not working or recovering from work, I reached out to people for marketing gigs, made connections on LinkedIn, responded to more Craigslist ads for marketing positions, and plugged away at my business.

These weren't Hail Mary throws to land some fast cash—or I tried not to see them that way. I methodically tested every avenue to change my financial circumstances. Before my bankruptcy, I'd put most of my effort toward quick paydays. Now I was planting seeds for future revenue.

Someone introduced me to a potential client for writing advertising copy. We scheduled a Friday call. But how do you sell your services over the phone? On Wednesday, Wally sent me a recorded talk on how to sell. I listened to it the next day as I folded mats.

Before the call, I did the Immortal Post. The call's start-time crawled closer. Adrenaline filled my belly like cold steam. Would the potential client even pick up the phone?

I dialed and he picked up. He uttered every word as if he'd slotted two hours for our appointment instead of 30 minutes. I asked him questions, listened, and quoted him two prices for different amounts of work.

"I'll have to check with my business partner," he said.

"Can you get him on the phone now?"

"Let me try." He put me on hold. "I left him a message—he'll get back to me soon."

We hung up and I dreamed about the money I'd make if he accepted one of my offers. I'd earn the same amount as working almost two hundred hours loading trucks. Or was it two hundred and fifty hours?

Wait. How much did I quote him?

Oh no. I forgot. Okay. Think. What should you do? And next time, write down the offer.

I decided that when the potential client called back, I'd let him do the talking. Maybe he'd mention the price. I was pretty sure I'd given him the options of $2,000 or $2,500.

He called back. "Okay, we'll go with the $3,000 option."

Good thing I stayed quiet.

Even though the truck-loading job pushed me toward panic, I tuned into my gut-level intuitions. Another client copped an attitude when he heard my fee. I needed that money, but said I wasn't the writer for him.

Later, however, I would ignore my body's warnings just once and my life would get much worse.

Daoists were the scientists of their day. They meticulously measured the effects of herbs and minerals on the mind, body, and spirit. They mapped our energetic meridians and found how they correlated with organs and emotions. They even invented gunpowder. Calling them scientists seems like a paradox because Daoism is a spiritual practice, but **the Daoists discovered spiritual truths through scientific experimentation**. They understand that humans are most productive and balanced when operating creatively on a journey of self-discovery.

"He who learns but does not think is lost!
He who thinks but does not learn is in great danger."
— Confucius

In my fumbling way, I behaved like a scientist when trying to rid myself of sadness and improve my circumstances. When goal-setting didn't work, I threw it out, although I needed a few years to realize that particular bit of trash had to go. Same with the law of attraction, which stunk even worse. When I tested the Immortal Post, I had no blind faith that it would help me. Instead, the results had to speak for themselves. My only faith was that it was worth a test. And even when good results came, my work was far from over. I had no self-help checklist. I couldn't just do a standing meditation and observe my life falling into place. Making money required experiments with measurable results.

Why is experimentation so important? Here's something you won't find in virtually any self-help book. The gurus who look at you as a paycheck won't tell you this.

One of your greatest and most neglected powers to achieve the health you want, the relationships you want, and the financial status you want is to create your own ideas and solutions, test them, and learn from the feedback. To do this, you must be rational, objective, open to learn from the results you measure, and you must get those measurable results through experiments you push yourself to undertake through your own commitment and creative energy (pardon me while I gasp and inhale after that mouthful of a sentence).

This isn't a sexy, sellable idea. Outside of school, few people want to peer through a scientific lens. Plus, no business gets far teaching this because it soon runs out of customers willing to do the work.

None of that changes how vital this philosophy is, especially today. Global communication is as easy as pushing a button, making the world more competitive than ever. As Georgetown Professor Cal Newport wrote in *Deep Work*, "Once the talent market is made universally accessible, those at the peak of the market thrive while the rest suffer."

We're firmly in a Knowledge Economy, and machines have mopped up the jobs previously guaranteed to older generations. Technology and automation will replace, if they haven't already, every job that requires pure brute force. You may not like this trend, but neither did the Luddites who dismantled the textile machines in the 19th century. How'd it work out for them?

You can't thrive at the peak of the market just by putting your nose to the grindstone. Millions of other people are grinding away right now, even while you sleep, and more and more machines are too. You can, however, get ahead by constantly experimenting with your own creative ideas and objectively measuring the results. This doesn't just apply to your career. Cultivating a deep relationship with another person means constantly experimenting and measuring the results of how you interact. Putting it in such stark, scientific terms may inspire images of a couple attempting to relate by doing the robot dance in front of each other, but this idea is anything but cold and distant. "Working hard" on a relationship is a nebulous term. Working hard at what? How? You need to be able to figure out how you—a unique person—mesh with someone else—a unique person.

Unfortunately, as a culture, we've been programmed to plod forward and do as we're told. Schools force rote memorization down our throats, often causing a near-instant mental gag reflex. Even if we manage to keep down a bunch of memorized facts, they'll help us the least when competing against machines for jobs.

We love underdog stories where hard work, hope, and persistence pay off. We get a thrill out of watching people get hit with setback after setback until they overcome the odds. We cheer Rocky as he runs and hits the bag. I don't discount the message these stories can deliver, but something is missing. Focus, stick-to-itiveness, and a high pain tolerance alone won't guarantee you'll prosper in today's world.

College didn't teach me this and self-help books and courses were no better. They sell the dream and make the product simple and sexy, designed to keep the customer on the hook for more. I figured this out after wasting tens of thousands of dollars and realizing that my belief in these courses—and my self-blame when I failed to succeed with them—was the real problem. I needed to approach them as a scientist, questioning assumptions, testing things, and coming up with other ideas. Learning how to inquire and experiment separates us from other animals. So does how we imagine new possibilities, think long-term, and examine cause and effect. We have to piece together our own user manual, which requires intelligent action.

"This is the way of true happiness,
But because people prefer distractions and noise,
It is not a popular way."[48]

How do we experiment? We choose where to focus our efforts. We ask questions and open ourselves to new knowledge.

Here is a powerful sequence of questions:

1. **What is it?**
2. **Where does it come from?**
3. **How do I know it?**
4. **What should I do about it?**

I learned these from Peter Ragnar, a self-made millionaire who's been practicing meditation longer than most people have been alive. They're great go-to questions for life challenges.

Here are some hypothetical answers for getting out of debt:

1. **What is it?** Over $10,000 in credit card debt.
2. **Where does it come from?** I don't splurge on unneeded luxuries, but I did lean on my credit cards when some unexpected medical expenses came up.
3. **How do I know it?** Looking at my bill, I see that my unpaid balance comes from grocery shopping, gas for my car, and other basic items—not luxuries.
4. **What should I do about it?** I have a couple of choices. With my current income and spending, I can slowly chip away at this debt and eliminate it within a year. Or I

could rent out my spare bedroom and put the profit toward the debt and get rid of it faster.

You can customize these questions for a specific situation. If you wanted to learn more about building wealth, you could ask:

1. **What do self-made millionaires do to build wealth?**
2. **Where does this information come from?**
3. **How do I know it?**
4. **What should I do about it?**

Here are some hypothetical answers:

1. They live beneath their means, meticulously save, and invest portions of their income, get and stay married, and many are high-paid professionals or business owners. Proportionately few self-made millionaires are famous, but they get overrepresented as examples of wealth because of their fame.
2. *The Millionaire Next Door*, a book by Thomas Stanley.
3. I don't know for sure, so I can trust the research done by the author and back that up by doing research of my own.
4. I'll scale down my spending until it's less than I earn, get out of debt, invest my savings, and look into starting a business.

Notice how the answers require some research. When you challenge yourself with "Where does it come from?" you must break from your assumptions and hold space for learning something new. Here are some hypothetical answers from someone who neglects the research, but still has a logical conclusion:

1. **What do self-made millionaires do to build wealth?** According to the social media star whose videos I watched, it all comes down to the secrets they'll reveal in their videos and it's easy and simple to do.
2. **Where does this information come from?** Some random guy who made a bunch of videos sitting by his pool in a house that looks rented for the day.
3. **How do I know it?** I don't really know anything other than this person really wants me to watch his videos.
4. **What should I do about it?** Ignore the person, other than possibly studying how he markets.

These questions may seem too basic for you to use. However, when you struggle with a part of life, your mind almost certainly skips pertinent details and distracts you with a coping mechanism. You can expose it by asking and answering the right questions.

See if you can spot the coping mechanism in these answers:

1. **What do self-made millionaires do to build wealth?** They're all crooks.
2. **Where does this information come from?** Everyone knows that.
3. **How do I know it?** Because I'm not stupid.
4. **What should I do about it?** I'm going to post more on social media and then ignore the issue.

This person copes by closing their mind with anger.

At my truck-loading job, I worked with a temp who had an odd vibe. At a lunch break, he said he'd finished a five-year stint in prison for punching a cop. After getting out, he went to school for welding in Fort Collins, about an hour north of Denver.

"Things were going great until I went on a bender and ended up in Denver," he said. "The teacher even tried calling me a few times to help me, but I never answered him."

He was getting his life back together and threw it away with a drinking binge crazy enough that he ended up living in a different city.

"My ex is coming after me for child support," he said. "Sometimes it gets automatically taken out of my paycheck. If I don't come back Monday, it means they found me."

I never saw him again. That was a tragic example of not asking and answering the right questions. If he had questioned his behavior and choices more, he could have found a way out. It's an extreme example, but let's be honest—we all have these patterns. Whenever a part of our lives causes us pain, we often think and act like this. Humans are geniuses at ignoring, neglecting, glossing over. If you'd asked me in my early twenties why I wasn't in the relationship I wanted, I'd have grumbled some answers like the above or ignored your question. My anger created beliefs and behaviors that kept me in a comfort zone of familiar misery.

If there's a part of life where we excel, we don't bother asking these questions because the answers seem obvious. If there's a part of life where we struggle, we don't bother asking these questions because the answers seem too painful.

Sometimes, it's difficult to identify our worst pain points because we do a great job of avoiding them. Here's how to shed some light on them. Imagine yourself in a room surrounded by people you respect, and they start asking you questions. Which questions would you *not* want them to ask you? Which questions would embarrass you? Which would you never dare tell them to ask? Which questions would you avoid because you want to look good? Which questions would trigger an instant shutdown from you? These are the questions to sprint toward because your aversion means there's a coping mechanism built around them. Whatever the coping mechanism is, you constructed it to feel psychologically safe, but it's gumming up your life and costing you chi. Questions can start dissolving the gum, if you're willing to ask them.

Around the time of my bankruptcy, I began asking myself what was truly required of me to become financially prosperous. I had to acknowledge that, for me, this meant becoming stable first. After asking more questions, I applied to manual labor jobs that allowed my mind to remain free for thinking creatively about my business. I would have pulled myself out of my financial hole faster if I'd asked myself more questions.

Same with my spiritual path. To progress, I thought this way:

1. **What is it?** The idea that energy like chi exists and that there's a spiritual dimension to everything.
2. **Where does it come from?** I've read about it in books and heard about it from teachers.
3. **How do I know it?** I don't know it now, but can find out by practicing their teachings, get feedback from my senses, and rule out other possibilities. For instance, if I close my eyes and someone standing ten feet away emits chi and I feel it at the exact time they start, this shows there might be truth to the idea. If I don't feel anything, it could be because they're not effectively sending the chi or I'm not sensitive enough to feel it, so multiple rounds of practice are required.*

* This example is based on an exercise I've done many times with different people.

4. **What should I do about it?** Start practicing with the right people and keep an open mind.

I swear this didn't suck the fun out of my spiritual walk. Instead, it got more fun because I clearly proved how real my experiences were.

To change your life, you need clarity and direction. The first two questions make something clear. The next two questions push you to become clear about yourself. The third question is like a GPS targeting where you're at. The fourth question helps you map your route. It's the "put up or shut up" question, and if more people used it, their lives would change.

Once you answer your questions, the real work begins. You need to test your answers. Your tests must have measurable results. There's an old adage supposedly said by retailer John Wanamaker in the 19th century: "Half the money I spend on advertising is wasted; the trouble is I don't know which half."

Here are steps to create a worthwhile experiment:

1. **Choose an action you will take.**
2. **Decide what long-term results you want to measure.**
3. **Decide what short-term markers you'll watch for.**
4. **Take your action and observe the result.**
5. **Repeat to see if you get the same results.**

Is it me or is this advice boring? And obvious? I mean, who would have thought a major key to success would be doing something and then seeing what happens and then doing more stuff? Shocking!

In my defense, the *Dao De Jing* states:

"Profound words are not clever.
Clever words are not profound."[49]

The method may be as unsexy as the time I attempted to dance, like actually dance, during a sign-spinning shift, resulting in merely wagging my butt side to side (I could feel the aghast looks from drivers and, when I came inside, the two women managing the store admitted they laughed the whole time). But the results of this method, unlike my dancing, are most certainly *not* unsexy. In fact, if it weren't for all the slow, plodding work involved, the results would seem downright miraculous.

Here's how to apply questions to the Immortal Post. First, observe something about yourself. For instance, while in the Immortal Post, you might feel some pain and tension at the bottom of your lower back. Ask questions about what you observe.

1. **What am I feeling?**
2. **How do I know it?**
3. **Where exactly is it?**
4. **What do I want to do about it?**

Here are hypothetical answers:

1. **What am I feeling?** I'm feeling tension in my sacrum (in this example, tuning in revealed there wasn't actual pain, but mere tension).
2. **How do I know it?** It feels cramped and stiff, but everything around my sacrum feels okay (you're making sure you're not just fatigued or that the tension isn't coming from somewhere else).
3. **Where exactly is it?** I can feel the tension right below

my lower back area behind my hips (it's important to be specific so you learn more about your body).

4. **What do I want to do about it?** I want to relax it (you're getting clear on what you want, owning it, and getting consent from your consciousness, which is more important than most people would imagine).

Form an idea to test. You've learned plenty of techniques to relax tension. Choose one for your experiment. Let's say it's imagining breathing through your sacrum, flexing as you inhale, and relaxing as you exhale. You predict this will help relieve tension. Settle into the Immortal Post and begin the breathing technique. Pay attention to the outcome. Go a few rounds if you need to collect more data. Did you relieve your tension? Is the technique worth more testing? Or is something different needed? Form another idea for next time.

I performed round after round of experiments and chipped away at the tension in my sacrum. It was frustrating, but I remained devoted to testing out new things, because science never stops. This attitude helps stave off discouragement when nothing seems to work because there's always something to test. You need to figure out what it is and try it. Eventually, when I explored more emotional hang-ups, I resolved the tension. To get there, I had to drop my assumptions about the tension having a physical root cause. **Often in your experiments, you'll find that your most nagging, long-suffering problems have a surprising cause and solution.**

Here's a paradox about using questions to discover the proper action to take. The answer to "What should I do about it?" is often "Nothing." You might be surprised by no response being the best response. The ancient Daoists observed how, as the cycles of nature flow without our effort, our mind grows peaceful when we don't fight it. Your body can be the same. For tension to dissipate, it often requires that you simply relax into your motionless stance and do nothing else—especially in the beginning, when you're most tempted to do *anything* else. One of the most maddening things during the Immortal Post is when your legs and shoulders are burning and the answer to "What should I do about it?" is to grin it and bear it. Non-action can be the same paradoxical answer to struggles in our relationships. Here's an example:

1. **What is it?** My cousin is lashing out at me and trying to make me feel guilty.
2. **Where does it come from?** She's always been able to emotionally hook me to get me to do her a favor so she's running that pattern again.
3. **How do I know it?** I've worked with a therapist to understand how my cousin's interactions with me are a form of abuse and we've figured out the root cause. A trusted friend agrees with this explanation and my intuition does too.
4. **What should I do about it?** Nothing. I've attempted to set boundaries through my communication, but she's proven that she won't respect boundaries that allow for open communication. I won't respond to her message. If this continues, I'll revisit my options and consider blocking her.

The Daoists often used the metaphor of a rock splashing in a lake and creating waves to represent the chattering mind and the emotional upheavals it creates. You must wait for the waves to dissipate so the lake's surface can become still again. Imagine two people on opposite sides of the lake, lobbing rocks into the water whenever they see the waves splashing their way. The lake will never be still. The peace will never come. In codependent relationships, we think we're stuck trying to manage ourselves and the other person, and it's as useless as trying to still a lake's surface by splashing the perfect amount of rocks into it at the perfect moment. Instead, distance and time are required for peace to return.

In the spirit of this chapter, here's some more boring advice:

In her book *Grit*, Angela Duckworth quotes sociologist Dan Chambliss: "Superlative performance is really a confluence of dozens of small skills or activities, each one learned or stumbled upon, which have been carefully drilled into habit and then are fitted together in a synthesized whole. There is nothing extraordinary or superhuman in any one of those actions; only the fact that they are done consistently and correctly, and all together, produce excellence."

You could say the same about all breakthroughs. They may seem like the result of luck or talent, but if you could travel through time and space and see how they formed, you'd see someone testing things out, learning from the results, and making discoveries until everything fits to produce an excellent outcome.

This boring stuff can make the difference between needing an additional part-time job in your middle-age years and planning an early retirement. It can make the difference between a divorce and a happy marriage. It can make the difference between building a lucrative business and burning through tens of thousands and maybe hundreds of thousands of dollars of your savings, if not more (I know this personally).

It can also mean the difference between changing your life with the Immortal Post or growing frustrated and giving up because you didn't feel a difference.

Absorbing information is a pit stop on the road of self-discovery. Most of the journey requires you to mesh together what you learn, and figure out what works best for you, without someone else confirming if you're right or wrong, and with no guarantee of success. This journey is less about getting answers and more about asking better questions. Very few people can accept this, which is why self-help books won't end a section with, "Ultimately, you need to figure out your life for yourself."

CHAPTER EIGHTEEN

SEE WITHOUT JUDGMENT

One Saturday in early 2014, I sat at my desk at home and buried my head in my hands, emitting something like a scream. An hour earlier, when I'd gotten out of bed to do my standing meditation, something in the air felt strange.

If my years as a sign-spinner were like growing in a peaceful womb, this job loading trucks was like getting yanked into the screaming din of a hospital delivery room. It was a nightmare of 10+ hour shifts where I hauled 275+ pound cages on wheels, plunged headfirst into refrigerator-sized baskets of dirty laundry, folded thousands of rubber mats, and packed empty trucks to the brim with fresh supplies. Washers and dryers the size of elephants hissed from one wall and idling trucks rumbled from another. Even the roof held surprises, sometimes dropping a laundry bag heavier than an adult from forty feet up, almost killing my supervisor. Once, I accidentally hooked a metal cage onto a bag I was sending up a conveyor belt and, as I stepped away, the cage crashed onto my shoulder. After I yelped and doubled over, I realized that if I hadn't stepped aside, the cage would have slammed on my skull and paralyzed or killed me.

Gone were my days of contemplation when I stood outside waving a sign. The good part was that the workweek lasted only four days; I needed the whole three-day weekend to hide in my condo and lick my wounds.

Every workday, I got up at 11AM, did my standing meditation, baked a flatbread or made a concoction of gruel, and drove to work. Shifts started at 2PM and were supposed to end around midnight, but often went until 2AM. The latest I ever stumbled back to my car was close to 5AM—and that was yet another time when the car wouldn't start. I fixed it by sprinting back to the warehouse, where I mimed using a pair of pliers to the morning shift worker who didn't speak English, and then borrowed some pliers to tighten the bolts on my battery.

I was trying to land gigs in the marketing world and had been working on a letter to send to Doberman Dan, proposing he subcontract some of his client work to me. It was a win-win deal, and sending him a printed letter would get his attention. For whatever reason, I didn't send it. The idea festered as another half-finished project.

That Saturday morning, life needle-jabbed me to get going again. After finishing my meditation, I checked my bank account. It was over $100 in the negative. A cold front blew into my torso. I called my bank. They told me I'd overdrawn my account and hit me with four overdraft fees.

I asked to speak with a manager. He said he could remove only one. "I—I understand," I said, "but I'd appreciate if you removed three. I understand one fee, but I need that money for food and rent."

"Gosh I'm sorry. It sounds like you're facing tough times over there, but that's all we can do."

I thanked him and hung up, buried my face in my hands, and shouted against my palms.

Then my energy shifted. Screw it. I'm going to climb out of this.

Within 60 seconds, I pulled on my shoes, darted out my door, jumped in my car, and drove north.

I recalled an ancient Daoist tale Peter Ragnar told that goes like this:

Once there was an old farmer working a field with his horse. One day, the horse ran away. Some townspeople approached and lamented what bad luck it was: "We're so sorry your horse ran away! Now you don't have its help anymore. It's too bad!"

"Don't say good, don't say bad," the old farmer replied. "You can simply say my horse ran away."

The townspeople shrugged their shoulders, shook their heads, and left. A couple of days later, the horse returned with a pack of wild horses in tow. The townspeople returned and said, "Oh, what good luck! Your horse returned with many other horses. This is so good."

"Don't say good, don't say bad," the old farmer said. "You can simply say I have many horses."

Again, the townsfolk left, shaking their heads. The farmer's son began to tame the wild horses and one of them threw the boy. The fall broke his leg.

The townspeople saw this and said, "Oh, what terrible luck! Your son broke his leg and now he can't work your farm. That's too bad."

"Don't say good, don't say bad," the old farmer repeated. "You can simply say my son broke his leg."

The townspeople slapped their foreheads. A war broke out. The army recruited every young man in the area to fight. Their first battle was a slaughter and all the recruits were killed. But the old farmer's son wasn't recruited, because of his broken leg.

The townspeople returned and said, "Oh, you're so lucky! The war has killed so many of our sons, but yours remains alive. That's so good."

"Don't say good, don't say bad," the old farmer said. "You can simply say I have my son."

What to make of this story? I can't speak for the storyteller's intent, but I doubt it's about drifting through life with sociopathic detachment. It's not about divorcing yourself from emotion or love and plodding forward like a robot, never acknowledging pleasure or good fortune. I choose to interpret the story as not letting your judgments give you tunnel vision. This story reminds us to see the facts nakedly. Then you can use what life gives you to your best advantage.

When I was on the phone with my bank, I felt helpless. When the money got deleted from my savings, it opened a wound that gushed every hardship I'd slogged through for the past four years and flashed every failure in front of my eyes. Then something broke.

The bank had simply taken some of my money, but my ideas could bring me more income. As my perception expanded, I remembered I could choose how to respond. I stood up and busted out the door.

The money disappeared but, taking a cue from the old farmer, I didn't curl up in bed, punch the wall, or stuff my emotions. Back when my advertising campaign had gotten me almost drug-like high, I wished I'd had the old farmer's wisdom. Overexcitement can sabotage you as much as fear. Both spike your adrenaline, which shrinks your perception.

Imagine the old Daoist farmer saying, "Don't say good, don't say bad," with a smile on his face, while thinking, "Instead of wasting energy judging a situation, I'm going to relish every moment of this sumptuous life and keep my perceptions open to possibilities that help me thrive."

How can you apply this attitude? Think through the last five to ten years and choose five events that seemed spectacular or catastrophic. Write them down. They may look something like this:

1. Graduated college—seemed spectacular.
2. Got married—seemed spectacular.
3. Lost job—seemed catastrophic.
4. Got divorced—seemed catastrophic.
5. Investments in the stock market collapsed—seemed catastrophic.

Apply the Daoist farmer's wisdom. Don't say good, don't say bad. Simply say you got married. You can say that.

Seems pretty vacant, doesn't it? We're not striving to be a robot, but to view life without delirium. We're clearing the fog created by our judgments, to let rationality and objectivity shine through. Rationality and objectivity often get a bad rap because they are conflated with cold-heartedness. Acting rationally isn't driven by cold-heartedness even if some people happen to be both. Instead, rationality helps you discern and do the right thing without self-sabotage. You can mentally step back from your life and observe it. This is how good scientists work—they're detached from the experiments they create. Scientists don't want involvement; they want measurable results, and they're open to learn no matter what the result is.

Being rational means being aligned with nature's laws, dropping dogma, and letting your emotions process without stagnation. It doesn't mean becoming a robot. If you see someone acting like a robot and claiming to be rational, understand that he or she is stuffing their emotions. Superficial rationality has become their coping mechanism.

What happens when losing a job isn't good or bad? It means you can more clearly see your next step. It positions you to find something better, or to let it find you.

Earlier in 2014, just days away from losing my sign-spinning job, I drove one of my supervisors, Kelly, home.

Kelly was her Americanized name because most people couldn't pronounce her Russian one. She emigrated when she was 18 and knew exactly two sentences of English. Since then, she propelled through life like an icebreaker ship, marching her 95-pound, 5' 1" frame toward whatever she wanted. Kelly's machine-like focus had long ago trampled over her empathy. Hearing her say, "My stupid husband!" in her accent was funny until I remembered she wasn't being humorous.

She was getting axed from her job too, but on the ride home she practically squealed with glee, darting her head toward me as she said how curious she was about her *next* potential job.

She embodied "Don't say good, don't say bad" but I still hadn't learned my lesson. The more she gushed, the harder I clenched the steering wheel. I bet her curiosity led her to a better gig than loading trucks.

Let's try one more from our hypothetical list:

"Don't say good, don't say bad. Simply say you got divorced. You can say that."

We're starting to see the Daoist farmer's wisdom. If you hadn't gotten married—which felt spectacular—you wouldn't get divorced—which felt catastrophic. What matters more, the beautiful memories or the pain? Why torture yourself trying to measure something that you can't? If you're trapped comparing everything, you'll find more reasons to be miserable.

What if you've been so busy measuring the meaning of situations that you forgot *that you get to determine their meaning?*

When you don't dwell on good and bad, you keep your mind focused on cultivating fulfillment, which you *can* control. That's not being a robot, but allowing yourself to grow to your full potential. Go through the final two items on your list to see how "Don't say good, don't say bad" applies. Apply it to your future. If nothing's good or bad, then you have nothing to fear or dread.

Losing money from my bank account wasn't the only time I had to keep my perspective from becoming my enemy. Years earlier, in the late winter months before I filed for bankruptcy, I sat in my apartment sick with fear, wondering how I'd afford the payments my debt collectors demanded.

When pondering filing for bankruptcy, I hesitated. Could I dare see this as a fresh start? For some reason, my love of the movie "Dumb & Dumber" popped up and I searched YouTube for Todd Rundgren's song *Can We Still Be Friends*. The haunting tone and lyrics mixed with regret and hope echoed through my mind as I imagined shuffling out of a bankruptcy meeting looking melancholy, but not ready to quit. As I played the song, relief washed over me. I didn't need to judge my life as hopeless.

Let's see how we can practice "Don't say good, don't say bad" with the Immortal Post. Say you've set fifteen minutes on your timer, relaxed into your stance, and, when the meditation's over, you feel more agitated than ever. Your shoulder muscles feel tighter than a Gordian knot. You figure you've wasted your time.

That's the perfect invitation to quote the old farmer's "Don't say good, don't say bad." You can say, "I did my fifteen-minute meditation. You can say that." Then move on with your day. Instead of beating yourself up, you're setting yourself up for an unseen blessing. You can even use the old farmer's wisdom before your fifteen minutes are up. Here are phrases you can employ during your meditation:

"Don't say good, don't say bad. Simply say your mind has been really loud up until now. You can say that."

"Don't say good, don't say bad. Simply say your shoulders have felt really tense up until now. You can say that."

Don't be surprised if your mind quiets and your shoulders relax.

Here's a caveat. Sometimes, the old farmer's wisdom is the wrong tool for the job. An example of that:

"Don't say good, don't say bad. Simply say you feel sharp, stabbing pain in your left knee. You can say that."

No, don't just say that. Stop your meditation! Learn to discern between harmful judgments and responding appropriately to an emergency. In the story, the farmer refused to judge the parts of life outside his control. However, if someone tried to steal his horse in front of him, he wouldn't mutter something about good or bad. He'd clean the would-be robber's clock with some badass Daoist martial arts move.

When his son fell and broke his leg, I doubt the farmer stood there quoting Daoist wisdom. He probably jumped to help his son. Only later, when the townspeople passed judgment, did he impart nonjudgmental wisdom.

If someone abuses you, it's not an invitation to reflect on life with an open perspective. Abuse is a sign to get the hell away from your abuser, even if it means ripping up deep roots. Once you're safe, you can detach yourself from good and bad and open your perspective.

When the bank overdrew my account, I bolted out the door because I remembered the draft letter I'd written for Dan. Driving to a FedEx Office to print the letter, I laughed. Nothing in my outside world changed, but I seemed to be floating. Everything shifted, as if something had reached down and turned a dial. I sent the letter, one of the most important letters I'd ever send—but I didn't know that, yet.

A few days later, Dan contacted me and I continued to take cues from the Daoist tale, reminding myself that Dan responding was simply Dan responding—that's all. He said he might have some leads. One became a client worth $3,000—more than a month's pay as a truck loader, with fewer hours of work. But the life-changing event wouldn't happen for a few more months. Today, I can look back on those months without judging them good or bad, but they did nearly destroy my body and teach me what hard work truly is.

CHAPTER NINETEEN

EFFORT

I grabbed the oozing bag, tore the plastic open like ripping apart a half-healed wound, flipped it, and let oil-soaked rags spill into the giant basket.

I was working the shift called "The Sling" at the truck-loading job. When a crew unloaded a truck, they threw the dirty pants, shirts, and floor mats into baskets. I hauled them to a sling, tagged them, and sent them up to a conveyor belt. I also had to rip open dozens of plastic bags stuffed with rags soaked in oil, body fluids, ammonia, and who knows what else.

As the stench radiated, I grabbed the next bag. White towels with green stripes. I waded through the chest-deep swamp of baskets, metal rims grinding at my arms.

The crew working the truck unloaded as fast as they could. If I didn't drag everything away in time, the 275-pound metal baskets crowded into a traffic-jam. Then the crew sat on the edge of the truck and stared at me.

One day, while I staggered around the baskets, searching and panicking as if I'd lost a child in a crowd, a co-worker sauntered over.

"Let me give you some advice," he said, smirking. "If you fall behind and they want you to speed up, just go as slow as you like. It doesn't matter—they'll just have to wait."

Yeah, why not? This was way too hard. Screw it. Holding one bag at a time, I moseyed around the baskets. More arrived and their rims clanged as they bunched together. Soon, nobody could squeeze through the sea of baskets.

My other co-workers sat on the edge of the mostly empty truck, folded their arms, and stared at me.

My boss, a former wrestler in college and now balding at age 24 with arms the size of my legs, said, "I need to see a sense of urgency from you."

I filled in the rest: "…or I'll fire you."

But how could I keep up? They're unloading the trucks too fast. It's too much work. It's impossible. Then I turned things around. I didn't want to spend the three-day weekend wondering if I'd get canned, nor did I want to let down my co-workers.

Peter Ragnar taught that two of his favorite words are *alacrity*, which means a cheerful readiness, and *celerity*, which means moving swiftly. Alacrity and celerity evoke a balance of effort and effortlessness, working with vigor yet without strain.

I came up with a mantra. *Earn your weekend*. I told this to myself after my shift was over, prepping myself to march back the next day and kick those baskets' asses.

"Earn your weekend. Earn your weekend," I said as I drove to work.

That mantra was different from any affirmations I'd used before going bankrupt—back when I tried to visualize myself rich. I wasn't demanding something that was out of my control; I was inspiring myself to be a better person. I believed I could do it.

When the truck backed into the bay, I glared at it, flexed my hands, and breathed deeper. After my co-workers dumped pants into the first basket, I clamped my arms around the metal rim and wrenched it to the sling. When they pushed a basket overflowing with plastic bags to me, I grabbed each bag and ran as if it were a wet, half-deflated, oversized football. I hurried, even when the coast seemed clear. I tried to never let my co-workers get ahead of me.

When the shift ended, I smiled. *You earned your weekend.* Paradoxically, I felt less tired and, later, I'll show how the ancient Daoists were very familiar with this phenomenon. It was an essential part of their training.

My truck-loading job redefined what I thought the human body was capable of. That's a nice way of putting it. It forced my body through twelve-hour meat grinders, where I thought half an hour of meat-grinding was all I could handle before collapse.

I'd be impressed with how I hoisted barbells and dumbbells for a 45-minute workout. If someone stepped into the gym and told me to do the same workout—over and over—for at least ten hours with one break, I'd have said that's impossible. But when I started the truck loading job, nobody said the work was impossible. Everyone acknowledged it would suck—all the new employees lost up to 30 pounds of bodyweight in their first couple of months—and I'd be slow at first, but the egregore of the warehouse reinforced that the impossible was indeed possible, and even normal. My body and mind adapted. As I learned the tricks—pulling on a 275-pound cage the right way to avoid the dinged-up wheel and grabbing and folding mats with no wasted movement—the impossible became possible.

During one of my first shifts folding floor mats, I could barely lift my hands or shuffle to the wheeled rack where I tossed the mats. A couple of co-workers joined me and we grabbed mats from the basket, folded them on a table, and turned to let them drop on the rack. For the next two hours, we marched in a counterclockwise circle until the mats were folded.

We didn't take breaks because that meant delaying our finish. It didn't matter how tired we were, what feelings came up, or if we finished at midnight or 5AM.The trucks were either loaded or they weren't.

Your inner growth is like those trucks. You either grow or you don't. The spirit world knows. Only you can fool yourself. If you want spiritual growth—I mean, if you *really* want it—then you need to redefine your beliefs of hard work, commitment, and consistency.

The ancient Daoists taught a paradoxical concept called effortless effort. When you get into the flow of the Dao, you work without strain or struggle, yet you accomplish everything you want. I'll cover **effort** first because it's easy to use effortless effort to justify a lackadaisical attitude.

"Without faltering
fully choose to do what you must do.
This is to live without forcing
to overcome without conquering."[50]

You probably don't need to haul tens of thousands of pounds of dirty clothes or boxes. However, if you want to change your life—especially if you want to uproot and transform negative feelings and coping mechanisms or if you want to increase your income by a significant margin—you must adopt a professional's attitude and standards toward work. Professionals work until the job is done, and done well.

The average person struggles to show up at the gym for more than a few weeks after January 1st. The professional ultra-marathoner struggles with how to properly navigate terrain and feed themselves as they do something that would kill the average person.

Changing your life is an ultra-marathon task and you must become professional about it. When you follow the Daoist path and rid yourself of emotional stagnation and coping mechanisms, the effort can become effortless, but you need to redefine what effort is for you. I started by practicing the Immortal Post for 60 seconds, but if I'd limited myself to that, I'd still be broke and drinking my days away.

When you apply the right amount of effort at the right time, it will feel effortless, just as I felt less tired after maneuvering the baskets with celerity.

Before your practice of the Immortal Post can become effortless effort, you must earn it by breaking through the mental barrier of your burning muscles.

The Immortal Post, all spiritual hubbub aside, is a test of stamina. You must push your way through the trial by fire of adapting your muscles to the slight knee-bend. Think of it as the initiation to a higher level of health and human performance. This is how new students have been tested for thousands of years. Once your body adapts, your muscles will no longer feel taxed. Then the transition to relaxing in your meditation accelerates.

This is my fancy way of saying that it's going to hurt. Ache. *Burn*. Once you advance beyond the stage of strengthening your muscles, you'll run into different challenges because your deep tension will be exposed. If your shoulders are tense, they'll ache. If your hamstrings are tense, they'll throb. In this case, they don't need to get stronger. They must let go. Feeling the pain is your first step to freedom.

Remember that you've lived with tension for years, but it seeped beneath your conscious awareness. The standing meditation is exposing something that was quietly holding you back all this time. Within the tension is emotional stagnation, woven together like DNA's double-helix. It's painful to unravel these patterns, but the results are worth it.

When you feel dull aches, general discomfort or just plain weird, run through this checklist:

1. **How is my structure? Am I aligned? Am I relaxed in my position?**
2. **How is my breathing? Is it slow, relaxed, and deep?**

If your structure and breathing are good, chances are the energy is breaking through some stagnation and you must accept the discomfort to continue your progress. Many people stall their progress right before a breakthrough because they think "this isn't working." Push yourself past this mental plateau and you might discover your breakthrough waiting on the other side.

Pain is the price of admission for benefiting from the Immortal Post. When you begin the standing meditation, your body will feel stiff, awkward, and lactic acid will pulse burning bolts of pain through your leg muscles.

Part of your brain will start negotiating for your surrender. A voice in your head will innocently mention that this standing meditation isn't right for you and not what it's cracked up to be. *After all, you're just standing there. You're busy. Why not move onto something else and revisit this another day? What would other people think, anyway? Isn't it weird to do something like this? And what are the chances you'll get any benefits? So why bother?*

The voice sounds so reasonable and so knowledgeable that it makes sense to listen. Does any of this sound familiar? It might, because this same subtly negative self-talk seduces you out of any worthwhile endeavor. This is the voice that moves people away from exercising or working on their marriage. It conspires with television and social media to keep you glued to them. It keeps you in your comfort zone and has no shortage of logical reasons for you to accept failure.

In her book *Grit*, MacArthur Fellow winner Dr. Angela Duckworth studied West Point cadets, Green Berets, NFL football teams, famous historical figures, CEOs, authors, and even National Spelling Bee champions. She found the genesis of their success came down to one word: the title of her book.

Dr. Duckworth measured grit with tests containing statements like, "I have overcome setbacks to conquer an important challenge." Other questions measured how long someone was committed to building a skill rather than jumping from activity to activity.

People who could say "Yes" to those statements and spend long stretches working on skills were the ones who succeeded, not just in their achievements, but in how fulfilled they felt.

In *Grit*'s conclusion, she writes, "...you can grow your grit 'from the inside out': You can cultivate your interests. You can develop a habit of daily challenge-exceeding-skill practice. You can connect your work to a purpose beyond yourself. And you can learn to hope when all seems lost."

When you begin the Immortal Post, you're training in a grit-building arena. No matter how advanced you become, the Immortal Post can be a challenge-exceeding-skill practice. You can connect it to a purpose beyond yourself and you can choose to feel hope even when your legs quake from the effort and your mind feels like your worst enemy. You can cheer yourself on, work through pain, and, as you get stronger, find that the pain fades and you can forever look back on your success. What sets the standing meditation apart from other skills is balancing grit and relaxation. You can't gnash your teeth and get it over with. You must relax into the pain.

As I practiced and experimented with the standing meditation, I had to remind myself to relax. My body's tension unwound slowly, and some days it jerked back into place like an animal fleeing in fear. I kept going because of how my inner life had already changed and from the grit I'd built up along the way.

Part of your mind will try to talk you out of pain, even if it means sacrificing your dreams. When you begin the standing meditation, you'll get a perfect opportunity to practice mental toughness and reject self-sabotaging seductive pleas. Once your body gets stronger, you'll be living proof that you can master your mind. That's when the rest of the benefits begin manifesting.

Think of it like lifting weights. If you start by bench pressing 100 pounds and then march back into the gym the next day and attempt 200 pounds, you'll probably fail and maybe quit, thinking, "Lifting weights doesn't work!" But your body was adapting; if you had waited a couple of days and attempted 101 pounds, you might have been surprised by how easy the heavier weight felt. This is spiritual weight training. Commit yourself to the long haul.

The good news is, once you get past the barrier of burning muscles—usually when you can hold the standing meditation for ten minutes—you can practice effortless effort. The same is true in the rest of your life. When I hit the right balance of effortless effort, like nailing a musical note, my life transformed.

While enduring the truck-loading job's pain, I emailed Peter Ragnar some photos of the Denver apartment I'd moved out of. I told him that I wanted to move back. Little did I realize what life had in store for me.

In the meantime, I was about to learn the power of effortless effort, but first life had to put me through even worse pain.

CHAPTER TWENTY

EFFORTLESS EFFORT

"I can quit any time I want! I can get a job across the street bagging groceries!"

I stood in my condo, trembling, soaked in a cold and sour sweat, shouting my threat to an empty room.

For a couple of months, my truck-loading job had beaten me down further and further. It was testing me, but was the answer to push through the pain or find a different job? I begged for a transfer—something less exhausting. My boss said I needed to meet certain efficiency numbers so I pushed myself even harder. My shift partner and I got fast enough that we finished our work early and helped other positions in the warehouse.

"There's an opening for the Order Puller position," my boss said. "You've got a pretty good memory so I think you could do it."

Why was having a good memory important? The thought flickered on and off my mental screen like a moth under a light. For the next few days, I told myself *of course* it'd be easier than what I was doing now.

One night a little after 12:30AM, as I stood outside the warehouse's bay doors, surrounded by buckets of dirty mop heads, my boss said he could transfer me.

"Are you sure about this?" he said. "Once you go, there's no coming back."

My intuition fired a distinctive warning pulse through my body, but I ignored it.

"Yes, I'm sure."

A few days later, he texted me to confirm the change, and at 4:30AM the next day—my new wake-up time—the intuitive pulse intensified into a shriek. I'd screwed up. Bad.

The new job was order-pulling, which meant memorizing rows and rows of clothes in a warehouse section as big as a McMansion. It was like solving a life-sized maze for eight hours while someone keeps growling about how you're screwing up. Actually, that *was* the job. My supervisor yelled contradicting orders at me. She loathed and dehumanized me, so I resented her, which intensified the dehumanization.

After I tried to lighten the mood with some humor, she said, "Leave the joking to the 10-year-olds. If you go through life making jokes, people will think you're a joke."

When I told this to the main supervisor for the shift, he said, "Uh, okay, I'll talk to her," as he gazed at some invisible object in the distance.

He did nothing so I complained again. And again. Then I cornered him in the break room at lunch. "Nothing's changed!" I said.

A temp, a woman in her sixties, had been working near me for a week. She marched next to me and said to the main supervisor, "She treats him worse than a dog!"

"She keeps yelling at me," I said.

"It's true!"

"Okay, okay," he said. The same glassy look poured over his face like a mist.

Even if it didn't help, I was grateful for the temp worker standing by me. Later that day, I bumped into her.

"Thank you," I said.

She squeezed my hand as she looked into my eyes and smiled.

After that day, her temp agency must have moved her elsewhere—I never saw her again

Every workday, I got up at 4:30AM, did a brief standing meditation, and made the dark drive to the warehouse. As the days turned into weeks, I reaffirmed that I'd use my mind power to excel at the job... until reality showed me that fantasizing and effort were no substitutes for rationality and strategic thinking. I began to break down.

As I drove to work in the eerie pre-sunrise dark, I tried to pretend every road would last forever. After work, I spent an hour looking for jobs before collapsing into bed. A haze of panic clouded my mind, until I screamed in my head. *What am I going to do?* After yet another failed attempt to find a new job, I screamed this out loud, clawing for any control, any way out, and declared that I could bag groceries. I craved my old sign-spinning job and my old life.

I visited the supermarket across the street, but discovered the only positions available were part-time, not enough to pay for my rent and food. I was trapped.

After working both positions in the company, I learned that it didn't matter how hard the job was. That's not where misery comes from. If I could do the work with a good team on my side, get a decent night's sleep, and sneak in a round of the Immortal Post and coffee, it was *game on*. But if I were stuck with hurtful people, no amount of meditation could keep me feeling wonderful all day. Fortunately, the way my energy was changing would help me escape.

I looked back on the times I'd scrambled nonstop for a result, but crashed and burned. The year before I went bankrupt, I pushed and pushed to create new product offerings, yet strange setbacks hit me. The post office would lose something I mailed. People would make promises, then disappear. So, I cranked up my scrambling.

The day after my job transfer at the truck-loading company, I tried transferring back, rushing to get my efficiency numbers high enough and skipping the morning break to do so. Nobody was even counting what I did.

I remembered times that I'd struggled yet allowed myself to surrender. Soon after getting the sign-spinning job, I'd prepared for what could have been the saddest New Year's Eve of my life—a designation with years and years of solid competition. I was tumbling toward bankruptcy, had gotten a low-paying, humiliating job, had no girlfriend to celebrate the new year with, and was taking stock of how my dreams in my early 20s had sunk into a joke.

I could stay home and sulk…or do something else. My friend Jim had given me a black-colored gift card, his way of hinting that one day I'd possess an actual black credit card, which has virtually no limit on purchasing power. I went to King Soopers and used it to buy everything needed to make a pizza.

This was revolutionary for me. I avoided spending even a few dollars unless I could tie them to achieving my goals. This time, I treated Jim's gift like a gift, and used it for something creative that would nourish me. I celebrated for the sake of celebrating.

When my ad campaign had bombed, and the next day I told myself this was just a bump in the road, it allowed me to celebrate that moment. Every time I picked up a penny, dime, or quarter on the street, I relished my riches.

I remembered my former co-worker from the gold-buying company, who'd been excited to get laid off. She regularly treated herself to little luxuries. With her example, the world was dangling something in front of me.

Peter Ragnar teaches that you have everything you need in this moment—and to always feel this way. I doubted that and pointed out times when I'd felt abundant and at peace, but then spiraled further into financial ruin. Yet what if there was something to it? Was it wrong to experiment with enjoying the present? What if the worst that could happen was getting more fun out of life?

Years earlier, I rode through the mountains on a snowy day. A traffic jam nudged me to take an unfamiliar road and as I got lost, I realized it was one of the most gorgeous drives I'd ever taken. I promised that, when I became wealthy, I'd return here whenever I wanted. But not **until** I'm wealthy.

That attitude was typical. Always chasing some nebulous result. Always putting life on hold until I got *this* or until I achieved *that*.

I'd burned through my late teens and most of my 20s turning the comforts of life into punishments. This withholding of rewards had withheld my greatest dreams from me. *What if I worked on myself and cultivated fulfillment in the present moment? What if I stopped pushing enjoyment out of reach?*

One Saturday, after another wretched week of work, I drove through that winding mountain road I'd fantasized about. I made that mini-vacation a tradition of driving in the Rockies, feeling that I was nestling in giant blankets and that I'd already made it, so I wasn't scrambling to change anything. Other days, I hiked to the top of South Table Mountain, a gentle foothill in Golden, and gazed at the view.*

During shifts at my new job, when I stumbled through aisles of clothes, I sneaked peeks out an open window facing the mountains. The opening was too low to see anything, but the springtime air breezing from the west filled my nose with sweetness and bathed my body in warmth. I inhaled, cleared my mind, and stopped time for five seconds before charging back into work. That pause deposited a bit more juju into my spiritual bank account.

But brief moments of re-generation weren't enough. After my shift, I searched for jobs. I found an ad for cargo handlers, unloading trucks and stacking the boxes in a warehouse. When I interviewed, I probably asked more questions than any other prospective cargo handler in history; I wasn't going to make my life worse by switching jobs again. My gut told me to accept the position. I gave the old warehouse notice and they allowed me to leave within a week. I started my new position the next day.

The warehouse was north of Denver, close to I-70. As I parked and walked to the stadium-sized building, the grounds were eerily silent. The perfectly manicured grass and the glass walls, which almost looked like a tech office space, seemed too nice and neat.

When I entered the front office, the security guard put down his phone. As he looked up my name, I glanced at his phone's screen—the video was playing porn. He let me through.

---

* A year ago, I bought a house in Golden within walking distance of those foothills.

Inside the warehouse, the buffed cement floors were nearly slippery and the walls stretched so far away I could hardly make out the details. It looked like the subterranean chamber in *Batman Begins* when Bruce Wayne tested the tumbler vehicle with Mr. Fox.

Lurking in one corner was a bay door with a conveyor belt laid out like a long, thin, metal tongue. It ran to the other side of the warehouse and forked hard right, stretching along the opposite wall from the bay door.

The mechanism was as sinister as it was simple. Trucks—monster 53-foot trailers—backed into the bay door, like a giant slowly positioning itself over a toilet. Then we'd unlock the back doors, revealing the truck was pregnant with boxes. My job was to square off with the 10-foot-high wall of boxes, grab them one by one, and throw them onto the conveyor belt, until the truck was empty. The position was called *throwing*, giving you an idea of how gently we handled the merchandise.

The first day was deceptively easy—just one truck trailer. The second day was eighteen hours of unloading nine truck trailers. After three I told my supervisor, "I'm feeling good. I could throw all day."

"Oh, yeah?" he said.

I marched into the fourth trailer. The boxes were smaller. Instead of the usual cardboard scent, the trailer was perfumed. I grabbed the first box and it almost wriggled out of my grip like an animal. *Oh, no.* The boxes were filled with perfume, lotion, and soap bottles. They felt so heavy that I might as well have been lifting iron. I bent and grabbed, bent and grabbed, journeying deeper into the dark trailer, the warehouse's light not daring to follow me, the truck's engine rumbling louder as I dug closer, dismantling an underworld box by box.

After unloading that truck, I was amazed my spine was still intact. I'll never look at mall displays of perfume and hand moisturizer the same way again.

When the day began, the football field-sized warehouse was empty. At the end, it resembled *Raiders of The Lost Ark*'s final scene where stacks of boxes tower beyond sight. My body trembled from exhaustion and I spent the final hours of my shift fantasizing about chocolate milkshakes.

That night, I crawled into bed, but my brain was so twisted with stress that I couldn't sleep, so I spent hours imagining marching back into the warehouse and roaring, "I quit!"

In my dark, silent bedroom, I decided to do it—damn the consequences. Then, as sunlight creeped into my condo, my bravado fled like a vampire, even as I tried convincing it not to return to its coffin. *No matter what, I'm going to quit…or maybe I'll give this a couple more days.*

I dozed for an hour before my alarm went off. As the tone blared, my last speck of rebellion fizzled out, and I trudged to work for another backbreaking fifteen-hour shift and another night of one-hour sleep. The next day, another shift and two hours of sleep.

After that, I told my supervisor, "I can't do this." Yet I didn't quit. Instead, I did something more strategic—something I'd done only a few times in my life.

Instead of crawling back to my job and accepting the insane amount of labor they expected, I negotiated. Negotiation can be a spiritual test. You must believe you deserve what you want, and your perspective must be open to what the other person wants, too. You can't be a bully *or* allow yourself to be bulldozed. You have to slog through uncomfortable communication and remain levelheaded. Many people are addicted to conflict or avoid it at all costs. Neither is emotionally nor spiritually mature.

In this negotiation, I had a couple of advantages. First, I still had the $3,000 from the contract job I'd landed a few weeks earlier. Plus, my dad sent me a check as a gift, for a bit more than that. Most of the money was earmarked for my business, but either way it meant I wasn't living hand-to-mouth. Besides, I was so desperate and crazed from lack of sleep that I didn't care if I ended up living out of my car. Something was breaking open in my life. Everything pointed to it: my spine adjusting all the way to the top, the gig I'd landed, the connections I was making, and my day jobs driving me crazy.

I sat in front of my manager and spilled out my demands. I wanted to work three days a week. I'd work the longest shifts—where they needed the most help and where I'd make the most money—but I wanted four days off in a row. They accepted; probably because I wasn't demanding much, and they struggled to hire anyone willing to destroy their body for $10.25 an hour.

This arrangement gave me the mental breathing room to move my business forward and enough cash to support myself...for three months. I let myself get crazier. On my days off, I booked a massage and chiropractor appointment. If there really is a connection between energy flowing through my channels and prosperity, I was going to find out.

Earlier in this book, you learned how your body and mind are influenced by a web of energy. My gut told me that getting chiropractic adjustments and massages—both physical changes—would help change this web of energy.

On the afternoon of my first day off, I entered a Starbucks and ordered the biggest, highest-calorie, most expensive chocolate/coffee/ice cream abomination to nutrition available. Then, as I ducked and weaved my car into the mountains, I sipped this drink and felt steeped in luxury.

It didn't matter that 24 hours earlier I'd sweated and stumbled through the back of a 53-foot trailer, throwing boxes onto a conveyor belt. Or that in a couple of days I'd do this all over again, like Sisyphus pushing the boulder uphill for eternity. What mattered was the inner peace I cultivated between my work shifts.

If I alternated working on my business and taking restorative rests, I'd break through—that was the message. Like the spiritual equivalent of *a watched pot never boils* (or checking your phone every two seconds for a text), I couldn't obsess all the time, but had to let the energy do its work. Little did I realize that my life was about to change.

Practicing a spiritual discipline will attract challenges which will, if you let them, help mold your character, granting you the things, people, and circumstances that fulfill you. Part of that process is the practice of what ancient Daoists called "non-doing."

"The more we are released
from vested fragments of knowledge,
the less we are compelled
to take vested actions,
until all is done without doing.

When the ego interferes
in the rhythms of process,
there is so much doing!

But nothing is done."[51]

This is one of Daoism's greatest paradoxes. How can there be so much doing when nothing is done? How can things get done without doing?

The first question is easier to answer. When emotional stagnation, old wounds, ego, and coping mechanisms drive your actions, you can work as hard as possible, but you'll self-sabotage. This sums up my early 20s and why planning, habit-forming, getting out of my comfort zone, taking action, and goal-setting didn't work for me. It's why I needed to work on my deepest energetic blocks—while standing still—before I could take steps toward changing my life.

Yes, there are exceptions to the concept of non-doing—people do seem to accumulate success by strain and struggle. Those exceptions bothered me because they seemed to prove this idea wrong. People do push themselves into exhaustion building a career for themselves and become wealthy. People, driven by self-hatred, do torture themselves with restrictive diets and brutal exercise regimens and become strong and slim. Yes, you can practically kill yourself to get what you want—maybe. But at what cost? And what if that's not the best way?

What if you could live a better life by not doing? And, when it comes to your work, what if you could get better results by straining less, by using effortless effort?

In my early 20s, part of me resisted going deeper with this idea because I feared becoming some spiritual slacker who lived a mediocre existence, but possessed some vague "peace of mind" or a "balanced lifestyle." My mind twisted in two directions like a pair of serpents with tails tied together. How do these lofty spiritual ideas mesh with what we can observe and achieve in the world?

When I negotiated my work schedule, I discovered how all can be done without doing. To the Daoists, **doing means actions that go against the Dao—actions driven by emotional stagnation, old wounds, ego, and coping mechanisms. This causes you to scramble.**

Before my bankruptcy, I was a stumbling mess of misguided action and lack of conscious awareness, spurred by the fear of going broke, the grief of being lonely, and comparing myself to other people. So much doing and nothing got done!

Daoists strip unfulfilling parts of their lives so they can act deliberately when intuition compels them to. This opens their perceptions and guides them to a better life. When it's time to recharge and process, they avoid distractions and relax into stillness.

If someone looked at both ways of living, they might fail to perceive a difference. Watching television may look like non-doing and taking frantic action may look like doing, but they're both *unconscious* versions of non-doing and effortless effort—similar to how someone sitting in meditation might appear the same as someone sitting with a chattering mind. One is "effortful effortlessness" versus "effortless effort."

The secret isn't to stop doing or to stop caring or wanting change. **It's to stop letting fear, anger, worry, overexcitement, and desperate actions interfere with your growth.**

Non-doing means not overreacting. When I felt desperate to escape my job loading trucks, I jumped at the first opportunity for a transfer and ended up more miserable. Without pausing to reflect, I ignored my intuition and warning signs. I let my emotions drag me around.

Non-doing is surrender—specifically, surrendering your ego's craving for everything to go your way, exactly as you want it, exactly when you want it, for exactly the reasons you want, with the exact people thinking and feeling exactly what you want them to feel, and that you should feel exactly a certain way after everything goes your way. How much energy do you think those demands burn? In my early 20s, I wrote detailed plans of how I was going to become wealthy and successful; the universe shoved those plans through the galactic paper shredder and dumped the strips over my head like spiritual confetti. Because I didn't figure out how to surrender, the universe was thoughtful enough to force the issue.

On the other hand, non-doing is *not* escapism. When you plug yourself into entertainment, that's doing. Even when you sit still and fantasize, you're doing something. You're using mental energy to hide from your problems. The waste of mental energy is a major reason why positive visualization sabotages people.

When you unravel your coping mechanisms and emotional stagnation, you can stop acting in ways that don't serve you. This might feel scary. "I need to do something or everything will fall apart!" "I can't get started—I'm too worried about how I'll fail!" Such thoughts are often buried too deeply to be heard, but they're lurking behind the compulsion to do more, more, more.

A life with less worry and grief and rage might seem like a risk, as if dropping negative feelings leaves you vulnerable for life to blindside you or those you love. This is absolutely true. Getting rid of your patterns and emotional armor leaves you more naked. Life might surprise you or your loved ones, but that might be the opportunity for growth that you need.

A lack of worry doesn't mean a lack of vigilance and a lack of bitterness doesn't mean a lack of boundaries. Drop your emotional armoring and unhealthy coping mechanisms to forge proper boundaries. Non-doing is essential for that.

The Daoists presented non-doing as a paradox (like "effortless effort") to show how non-doing coexists with doing, like the famous Taiji symbol (the yin/yang symbol).

When athletes perform perfectly—sometimes superhumanly—without conscious thought, they're combining doing and non-doing. Their bodies do everything needed to win while their minds shut off so they can observe. Athletes call this being in "the zone."

Too many people spend their lives doing the opposite. They *do* by worrying, obsessing, grieving, raging, distracting themselves, and reacting. They clutter their lives and push themselves into actions based on coping mechanisms and limited perceptions. Instead of processing their emotions, they go into denial and plug themselves into television shows or social media until they're paralyzed; a perverse version of *non-doing.*

Think of the last time you were in a creative flow, when your mental chatter ceased and you accomplished something remarkable. Time flew and you felt more energized when you finished, yet an observer would think you'd performed an exhausting amount of work.

This flow state isn't limited to creative endeavors. Surgeons report this while performing a 12-hour life-or-death operation. It needn't be dramatic, either. If you file your taxes without emotionally reacting, the Daoists would consider that effortless effort.

In my second job unloading trucks, one of my co-workers could unload the 53-foot trailer so quickly that he'd do handstand push-ups while waiting for everyone to catch up organizing the boxes. After I worked there a few weeks, I figured out how to twist the boxes in the perfect way so they'd spin midair and land where they needed to on the conveyor belt. I sensed how much—or how little—force I needed to grab, pull, and push with.

When I finished the truck and marched out, feeling that I'd conquered the empty trailer, my co-worker said, "Feels good, doesn't it?"

He was talking about effortless effort—doing without doing.

Seen from this perspective, non-doing isn't refraining from action and not necessarily meditation. If someone pontificates all day and claims they live a spiritual life, they're misguided. The Daoists call it effortless effort, not effortless sitting around and contemplating spirituality. When I sat at the top of the foothills and gazed at the Rocky

Mountains, I wasn't being lazy or "taking time to smell the roses." I was stripping away compulsive actions spurred by coping mechanisms.

The Daoists teach to flow like water, by the force of gravity. Water often appears still while moving—sometimes rapidly and with so much power that it carves through stone. You can admire a river one day and return a month later, and the water you originally saw might be hundreds of miles away. When you align with your soul and the spirit realm, you can do something that looks effortful on the outside but feels effortless.

As you change your energy, your life will match your internal state. Put more elegantly in the *Tao Te Ching*: "…each part is the whole, and the whole is in each part."[52]

This subtle concept of non-doing is why some people can take massive action and build their dream life, while others give up in a few weeks. Sometimes, the difference is simple willpower. Someone's coping mechanism might be to whip themselves into an action-taking frenzy and they stumble into success—workaholics tend to be wealthier. But often, successful people can tap into their personal version of effortless effort. The trouble comes when others try to mimic that and exhaust themselves with effortful effort.

"When we no longer live from the heart,
We search for clever strategies
To guide our actions."[53]

Before we move on, let's cover an important example of what is **not** non-doing. When someone abuses you and you don't stand up for yourself, get to safety or do something else to stop the abuse, that's not non-doing. You're still engaging a coping mechanism of choosing to be a victim. If you're getting abused, use non-doing to get yourself centered so you can rationally choose your best actions to stop the abuse.

The Immortal Post is designed for you to embody effortless effort. When you relax into the aligned position and quiet your mind, you do nothing, and yet your body is opened to the energy of Earth and the Heavens. You're not moving, yet all kinds of movement—both physical and energetic—happen inside and around you. When you stand correctly, someone can push your shoulder from the side and the force will transfer into the ground. You do nothing, yet your partner will get exhausted from pushing. It's also possible to relax and open to the energy from Earth so much that the energy transmits upward and bounces your partner off you. When Daoists refer to doing nothing, but everything getting done, they're also hinting at this martial arts application.

I regularly experience this energy transmission. Mostly, I use this technique for mystical practices and healing, where this energy is used for spiritual cultivation and improving another person's health. To do this, practitioners open themselves to energy from Heaven and the Earth and, instead of storing it in their bodies, they direct the energy into other people, which helps resolve their energetic stagnation. My teachers refer to it as "applied meditation" because meditation is literally being applied to another person.

The only way to harness this energy is to practice non-doing. The way to sabotage this flow of energy is to use muscular force to push harder—which is dysfunctional doing. When you swap effortless effort for hard work and try to push your opponent, he won't budge. You'll fail if you force your way into any result.

Doing is when you let your mind run wild about something you felt during your Immortal Post and ruminate whether it's good or bad, when you could just shrug and say, "Don't say good, don't say bad, simply say…"

Doing is when your tight thighs and shoulders tremble after holding the Immortal Post for five minutes. Non-doing is when your relaxed limbs hold the same position for over an hour.

Doing is when you demand your practice give you something specific. This includes setting goals for your practice, other than holding the stance for a certain amount of time. In Daoist alchemy, there's a special practice where you gather energy until it opens one of your body's major channels. The practice can take an hour per day for 100 days or more and requires strict lifestyle changes. It's like filling a swimming pool with a garden hose while wearing a blindfold. You can't grit your teeth and force open the channel. Even setting a goal is counterproductive. Trying to achieve a goal that's outside your conscious control stresses you, bouncing you away from what you want. You must let it happen when it's supposed to happen; non-doing. It took me 120 days and the result occurred when I wasn't thinking about it. The lack of concern provided an environment for the energy to do its thing. If you let the Immortal Post be what it is and focus on improving your practice, you'll open the spigot for the benefits.

End your training with at least 60 seconds of doing nothing. Don't try to relax your muscles and don't try to align your body better. Stand there and be quiet. It seems paradoxical, but the key is doing this at the end of your practice, *after* all your doing. This stillness can be one of the most nourishing things you do.

It's hard to believe in non-doing's power. When one of my teachers pushed me from the side as I stood in the Immortal Post, I tensed my shoulder and he toppled me over. Then he coached me through relaxing more in the face of opposition. Slowly, I was able to lead his force through my body and into the floor. The harder he pushed, the more I simply did nothing. He couldn't budge me. Later, he showed me how I could turn and relax my body even more as he pushed until he flew staggering across the room.

Next, I'll show how to use one of nature's most powerful laws to live with more effortless effort and do without doing. This law was key to me breaking through and building wealth.

CHAPTER TWENTY-ONE

CHAOS

In springtime of 2014, I felt as if I were living a double life. For the first three days of each week, I unloaded boxes from truck after truck, staggering out of the empty trailers to gulp down as much Gatorade as my stomach could handle and always thinking I couldn't do any more, before trudging back into the next full trailer. Hours of dripping sweat and smelling cardboard as the truck's engine—always on—rumbled around me like a thunderstorm. The rest of the week, I sipped coffee while enjoying mountain views, got a chiropractic adjustment and massage, and pursued leads for contract work. Part of me knew something was about to shift, but another part was at the breaking point.

One Saturday afternoon, I walked through the buildings in my condo complex and grabbed my mail. Bills. Ads. Maybe a product order from a marketing campaign I was running. And a big envelope containing Doberman Dan's monthly newsletter.

That night, I tore open Dan's envelope, pulled it out, and read it. Something about this newsletter issue was odd. Dan took a couple of pages to describe how a major company on the east coast was looking to hire copywriters to write their advertisements. That just happened to be my specialty. Dan wrote that maybe—maybe—someone had a chance to get the job if they sent in some writing samples.

I dropped the newsletter, jumped to my computer, wrote an email, attached four or five writing samples, and sent it to the address he'd given. After I clicked the button, questions reverberated through my brain.

Did they get the email?

Will I make it?

Don't think about it. You've got work tomorrow and the day after. You'll torture yourself if you dwell on this.

An hour later, Dan's assistant replied, acknowledging she had received the email.

Yes! But keep your cool. It's just someone saying she got the email.

The next day, after work, I checked my email. Doberman Dan had replied, thanking me for my submission.

Yes! But keep your cool. Dan only said that he got my samples.

That Friday evening, I trudged through my condo's front door, irritated after slogging through two hours of traffic jams. I wasn't thinking about the samples I'd sent when I sank into my chair and checked my email. My inbox had a new email with the subject line **"Nate, meet Jed."** It was the most life-changing email I ever received.

Let's examine effortless effort from a higher level. Getting in the zone is wonderful, but how do we sustain efforts long-term, when the zone disappears? How do we live a life of non-doing when we get roped back into the grind? The secret is to harness one of nature's most powerful laws for multiplying the power of actions. It starts with something called the 80/20 Principle, which originated with a scientist named Vilfredo Pareto. He discovered 80% of the land in Italy was owned by 20% of the people.

This inspired him to discover the 80/20 pattern in other areas of life. For instance, 20% of Americans paid[54] an estimated 87% of tax revenues in 2018. Statistics show the 80/20 rule in everything from ecology to economics. Consider your own life. If you have a network of 100 people, you probably don't spend exactly 1% of your time with each person. Instead, you probably spend a disproportionate amount of time with a smaller group within those 100 people—your closer friends. Twenty people in that group likely get 80% of your time.

It's the same with where you live. You probably don't spend an equal amount of time in all the square footage of your home, but 80% of your time in 20% of the area—your bedroom and perhaps the living room.

Here's why we're running mathematical figures about your home and relationships. The 80/20 law weaves its way through nature. You'll see it in architecture, wealth distribution, healthcare, the weather, and more. It's like streaming code, hiding in plain sight while helping support The Matrix.

Decades after Vilfredo Pareto shed light on this phenomenon, author and management expert Richard Koch took things a step further. He wrote how 80/20 applies not just to nature or our behavior, but the results we get from our behaviors. He published a book about how 20% of your activities give you 80% of your results—both positive and negative. Let's say you go to the gym to lift weights for an hour. Even though you might say, "Oh yeah, I exercised for an hour," that's probably not true. First you found the proper set of weights to use, did some warm-ups, rested a bit, and then did some actual sets with a challenging weight. Then you rested, got a drink of water, daydreamed a bit, checked your phone, and did some more sets. When you add up the time it takes to change clothes and adjust the equipment you use, you're lucky if 20% of your time in the gym is spent triggering muscle growth. This isn't a knock on your productivity—it's how life works until we adjust how we live.

Let's dive deeper. Think back to your closer circle of 20 friends. Do you spend equal amounts of time with all of them? Or is there a closer circle within that group of friends? Perhaps it's only four people—which is 20% of 20. And they might get 64% of your time, which is 80% of 80%. If you're married, you might spend half your time with your spouse. Stay with me here because the math is about to get weirder. 20% of 20% of 20% is 0.8%, which is close to 1%. And 80% of 80% of 80% is 51.2%, which is roughly half. The 80/20 law holds up even when we drill further into it.

If we zoom in on your home habits even more, we could probably find that you spend many hours on one side of your bed. Plus, you might prefer sitting on one part of your couch in your living room. Those parts of your home might make up only 1% of the square footage, yet you might occupy them for almost half your home life.

This is because 80/20 patterns are *fractal*, meaning you can drill down (or up) and whatever part you're looking at will have the same statistical character. Here's a computer-generated image of fractal lines. As they split, they form smaller versions of themselves:

If you look closely at these branches, you see that the offshoots look like the original. Videos online show how you can zoom in on the branches in this image indefinitely and the pattern remains the same. Just as you can zoom in on the patterns of your friends or your home and the math still works. "…each part is the whole, and the whole is in each part."[55]

Does the computer-generated pattern of branches look familiar? It should because it's all around you:

When it comes to your behavior and your outcomes, 80/20 is still fractal. That means you can go beyond 20% of your efforts to create 80% of your results. What's 20% of 20%? A tiny 4%. What's 80% of 80%? 64%.

Therefore, 4% of your efforts can produce 64% of your results.

You can use the 80/20 Principle within the Immortal Post to accelerate your results. You've learned many techniques in this book. Chances are, 20% of them will give you better results than the other 80%. Discover what that 20% is, and the 20% within that 20%, and you'll multiply your benefits.

Search for the 20% in the rest of your life. When I wanted clients, I tested LinkedIn, Craigslist, and referrals from other people. For me, the 20% of the 20% of the 20% was Doberman Dan making a single introduction for me. Your life has an 80/20 array and it is fractal. Dive deeper to discover those small leverage points, and the "20/20/20", to amplify them.

Take it one step further. Less than 1% of your efforts can produce more than half of your results. Hard to believe? I'll show how in a bit.

Author and marketing expert Perry Marshall describes how the 80/20 Principle—and especially its fractal nature—work because of *feedback* and *chaos*. He uses this example: the Grand Canyon began as a slab of rock. Water fell on it and flowed over the rock's rough surface, taking the path of least resistance. As the water flowed, it eventually wore a channel on the surface, which became a deeper path of least resistance. More water flowed along that channel, which created a deeper channel, which caused more water to flow in it. This is feedback: an action amplifying itself. This cycle of ***amplifying feedback*** was microscopic at first, but after millions of years it sculpted the Grand Canyon.

Amplifying feedback doesn't need to take millions of years. Think of the last time someone talked into a microphone that was too close to the speaker. Within a second, amplifying feedback turned a regular voice into an ear-piercing shriek.

Your brain gets sculpted the same way as a canyon. It wires and rewires itself every moment of your life—including as you read these words—upgrading its neural pathways. As habits become ingrained,[56] the neural pathways automatically shift throughout our brains. Have you ever complained to your friends that you can't seem to get motivated to brush your teeth? Ever made a New Year's Resolution to take regular showers? Probably not, because amplifying feedback loops have sculpted your daily sanitary habits as thoroughly as the Grand Canyon. They've also sculpted your beliefs and coping mechanisms. If your brain gets installed with the belief that you're a poor person, your savings and investment habits will reflect that belief, creating more poverty, which deepens the wiring in your brain that your belief was correct. The amplifying feedback helps create the self-fulfilling prophecy.

Here's why this is important:

Amplifying feedback powers the 80/20 effect.

As you choose the "1%" efforts that give you more than half of your results, you want to choose efforts that have *amplifying feedback* built in.

Amplifying feedback gives your effort the snowball effect...causing your 20% to bring you 80% results...4% to give you 64% of results...and 1% to give you over half your results. For example, if you make an effort to save some of your income, you can build in amplifying feedback if you choose to invest your savings. Over time, the money will grow. Same effort—snowballed results.

The other kind of feedback is balancing feedback. Here's an example of ***balancing feedback***. If you have young children and take them bowling, you might play on a bowling lane without gutters, one lined with rubber edges to keep the bowling ball in play. These rubber barriers provide balancing feedback. If the ball strays toward the edge instead of the pins, it bounces off the barrier and keeps barreling toward the pins. If you decide your children have had enough sissy bowling, you'll put them in a lane with gutters on either side. When you throw the ball down this lane and it rolls against the gutter, it doesn't bounce off. Instead, the ball receives amplifying feedback. The slope of the gutter—with help from gravity—causes the ball to fall in. More amplifying feedback keeps the bowling ball in the gutter until it rolls out of play and the bowling pins remain untouched. Then you can tell your children that your gutter ball was because of too much amplifying feedback.

This example is to clarify how amplifying and balancing feedback work—not to make a judgment on whether they are good or bad. They are forces of nature and they can be healthy or unhealthy depending on the context.

Let's dive deeper into the effects these forces of nature have:

Balancing feedback slams the brakes on 80/20.

As you choose the "1%" efforts that give you more than half of your results, you want to choose efforts that minimize *balancing feedback*.

Balancing feedback prevents your effort from getting the snowball effect. For example, if you make a purchase on credit with a high interest rate, not only do you spend instead of save, you force yourself into future spending. Over time, the debt will grow. Same effort, but with results that push you further from wealth. It's like 80/20 in reverse.

You can watch both amplifying and balancing feedback when a product is sold on Amazon or any other site with a user review system. If the product is purchased by enough customers and satisfies them, it accumulates five-star reviews, which help compel prospective customers to purchase the product, leading to more five-star reviews, leading to more purchases, helping the product dominate competition. If reviews are good, the system provides amplifying feedback for sales. If reviews are bad, it provides balancing feedback for sales. In a world of feedback and fractal 80/20 patterns, there's no such thing as a superior product doing slightly better than competition. Instead, you have Harry Potter sitting on almost every bookshelf in existence while most book printings get thrown out, unread. Think about it: if you see two similar products listed for a similar price and one has five-star reviews and the other has two-star reviews, do you usually purchase the five-star product...or *always*?

Those are simple examples, but life isn't a simple game. It's complex beyond comprehension, and this is where *chaos* comes into play and how to use 80/20 and feedback to transform your life.

Many people think of chaos as randomness, but chaos has a different meaning in physics. It's when a complex system builds upon itself because of amplifying feedback. Think of a snowflake falling on a mountain peak and triggering an avalanche.

Your energy, your brain, your family, your friends, your job, the world around you, and how they interplay is so complex that no computer could predict what your future holds. Tiny changes can swing your life course because of amplifying feedback. It's called the Butterfly

Effect, with the example of a butterfly flapping its wings and transforming weather patterns in another part of the world.

Negative actions that create amplifying feedback can destroy your life. Think of trying an addictive drug like cocaine. As you crave the high, your brain requires the drug to feel good. The more you use cocaine, the more you depend on it, until you're like the bowling ball stuck in the gutter. If you're lucky, you'll hit a personal rock bottom, which can provide balancing feedback, bouncing you away from the unhealthy habit.

A positive action like exercise also creates amplifying feedback. When you exercise, you practice a healthy habit and your brain releases pleasure chemicals that push you toward a healthy addiction to exercise. You start craving exercise, which causes you to do more, which reinforces the high until you're like the bowling ball in the gutter—but *this* gutter might lead to washboard abs or at least fewer lectures from your doctor during a checkup. If you're unlucky, your exercise might injure you, which can provide balancing feedback, again bouncing you away from the healthy habit.

If you want to live a life of effortless effort, where everything gets done without doing, then **you must maximize the amplifying feedback of your healthy habits and maximize the balancing feedback of your unhealthy habits**. This is how you harness the power of chaos.

You want healthy habits to ingrain themselves deeper, to spread wider, to have a more powerful impact. You want the results to multiply and come back to you. You *don't* want to bounce away from healthy habits and for their impact to grow weak and disappear.

It's the opposite for unhealthy habits. You *don't* want unhealthy habits to ingrain themselves deeper, to spread wider, to have a more powerful impact. You *don't* want the results to multiply and come back to you. You want to bounce away from unhealthy habits and for their impact to grow weak and disappear.

For instance, your choice of spouse and close friends give you feedback. When you choose your spouse well, they will support and encourage you when you make positive changes in your life. This amplifying feedback will help you change even more. If your spouse resents your changes, they will provide balancing feedback. For example, if you try to eat healthier, they'll cook foods you're attempting to avoid. Because you care about your marriage, you might abandon your plans to eat healthier. Your spouse acted like the rubber barrier to the bowling lane, bouncing you from where your momentum was taking you. A supportive spouse might see you making changes to your diet and cook healthier foods, praise your improved appearance, and join your efforts, creating amplifying feedback and keeping your new habits going.

Your relationships create an egregore and egregores create feedback. Which way will the feedback propel you? I've seen this effect when it comes to meditation and marriage. If someone's spouse isn't on board with the habit of meditation, the balancing feedback hinders or even destroys the person's progress.

Your close friends do the same, so your Friends of the Dao—your "inner circle"—must support the changes you want to make. They can bolster your momentum or squash it.

When I went bankrupt and worked as a sign-spinner, I was fortunate to spend my time in solitude. I didn't have someone sneering at me and saying I was a fool for trying to build a business. I didn't get hit with balancing feedback, but also failed to surround myself with supportive friends, so I missed out on amplifying feedback—a mistake I corrected a few years later.

Investments can harness amplifying feedback. So can debt. Before I went bankrupt, the interest on my debt climbed so high that, unless I won the lottery or signed an MLB contract, the amplifying feedback was too powerful to overcome.

When you get rid of every unhealthy food in your home, uninstall social media apps from your phone and cancel your cable subscription, that's healthy balancing feedback. It doesn't mean you won't enjoy those indulgences—it means you'll need to work a bit harder to get your fix of each one. When you give yourself a barrier to entry—even a slight one—you prevent yourself from falling into a bingeing and scrolling stupor.

One of the most powerful forms of amplifying feedback is your attention, which is why it's one of the four pillars of Daoist meditation. Wherever you place your attention, you program your brain to see more of that.

When I walked through downtown Denver to my bankruptcy hearing, I spotted a couple of coins on the sidewalk. They were a dime and a quarter—a sum larger than the usual penny. I chose to see it as a good sign. Some could call that superstitious. I chose to see it as a reward for redirecting my focus and proof that I was building wealth in challenging circumstances. I was also training my brain to observe more of the same.

Later, I experienced the dark side of redirecting my focus. During my second job unloading trucks, when I was inside a rumbling, dark 53-foot trailer, exhausted from grabbing and throwing several hundred cardboard boxes, I jumped on a plastic footstool to peer over the top of the 10-foot box stack. I wanted to see the far end of the trailer. The closer it was, the sooner I was to finishing.

It was usually an exercise in self-torture because when I peered over the mountain range of boxes, I could see only a blur of darkness. There were so many boxes to go that I literally couldn't see the end of the trailer. Guess where my focus shifted? Not on how much I'd accomplished, but how far I had to trudge.

A few weeks before my life transformed, I focused on the brief moments of rest I got between grabbing boxes, which bolstered my energy.

Here's an exercise I learned from a copywriter named Gary Bencivenga. The first step is to close your eyes, but you can't do it yet because you need to be able to read the second step (Bencivenga took a live audience through this exercise). When you get to the second step, immediately close your eyes. Here goes: As your eyes are closed, mentally list all the things in your surroundings that are colored red. Now close your eyes and do it without glancing around first.

Okay, now that you're reading this, I assume you closed your eyes, counted every object with the color red, and made a mental tally. Maybe you remembered 3 or 7 things.

Here's step three. Look around the room for 30 seconds and pick out everything red. Close your eyes and repeat the mental count.

It's likely your tally this time was higher—perhaps much higher. Your attention commands power. The more you focus it, the more it turns from a flashlight into a laser. When you focus on certain things to the exclusion of others, your perception becomes skewed, and you train your perception to skew in that way—in this case, your perception skewed toward the color red. This is where amplifying feedback comes in. When you skew your perception and don't consciously correct it, your brain will focus on certain things more, and skew your perception more, which narrows and intensifies your focus even more, and so on.

This is how people end up complaining, "Such-and-such *always* happens to me." Their brain literally doesn't show them the exceptions to their statement.

Think of the last time you were worried about an upcoming event and it consumed your mind like a thick cloud of smoke, choking off your thoughts of anything else for more than a second. Your worry made the event seem bigger and scarier until it towered over you like the Wizard of Oz's swollen green head. After the event, you wonder why you got so worried.

The media's relentless coverage of bad news, and our access to this news 24 hours a day, creates a skewed perception of a more dangerous world, which makes us more paranoid, which trains our brains to focus more on danger. We can flip our perception by ignoring bad global and national news and focus on our surroundings and local community.

Here's a habit I picked up from Joshua Kennon, a brilliant investor and author. Whenever I drive across town and see a building that's part of a company in which I hold stock, I cheer for that building and celebrate how much business it's getting, and how a fraction of the revenue generated by its customers will show up in my investment account. This skewed perception is a fun game and makes traffic jams slightly less awful. It also shows how my brain is wired to observe growing wealthy and feeling joy.*

* If you think this attitude is elitist or off-putting, I challenge you to pay attention to your skewed perception and to keep in mind you can buy stock in many valuable companies for less than $50, so this game is open to virtually anyone.

This Pollyannaish focus has a downside, which happens when objective reality bites you in the ass. Skewing your perception toward opportunity can help you grab it, but danger exists and changing your focus won't dissolve it.

So, what do you do? When you need awareness of dangers as you analyze business competition in a crowded market, focus on that. Turn off that focus when you want to find creative solutions. You must be able to switch perceptions. Otherwise, you'll grow more paranoid, anxious about looming dangers, and your creativity will shrink to imagining scenarios of your doom. Some people can thrive being paranoid all the time; they're called a company's in-house legal counsel. But not a single member of that legal department focused 100% on danger when they strove to land their job in the first place.

When you must be aware of all feedback, as when doing the Immortal Post, focus on everything without judgment because judgment will skew your focus. When you don't filter your experiences through the lens of judgment, amplifying feedback will make you more and more aware of sensations. This helps you feel and direct chi.

Uncover all amplifying and balancing feedback in your life because it will act as a greased slide or sandpaper on your path. Map out actions that put amplifying feedback and balancing feedback to work for you. When I saved $30 per week, I was starting the cycle of feedback. It didn't matter that my savings were a trickle of water pouring over an uncarved Grand Canyon. As I reinforced the savings habit, worked on my career, and learned more about investing, the trickle turned into a torrent and finally into an unstoppable river that carved through rock.

Consider again the line from the *Tao Te Ching* "...each part is the whole, and the whole is in each part." When I saved $30 a week, I proved to myself that I was growing wealthier. Even if the dollar amount was small, the universe operates in a fractal way. *Each part is the whole.* Saving $30 per week was like making a tweak to one of my financial life's branches. As a result, all the branches rearranged themselves.

To summarize:

- Your actions and their results can be measured with the 80/20 principle.
- The 80/20 principle is fractal. You can zoom in and make the 20% of the 20% of your actions give you 80% of the 80% of your results.
- This is possible because of amplifying feedback. It powers small actions (the 20% of the 20%) to create big results (80% of 80%).
- On the other hand, balancing feedback pulls everything back. When your actions get resisted in the form of balancing feedback, you'll waste time and energy. 80% of your actions will get you only 20% of potential results.
- Take advantage of amplifying feedback to enhance the results of healthy habits.
- Take advantage of balancing feedback to eliminate unhealthy habits.

Here are some questions to help you uncover amplifying and balancing feedback:

1. **What do I want?**
2. **What balancing feedback could prevent me from getting what I want?**
3. **What amplifying feedback can propel me toward what I want with effortless effort?**

4. **How can I minimize the balancing feedback and maximize the amplifying feedback?**

Now that I understand the universe arranges itself in a fractal way, what small actions can I take to show I already possess what I want so I can affect the array of the universe?

Here are some example answers:

1. **What do I want?** I want to lose 30 pounds and look great naked.
2. **What balancing feedback could prevent me from getting what I want?** Every time I try to do a regular workout routine and eat healthier, my boyfriend/girlfriend mocks my efforts, waves food in my face, and complains I'm spending less time with him/her because of my short daily workout.
3. **What amplifying feedback can propel me toward what I want with effortless effort?** One of my friends is training for a triathlon and we've grown distant. By exercising together and sharing ideas and encouragement, we'll become closer, which will reinforce our healthy habits, which will boost our confidence, which will strengthen our bond more, etc.*
4. **How can I minimize the balancing feedback and maximize the amplifying feedback?** I can set healthy boundaries in my relationship. I won't try to change the other person or negotiate with them. If that doesn't

* Any time you can describe a chain of events like, "Which causes this...which means this will happen...which will make this first thing even stronger...etc.," you're describing an amplifying feedback loop.

work, I can end it and let this be a new, healthier chapter in my life. This makes room to spend more time around healthier people, which amplifies my efforts.

5. **Now that I understand the universe arranges itself in a fractal way, what small actions can I take to show I already possess what I want so I can affect the array of the universe?** I can start exercising every day, even if it's just holding myself in a push-up position for 20 seconds, to show I am now someone who exercises daily. I can pick three things I've wanted to do once I get in shape and do a reasonable version of them, to get a taste of success.

When you choose your small actions wisely, they'll feel more effortless. When you have a supportive spouse and friends, your effort will feel more effortless. When your home is arranged to support your health, your efforts to improve your health will feel more effortless. Even something as mundane as an automatic withdrawal from your paycheck to bolster your 401K would get a thumbs up from an ancient Daoist for being "done without doing."

"Map difficult through easy
Approach great through narrow.
The most difficult things in the world
Must be accomplished through the easiest.
The greatest things in the world
Must be accomplished through the smallest.

Therefore the Sage

Never attempts great things
And so accomplishes them."[57]

Meditation delivers you an exponential return on investment. If you meditate for ten minutes, you don't just experience a better brain for ten minutes after you finish. A study published in Frontiers in Human Neuroscience[58] showed meditation changes the way your brain works, even when you're not practicing. The scientists found that, after the participants meditated for eight weeks, they had calmer reactions to negative images. A controlled study out of UC Davis[59] showed three months of meditation training improved focus and the participants reported *this superior focus improved their self-control, even five months later.*

The ultimate example of amplifying feedback is the Immortal Post. When you relax your muscles during this standing meditation, you also enhance your alignment, which helps to quiet your mind, which helps you relax your muscles. This system of amplifying feedback is shown in this diagram:

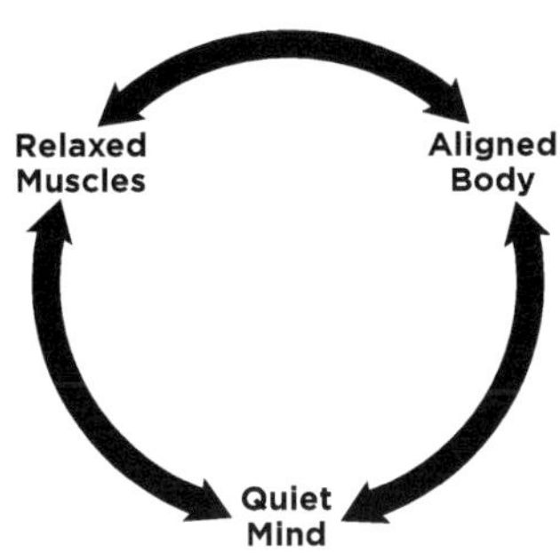

The arrows go both directions in the circle because the cycle can go multiple ways. As you quiet your mind, your breathing will slow, your stress will go down, your muscles will relax, and your body will align. Aligning your body allows your muscles to relax, which eases your stress, which slows your breathing, which quiets your mind. You can start anywhere and end up anywhere in this cycle, and you're going the right way.

Most of the time, when you begin the Immortal Post, you'll be a little tense, your mind will be filled to the brim with chatter, and your form will feel off in a way you can't put your finger on. It's easy to let frustration slip in, which makes your thoughts louder, which stresses you, which makes you tense, which can lead to this:

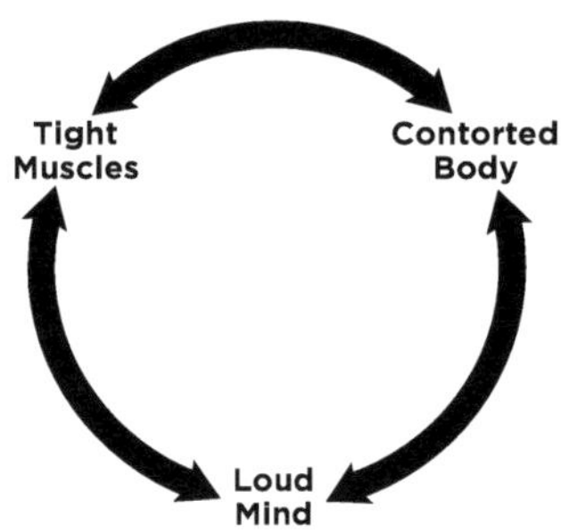

The difference between these two scenarios comes from your intention. The destructive cycle of amplifying feedback will loop if you let it happen. The healthy cycle will loop when you intend to make it happen. As you persevere, your success will build on itself and will build momentum. It will spill into other areas of your life.

Balancing feedback can prevent you from going deeper into your standing meditation practice. It often comes from your environment. Carve out time in your day so your meditation practice isn't at the mercy of the rest of your life. Switch your phone to Airplane Mode and practice in a room where you can lock the door, even if you're practicing for five minutes. This way, your brain won't be distracted—even by the potential for distraction.

Balancing feedback also shows up in how you begin your practice. Many people attempt to meditate when they're feeling sleepy, and the more relaxed they become, the more they self-sabotage by falling asleep. I've never been so sleepy when doing the standing meditation that I've face-planted on the floor, but it's happened with sitting meditation. Some see this as a positive—a nice way to fall asleep—but Daoists understood that it's a bad idea to mix the practices because you'll program your brain to associate meditation with sleep.

The standing meditation's power to put chaos on your side is why I wrote a book about it. **This tiny percentage of your life re-wires your flow of chi, which ripples changes throughout your environment. You're harnessing energetic chaos.**

If you want to live a good life with effortless effort, start your day with the Immortal Post.

"A tree that fills a man's embrace grows from a seedling
A tower nine stories high starts with one brick
A journey of a thousand miles begins with a single step"[60]

One more note on chaos. When I grew frustrated because I couldn't get money to flood my bank account with the same speed and ferocity with which the IRS vacuumed it out, I concluded that the mind has zero esoteric or mystical power. I believed disorder reigned.

When you change your body's chi—a change so subtle most people wouldn't feel the difference—this can compound into greater health, better relationships, peace of mind, and power and choice in your life. But why can't people jump into the Immortal Post, change their energy, and make it rain Ferraris with trunks full of cash? Why can't one practice the Immortal Post and get the exact same benefits every time? If something mystical is going on, why can't we predict exactly what the esoteric benefits will be for every person and guarantee a specific set of results?

Acclaimed theoretical physicist Stephen Hawking wrote the answer in his final book, *Short Answers To Large Questions*, when referring to the example of a butterfly in Australia changing the weather in Central Park: "The trouble is, it is not repeatable. The next time the butterfly flaps its wings a host of other things will be different, which will also influence the weather. This chaos factor is why weather forecasts can be so unreliable."

Your mind and your energy have power over your reality and its chaos. Your practice of the Immortal Post is flapping the butterfly's wings. No one can predict exactly how or when it will transform your life—but it will.

In the late spring of 2014, it was hard to believe I should get weekly chiropractic adjustments, massages, and enjoy trips to the mountains. Even weirder, every time I found a higher-paying job on Craigslist, my gut kept telling me to skip it and I listened. What was going on? Fear and a strange inner peace played musical chairs in my head.

Then, I came home one night, and when I checked my email and saw the subject line **“Nate, meet Jed.”** I clicked it open and stopped breathing.

CHAPTER TWENTY-TWO

BREAKING THROUGH

One email changed my life. Doberman Dan introduced me to one of the head honchos at a publishing company I'd admired for years. Before I freaked out in response to the email, the lessons and training from the last few years clicked in. I relaxed, pulled in deep breaths, asked myself how best to respond, and took time to craft my reply. After sending back an email, I affirmed that there were no guarantees and it wasn't good or bad.

Within a few days, the executive of the company and I hopped onto Skype for an interview. I reminded myself that the company probably needed only some contract work. This wasn't to discourage myself—I was just preparing for all possibilities. Before the interview, I did the Immortal Post. The call was like a relaxed conversation.

"We're looking for someone to move to Baltimore and work for us full-time," the executive named Jed said. "What do you think of that?"

My adrenaline lit up like a July 4th sparkler. But my mind's chatter jumped aside so I could talk from Jed's point of view and about what would benefit the company. I marveled at how in the flow I felt. He offered to fly me across the country to visit his offices and I accepted.

The days before the visit crawled by and I craved to get it over with and find out what would happen, but I reminded myself to breathe deeply and relax. I could take advantage of the delay—something that seemed like a setback—to improve my chances of getting hired. How could I show, rather than simply tell, the publishing company that I was serious about becoming a full-time asset?

I bought a few of their books, signed up for their email newsletters, and made sure the executives knew I did so. During lunch breaks at the job unloading trucks, I read the books. It was antifragility in action.

The travel day came. When I took the bus to Denver International Airport, part of me didn't expect a ticket to be waiting, but it was. After landing in Maryland, I took a train to downtown Baltimore, waves of nostalgia hitting me as the trees zoomed by, so much like the outdoors in my hometown. When the train doors rolled open and I stepped out, the earthy air hit me like a blanket.

I found their building nestled in the rows of Baltimore's brick homes, pillars of America's adolescence. Jed jumped around his desk when he greeted me in his office. He was wiry with a shaved head and spoke and moved with the darting energy of someone whose brain never turns off. The other executive was tall, lanky, and beamed like a kid who had matured from setting off fireworks to building businesses, but never lost his mischievousness.

They described how they were expanding, and were interested in hiring me for my marketing skill and my business failures; I could help them succeed and warn them about what didn't work. I hadn't thought of my failures as having that value. I'd also never thought of becoming a full-time employee. In my early 20s, people had often advised me that my biggest breakthroughs would come from surprising places. I'd doubted this was true in my business life because I obsessed over every possibility—but this one remained hidden. I gave a presentation about a project we could start with, trying to make sure my vision aligned with theirs. Mostly, I sat back and listened, knowing non-doing was as important as doing.

As the company visit neared its end, I got scared. *Would they make an offer? Or would I go back to unloading trucks?* Sitting with Jed and another executive, I said I'd love to work for them.

"That's a big decision," Jed said.

"It is," I said, "but you flew me out here for this and I've been thinking about it." I described how I was still young, single, and mobile.

"Well, we'll have to talk it through," Jed said, gesturing to the other executive, who interjected, "It's a yes from me!"

"Okay, great," Jed said. "Let me tell you about our 401K and all that..."

The rest of what he said got lost in the gale force of my excitement. I felt as if I were sitting in front of the ocean as a warm mist washed over me. I felt waves of excitement and relief—excitement because of how my life was going to change, and relief because this new career would allow me to thrive doing what I love.

I kept my cool and made sure to feel grateful and open to whatever happened. After returning home, I remembered a story Peter Ragnar told about when he was broke and jobless. He and a few other guys got hired for one morning to unload a truck full of steel. The other temps grumbled and complained, but as Peter worked, he practically jumped up and down with gratitude, whipped off his shirt, and relished the sunshine and sweet air.

After they unloaded the truck, the other temps were sent home, but the manager asked Peter, "Do you want to stick around and wash the company's vehicles?"

"I'd love to!" Peter said.

After lunch, the manager said, "Do you want to clean the office?"

"I'd love to!" Peter said.

Finally, the manager said, "Do you want to come back and work tomorrow?"

"I'd love to!" Peter said. He rose through the ranks until he was leading hundred-million-dollar construction projects for the company.

The morning after I returned home, I did my Immortal Post practice and checked my email. The official job offer was waiting for me. It included a salary and a royalty based on performance. I replied, "I'd love to!"

The next day when I went to my truck-unloading job, I gave my supervisor two weeks' notice and called my landlord to say I was moving. Fortunately, my lease was month-to-month.

At some point, I got Doberman Dan on the phone to thank him. "It's amazing how, after you told all your subscribers about the opportunity, I managed to nab it."

"You know, there were a bunch of submissions. But you were the only one who'd taken my advice in my newsletter and monthly webinars and applied it and kept coming back with results," Dan said, "So, I mentioned that when I gave your samples to the company. And, just so you know, I made sure you were at the top of the stack."

As I packed up my things, I found boxes of forgotten CD, DVD, and printed courses on everything from making more money to attracting women. I grabbed them by the armload, marched to the dumpster in front of my condo complex, and tossed them inside. I smiled as they clanked against the walls and garbage bags. I used to worship these courses like false idols. As they rested at the bottom of the dumpster, radiating its thick odor in the springtime sun, I paused to see if lightning would strike me. It didn't.

A couple of days before I moved, my landlord came over and we talked about his other job managing a caretaking facility for people with disabilities. He always looked for items that could be useful, like dishes or gardening equipment.

"Would my bed be useful? Or my lamps or desk?" I asked.

"Definitely!" he said.

"Take everything," I said. "If you want, I can just leave it all."

For seven years, my only decent piece of furniture was my bed. It felt good to pass it on.

On my last day in Colorado, I practiced the Immortal Post and marveled over how I'd never meditate in the Aurora condo again. I wouldn't be "a stone's throw from Kansas" anymore. I finished my packing and locked the door. I'd moved out of my previous apartment because I couldn't afford it and cried as I left. This time, I was smiling.

I went to Starbucks, bought a giant chocolate and coffee combo, and sipped it as I drove west on I-70 toward the next chapter of my life. Whenever traffic slowed down or I struggled to find a hotel, I reminded myself about "not good, not bad."

After four days, I made it to Baltimore and the townhome where the company was putting me up. I had a new career, home, bright future, and a new awareness, but I monitored how I reacted to this journey.

After the initial high had worn off, I found myself irritated or worried about the same tiny things—but now I knew what to do. My behavior didn't need to be dictated by the emotional roller coaster my brain strapped me into. It didn't need to dictate how I saw myself or how I felt. The morning after moving in, as I looked around the room from an unfamiliar bed, I felt groggy and irritated. My brain was recovering from a dopamine rush. The old Daoist farmer wouldn't let that bother him, so I didn't, either.

A day later, I walked into the office building where a desk awaited me. I got to work. As I used the Daoist lessons I'd learned the previous several years and combined it with my copywriting skill, my career blossomed more than I could have imagined.

Years before, I'd struggled to build businesses. **I failed because I chased a result. I should have focused on a craft and let the results take care of themselves.**

With the standing meditation, there is no finish line—only improvement.

This new job narrowed my role to marketing, especially writing advertisements. This was simplification and 80/20. The more I wrote and the more skillful I became, the more my income shot up. This was amplifying feedback. I worked every day, perhaps 60+ hours per week, but it was effortless effort.

That was over six years ago. Many, many times I've shaken my head and asked, *Did all that really happen? Did I really wave around a sign for almost three years, or was it all a strange dream?* Usually, I conclude the answer is *yes*.

I've met amazing friends and mentors, grown as a person, stumbled into more spectacular failures, and received more life-changing teachings. After working as an employee for eighteen months, I switched to doing contract work for the company and returned to Denver. In fact, I moved back into the apartment building I'd missed so much, the one I'd emailed Peter Ragnar about. I called the leasing office and asked if they had an apartment available on a high floor with a north-facing view. They did and, out of their three buildings, it was the one where I used to live.

It was fun to dig up the email thread with Peter. I first emailed him about the apartment on April 20th, 2014, lamenting how much I missed it. On February 8th, 2016, I replied again. Here's part of what I wrote:

"I asked about enjoying little things in the present moment, like driving in the mountains. Well, shortly before my financial life transformed for the better...I did begin doing that, a little bit. It was like a sprinkling of pepper on a nice meal—treating myself, while still working diligently.

And just so you know...the apartment photos I shared with you... I'm now living here."

As I reflected on my bankruptcy and long climb out of a financial sinkhole, I realized how isolated I'd been in those days, so I formed a Mastermind group of colleagues to support each other. It's like a business version of Friends of the Dao, and something I'll write about in the future.

By the time I could start chipping at my $50,000 IRS debt, the interest ballooned it to over $96,000 (see Figure 9, especially where the handy arrow points).

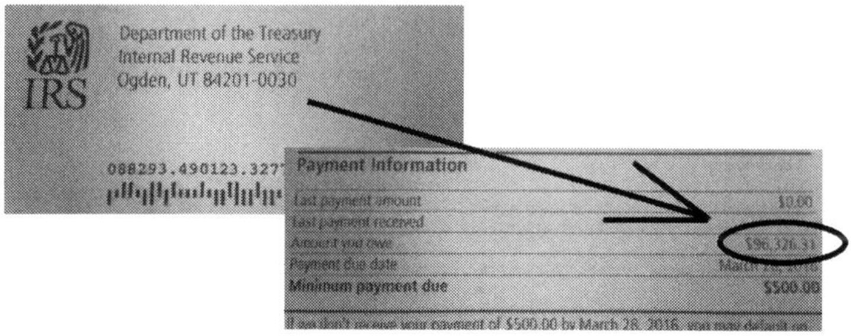

Figure 9

I paid off every penny and the IRS released the lien they'd placed on me. It amused me to know I was within shouting distance of the IRS's 10 Year Statute of Limitations—if I'd ignored them for a couple more years, they'd have wiped the debt from the books. But I was proud of making good on it (proud enough to take a photo, shown in Figure 10).

Figure 10

Even though I'd turned my life around spiritually and financially, I still yearned to deepen my exploration of esoteric Daoist training. I wrote a letter to my former mentor, Mike, to thank him for his teachings and asked if he would take me on as a student. Even though he had an unhealthy side, I didn't know where else to turn for deeper Daoist teachings. He never replied and, like the story of the old farmer, I affirmed that this wasn't good or bad. Later, I met another teacher with remarkable martial arts skills who helped me identify muscular tension that I was still carrying. For almost two years, I trained with him and got to know him and his live-in girlfriend. She eventually confessed to me that he had threatened to hit her. I rejected him as a teacher, but affirmed this wasn't good or bad.

Three years ago, with the help of a therapist, I faced my deepest issues surrounding relationships. As much as the Immortal Post changed me, it didn't transform my love life. It's a solitary activity and because my blockages were biggest surrounding relationships—even bigger than my financial life—the standing meditation wasn't enough. My therapist and I dove into the buried grime of programming I'd received from my parents, rewrote it, and, with the assistance of a friend who's an expert in online dating, I met the woman who's now my wife.

For almost a decade, I wondered about the standing meditation and Daoist energetic practices. How deep does the rabbit hole go? How many of the stories of ancient Daoists and their magical abilities are legends or actual truth? Is it possible to radically extend life, heal others, and explore a spirit realm? I had nowhere to turn for answers.

In 2019, my wife—then my girlfriend—and I deepened our practice of Daoism under the guidance of Daoist Abbot Dr. Jerry Alan Johnson, a master of this spiritual tradition with over four decades of experience, and other teachers in the lineage.

They taught me crucial aspects of the standing meditation which I didn't know; this book wouldn't have been possible without them. They've also helped me understand why the standing meditation delivers such amazing benefits, as a foundational pillar in the energetic architecture we can work with to enhance our mental, emotional, and physical health, and our spiritual development. They've helped me go deeper into the rabbit hole, setting me up with a rope, pickaxes, and a headlamp so I can explore the esoteric depths.

My wife, Dina, and I are learning how to work with the energy of someone's organs to transform their emotional state, purge negative stagnation, and power someone up with more chi, while they relax on a table. I've befriended a Daoist priest who can do this at a distance, and he works with my energy regularly as we sit in our homes hundreds of miles apart. At first, I could feel only subtle sensations, but now we're able to compare notes and match what I experience with what he's doing. I can feel exactly when he's focused on the energy centers in my brain, and have started seeing his projected image as he works on me.

On February 9, 2020, I poured wine into two shot glasses on our kitchen counter. My wife—then my fiancé—was in the living room, out of sight. I did a meditation to draw chi into my body and transmitted the chi into the wine glass on the right. I left the other wine glass alone.

"Okay, they're ready," I said.

Dina entered our kitchen and, after I closed my eyes, she handed me each glass. I sipped both and said, "The flavor of the second glass tastes 'harsher' or something like that. What do you think?"

She tasted both and said she was more drawn to a certain glass.

"Was it the glass on the left or the right?"

"The right," she said.

"That's the one I blessed."

Dina and I purge unwanted energy from the food we eat and enhance it with our chi; taste-tests confirm the flavor changes. This includes pouring three glasses of wine and altering the energy of two of them, while leaving one untouched. We've tested this on others who can determine which glasses were worked on and taste the difference. We've even changed the alcohol content of wine and whiskey, and confirmed the changes with a hydrometer.

One night, I brought a mylar balloon into our bedroom and turned off the AC, so there wasn't a hint of breeze in our apartment. The balloon was tied to a string about four feet long and I weighed the string's bottom end down. I sat on a corner of the bed, ten feet away from the motionless balloon. Dina sat on the other side of the bed and watched the balloon.

I breathed deeply and began a particular meditation. A few minutes later, I settled back into my body, turned, and looked back at Dina. She gave me a Mona Lisa smile and nodded.

"Really?" I said.

She nodded again.

"It moved?"

"It did," she said.

"Tell me what happened." I smiled. "In detail."

"The balloon was motionless for a few minutes. Then it suddenly jerked as if someone twisted it. Then it stopped. Then it twisted a little more, as if someone were turning it." She motioned the stop-and-go turning with her hands.

"Now," I said, "did the turning start a couple of minutes after I began the meditation?"

"No, it wasn't that quick," she said.

"Perfect," I said. "I didn't start immediately."

I had done a meditation where I projected myself outside of my body and I wanted to confirm if it was real. That night was just one of many tests I've done.

Before my bachelor party, my Best Man, Wally, drove over to pick me up. He sat at our dining room table and talked with Dina while I made coffee. I poured the coffee into two mugs and excused myself upstairs.

When I was out of sight and earshot, I did a set of Daoist meditations on one of the coffee mugs. I kept the other mug in another room. After a few minutes, I returned, gave both mugs to Wally, and asked him if he could taste a difference.

After several sips, he described one has having more of a Costa Rican coffee flavor. The other had a more subtle, smooth Hawaiian "Kona coffee" flavor. Then I asked him—and Dina, who hadn't even tasted the coffee—to guess which one I blessed. They both got it right; it was the one with the more subtle flavor.

These abilities aren't unnatural. We all have the potential for them in the same way we have the potential to train with weights until we can lift 400 pounds. It takes extreme dedication, but it's possible, as these abilities are built on a bedrock of emotional health and peace.

Just as it's natural to grow abilities beyond the comprehension of most people, it's natural to reroute the course of your life no matter how deeply it's swung in a painful direction. In the fall of 2018, I ventured to Aspen, Colorado, with Dina. We wandered the streets, making our way off the sidewalks and onto a dirt trail, coming to a fork. One path continued through the manicured grass of nearby athletic playing fields.

The other, called Ajax trail, narrowed and weaved into the dense trees of the mountain. After a little debate, we took the narrow path.

As we ventured farther and farther up and into the mountain, the trees seemed to engulf us like cave walls. At a few spots, the branches pulled away, letting us admire distant mountains from greater heights. The fall season had reached its climax and the rich reds, spicy yellows and deep browns bathed our eyes. I admired my future wife as she added to her macro photography collection.

We stopped at another unfurling. I turned to Dina. "Want to keep hiking? I know we planned to drive home today. We'll have to leave soon. Or I can just get us a hotel room for tonight and we can keep going," I said.

"Can we?" she said.

"Absolutely." I booked a hotel with my phone and we continued our journey.

As we hiked, I was struck with a vision from my past. Almost three years earlier, I'd visited the Tao Garden in Chiang Mai, Thailand, where I took many photographs, but treasured one above all. It wasn't of a manicured bed of flowers or a clipped bonsai tree, but of another tree with a massive bend near its root. The tree had been knocked off course, but didn't die. It rerouted its trunk toward the sky, reaching the heights it was meant to.

In Aspen, on that hike, the same thing appeared over and over.

Tree after tree had sprung out of the mountain slope, risking death as they course-corrected to find the sun. The perfect curves of their trunks were a testament to how they persevere, adapt, and attune to their nature.

I was grateful for the reminder. Maybe Mother Nature was looking out for me and making sure I'd notice.

When we get knocked off course, we have the chance to correct ourselves. We can change our energy, relax, and align ourselves, quiet the mind and make it an ally, harness our antifragile nature, simplify our lives, temper our emotions, seek solitude when we need it, practice patience, journey into self-discovery, let go of judgments, push ourselves, allow the energy to change us when the time is right, and empower ourselves with chaos. We can compare our challenges and setbacks to the trunks of these trees as part of our journey. We can even find that the key to do this, in the modern world, is with an ancient practice.

The beginning of the *Dao De Jing* states, "The Dao that can be spoken of is not the true Dao." The words that describe the way are not the way itself.

I've told my story, but the true Dao is what you explore on your own. I hope I've given some useful directions for your journey. I wish for you the peace I felt as I walked the winding path with the woman I love, the leaves shimmering and blazing their colors, as light shone from above and moved over the face of the mountains.

JOURNEY DEEPER ALONG THE PATH

In my third semester of college, after I stopped going to classes and became a ghost on campus, I studied marketing, huddling in my dorm room in front of my computer, scouring the internet for information. One company offered a 3-day seminar at the Crowne Plaza Hotel in Manhattan. I signed up. Then I called the hotel. They wouldn't rent a room to anyone under 21. After searching online, I got the impression that no hotel in New York City would rent a room to me.

Now what?

I could stay in my dorm. Or I could start the journey and figure things out when I got there.

I bought a Greyhound bus ticket from Amherst, Massachusetts, to the Port Authority Bus Terminal in New York City. Maybe I could sleep at the bus station?

I sat on the bus, staring out the window as it chugged through the blocks of Manhattan and people charged along the sidewalks, a sea of thousands of pedestrians, seeming to generate electric sparks as they passed by each other. I took deeper breaths. The fall air mixed with burnt rubber, spicy kebabs from street vendors, and the sweat of hustling New Yorkers was like snorting freshly shredded coffee grounds. When the bus lurched to a stop at the station, I jumped out, almost pumping my fists forward like Superman.

The first night of the event was a meet-and-greet and I attempted to consume the entire value of the ticket price at the buffet. After the first night ended, I weaved through the Manhattan streets to the bus station. Downstairs, I saw cops every 25 yards, stalking the waiting areas. Were they there to kick out vagrants? Protect them? Did I want to find out?

Shyness sucked at my torso like a vacuum. I plodded back up the stairs. As I reached the surface, the fluorescent lights disappeared and I looked around the dark Manhattan skyline.

Now what?

My gut told me that, if I started pacing around the streets and avenues, I'd find a hotel with lower guest standards. I marched in a counterclockwise spiral from 42nd street. Fifteen minutes later, a blood red neon sign blared at me: *Hotel Carter.**

The closer I got, the sleazier it looked. Maybe I had a chance. Inside the lobby were a couple of couches that looked like they'd been dragged, facedown, half a mile from the nearest dump. The front desk was encased in glass with a little slit at the bottom like a bank teller station.

I bent down to talk through the intercom. "Hi, I'd like a room for three nights."

I passed cash through the slit. They slipped me a keycard. The

* Google the Hotel Carter in Manhattan if you want to read about how creepy this place is.

closet-sized elevator squealed and hummed as it hauled me upward. *Please don't break. Don't plummet 20 stories down.* When the doors sputtered open, I hopped out, relieved.

As I roamed the narrow hallway, my shoes squelched on a green carpet, hidden somewhere beneath an advanced ecosystem of mildew, until I found my room. My room's bathroom had a basketball-sized hole in the wall. I eased my head halfway into it and looked down into the blackness. I dragged a loveseat to my door and propped it under the knob, in case nefarious characters squelched down the hallway to my room.

The bedsheets were stained, but seemed washed. Outside the window, over 20 floors down, people roamed, weaved past each other, still generating an electrical current that sparked me. The ambulance sirens were dim enough to calm me like an ocean's rumble. *I'm here. I'm doing it.*

The next evening, I wandered around Manhattan until I found Bryant Park in front of the New York Public Library. I sat at a black metal table near the thick, grainy, white, stone fencing. The bustling street was just a few feet away, but I felt like I'd found a secluded vortex where I could channel the energy around me. I scribbled notes and ideas onto some Crowne Plaza stationary.

The marketing seminar wasn't important, but making my decision to go was. Instead of languishing in my dorm room, I said yes to an adventure.

Years later, the night I felt my body glow like a sun after doing the Immortal Post, I said yes to another adventure. I devoted myself to practicing the standing meditation.

A decade after that, when I had the opportunity to study Chinese

Energetic Medicine, Daoist mysticism, and other forms of mysticism, I said yes again.

I have an invitation for you. At the following URL, you can sign up to receive a video of how to do the Immortal Post. When you see the standing meditation demonstrated in a video, you'll deepen your understanding and you'll double your results:

NateRifkin.com/journey

There's a reason I use the word *journey* in the URL. In addition to receiving the instructional video, you'll also get on my announcement list, reserved only for readers of this book. Announcement list for what? I don't know yet. It could be for live events. I might create some videos. Or I might publish a monthly newsletter that's mailed to your door. Whatever it turns out to be, you'll have a chance to dive deeper into Daoist mysticism. It won't be a gentle or easy ride. It won't be pain-free. But it will change you.

You don't need to say yes. Everything you learned in this book will help you live a wonderful life. Practice the Immortal Post and feel how it resonates with you. It might be all you need—it's the only Daoist practice I needed to turn my life around. But if you want to go deeper…

See if Daoist training gets in your blood. If it does, you might grow hungry for more. You might yearn for an adventure to explore how far this journey can take you. I'd be honored to help.

APPENDIX A

THINGS YOU'LL NOTICE AS YOU PRACTICE

Everything below can serve as guideposts for your progress. This list can relieve the feeling that something is wrong if you experience unusual things such as:

1. SHAKING

More than once during my Immortal Post practice, I've thought, "What the #$%& is going on?" as I flailed my arms and rocked my hips. My hand twitched back and forth, as if trying to fan the air. My hips swiveled, my shoulders jumped and rolled. My body appeared to have decided that if I were to attempt to stand still and relax, it would entertain itself with the dorkiest interpretive dance imaginable.

Shaking is normal, even if it lasts throughout your practice. Shaking is good because it means you're discharging stagnant energy. Parts of my torso shook and swayed for a couple of years (only when I did the Immortal Post and not at the supermarket, where I'd have spilled eggs and kumquats on my fellow shoppers). A few times my head shook so violently, like a dog trying to dry off, that I feared I'd injure myself, so I actively resisted shaking. Otherwise, I let it rip.

Whenever part of your body shakes, trembles or waves around, don't resist it. The shaking will subside…and sometimes return. Let it come and go. Make sure not to indulge in the shaking.

"Movements of the soul are made known by movements of the body." Leon Battista Alberti, *On Painting*

2. MEMORIES WILL POP INTO YOUR MIND.

Recently, I settled into a standing meditation, breathed deeply…felt myself relax…and remembered an awkward exchange with a friend from the day before. *Perfect*, I thought without any sarcasm, and let the memory come and go. Other times, memories from previous decades of my life bubbled up. Embarrassing situations, regrets, resentments, and, occasionally, memories I wasn't consciously aware of.

Get ready for weird stuff to pop up, and when it does, let it roll. Instead of remaining buried in your body, the emotional charge behind the thoughts is dissipating. Memories can crop up over and over again, so don't get concerned if one keeps throwing itself in front of you. It could be the archetype for a negative emotion in your life. One memory of getting yelled at could be your imprint for feelings of being victimized. Un-root your feelings of victimhood by allowing this memory to bubble up while you relax in the Immortal Post.

3. YOU'LL COUGH EVEN IF YOU'RE NOT SICK AND DON'T NEED TO CLEAR YOUR THROAT.

I'm sure I've convinced apartment neighbors that I've been on the verge of death when they heard me sputtering through the walls. I've coughed more while doing the Immortal Post than in any other situation. According to Traditional Chinese Medicine, the lungs house grief. If true, then I was clearing out the grief for me and my family lineage.

Other people report belching and passing gas. Celebrate this. It's a physical manifestation of you clearing emotional and psychological gunk from your system.

4. YOU'LL GRUNT, GROAN, AND MOAN.

"Oh, so that's what...you...were doing," a skeptical roommate said to me in Baltimore. I was trying to explain that, as I meditate, I sometimes groan.

That was over five years ago; later my grunting and groaning settled into something more like humming. Don't get concerned if you keep coughing or humming or anything else. Think of it as a signal of inner evolving.

The ancient Daoists believed that these sounds are a sign of releasing emotional trauma. They also connected certain sounds to organs, like laughter to the heart, which is connected to overexcitement, or groaning to the kidneys, which are connected to fear. Let the sounds come up without getting caught in the feeling. If you feel you're getting too angry or sad, take a short break so you won't get trapped in a cycle that reinforces the emotion.

5. YOU MIGHT DRY-HEAVE.

Don't worry—you're not going to hurl as if you'd spent the night slamming back vodka shots. In all seriousness, don't expect the Immortal Post to make you nauseous. Once every few months, I dry heaved even if I didn't feel discomfort; I was clearing out some heavy emotional crap. Every time I've done this, I've felt fantastic afterwards, as if I'd gone through a dozen good therapy sessions at once.

There's no guarantee you'll dry heave, but I'd be remiss if I didn't mention it. If you're still concerned, think of it this way: you're releasing emotional gunk that's been rotting within you. Would you rather heave it up or keep it inside?

6. YOU'LL PRODUCE MORE SALIVA.

You might find your saliva glands pumping overtime, as if your favorite food was plopped in front of you.

7. YOU'LL REMEMBER FUNNY CLIPS FROM TV SHOWS, MOVIES, ONLINE VIDEOS, ETC.

You might giggle from a hilarious clip you saw a few days, years or decades ago. Enjoy the feel-good hormones and let it pass.

8. PARTS OF YOUR BODY WILL FEEL HOT OR COLD.

Your hands might become hot, or your belly, or one side of your face, or the tip of your nose. You might feel as if you're standing on hot coals. You might especially feel heat between the tip of your tongue and the roof of your mouth.

You might also feel cold. For years, my hands felt freezing.

You could simultaneously feel hot in some parts of your body and cold in other parts. Let the energy do its thing.

9. YOU MIGHT ITCH.

You'll desperately desire to scratch a certain part of your body. Resist the urge as best you can—but don't feel guilty if you give in. The itching is a sign of energy starting to flow where it was once stagnant.

10. YOU'LL FEEL FRUSTRATED.

Intense frustration might bubble up. Perhaps a specific reason will be involved or you might feel the frustration first and your consciousness will attach a plausible reason to it. Either way, let it arrive, do its thing, and leave on its own terms.

11. YOU'LL FEEL FEAR.

You might feel a wave of fear as your mind drifts to a potential event or perhaps a phobia. Breathe and relax. The beauty of negative emotions stirring is that you're releasing them from the deep recesses of your body. Like cleaning a refrigerator shelf. It's going to look and maybe smell nasty, but that's evidence that your fridge will be a whole lot cleaner.

12. YOU'LL FEEL ANGER.*

You might feel animosity toward friends, enemies, family, loved ones, and total strangers. You'll feel tempted to believe this is something you must deal with immediately or that something's gone wrong. Focus on breathing deeply and slowly, and on letting your energy settle into the bottom half of your body. Anger raises your energy toward your

* Anger is one of the more common emotions to boil up during the Immortal Post because the standing meditation exercises your tendons and, according to Daoism, your tendons are associated with your liver, which is associated with anger. If you're prone to anger, be careful when doing this meditation.

head, so when you mentally intend energy toward your legs, it can help stymie the feeling.

Use the same guidelines with other emotions. If you get a sense that they're not leaving, take a break and start over when you feel more neutral.

13. YOU'LL FEEL JOY.

You might bask in the splendor of life. It reminds me of the old Zen story. A student, after sitting in meditation for a long time, approaches his teacher and says, "Please help me! I keep feeling so angry!"

The teacher whacks him upside the head and says, "Let it go!"

Ah yes, the student thinks. He returns to his meditation. Later, he approaches his teacher and says to her, "Ah, I feel so much better! I'm filled with so much bliss and joy that I can barely focus!"

The teacher whacks him upside the head and says, "Let it go!"

Let positive emotions arrive, do their thing, and leave. This doesn't mean you're letting go of joy forever or that you won't get it back. You're simply not letting an uncontrolled emotion interfere with your practice. If you're still concerned, remember that by letting blissful emotions come and go without trying to cling to them, you're making yourself a more inviting vessel for them.

14. YOU'LL SMELL STRANGE SCENTS.

On occasion, when I've dug up some nasty stuff from my subconscious, I'll get overwhelmed by a scent like feces, but it goes away as quickly as it appears. More recently and—I'm thankful to say—more often, I've gotten scents of cookies, cakes, and other sweet treats. According to

Daoist lore, pleasant scents mean you're getting visits from your spiritual older brothers and sisters.

15. YOUR SPINE AND OTHER JOINTS WILL CRACK.

Your practice may feel like you're getting an extended, gentle chiropractic session, which you are. As tension releases around your spine, it will adjust and sometimes audibly crack. You might get the urge to facilitate this adjustment with a shift in your hips or between your shoulders. If it feels natural, go for it. But don't try to crack your spine every time you have the urge.

This doesn't mean you're going to land a big payday once the spinal adjustments stop—but you might be opening up to something. Focus on your practice and let the results be what they are.

16. YOU'LL GET VISUAL OR AUDIBLE CUES FROM YOUR ENVIRONMENT.

I can't count the number of times I've dropped into a deeper level of relaxation and peacefulness and then a chorus of birds began to chirp, as if they were congratulating my progress and enjoying my greater harmony.

It's not just nature. I've enjoyed car horns, cracks from walls, engines turning on, the refrigerator revving up, tires screeching, a faucet dripping, my phone buzzing when I've neglected to put it on "Airplane Mode", my computer screen flicking on (when it's in my field of vision), dogs barking, and police sirens. This list could go on and on.

Most of the time it's mere background noise, but sometimes it's a cue, which can fall into two categories. One is confirmation that you're on the right track. You relax more, feel in the flow, and are greeted by sudden—even startling—background noises or visuals. When this happens, keep meditating, or take a moment to acknowledge the sign and feel grateful. Don't feel discouraged or annoyed because these things distract you when you're getting in a good groove. Think of them as part of the groove. Enjoy them and let them go.

The second category is the sound or visual cue reminding you to get on the right track. At times, your mind might seem to go berserk. Your thoughts blare so loudly that you're closer to experiencing the meditation version of road rage than tranquility.

Sometimes, the universe will reach out, often with a car horn, to get your attention. When it does, take advantage of the pattern-interrupt. Focus on your breathing, thank the universe for the reminder, and don't feel bad—not even if you need three or four horn blasts within five minutes to get you back on track. There's always another chance to improve your practice.

APPENDIX B

COMMON MISTAKES WHEN PRACTICING THE IMMORTAL POST

A. STICKING THE FRONT OF YOUR HEAD UP

When I taught the standing meditation to a new friend in California, he jumped into what looked like a sumo wrestler's stance, flexing his arms in front of him and sticking out his chin. He looked powerful...but when I began making adjustments, he could actually *be empowered.*

"Raise your head up," I said.

He pushed his forehead up and stuck his chin out even more. I made a mental note to work on my directions.

"I mean, raise your skull straight up, so it's neutral. Here, let me show you."

I pinched a bit of his hair near the back of his head and pulled straight up. That did the trick. But today, I'd teach this a different way. First, I'd ask:

"Where is the top of your head?"

Touch it with your fingers and then stand next to a mirror to confirm. You'll discover that the real top of your head—directly over your spinal cord—is farther back than you probably thought. An easy way to feel the top is to pull your ears up, which are in line with the crown of your skull.

As you practice, you'll discover that you'll achieve maximum height only if you rid yourself of tension in your neck, shoulders, and along your spinal column, because any tension will subtly pull your head in some direction other than straight up.

B. BENDING YOUR KNEES TOO MUCH

Whenever I correct someone's form, I tell them to bend their knees less. I've never seen someone bend their knees too little.

C. NOT TUCKING YOUR BUTT ENOUGH

I asked one of my teachers, Dr. Diego Sanmiquel, who's been training people for over two decades, if it were possible to tuck your pelvis too much.

He thought about it for a moment and said, "No, I don't think it's physically possible." Unless you compromise something else in your form, like bending your knees too much or not keeping your spine straight, it's impossible to tuck your butt too much. Just don't force anything.

D. FOCUSING SO MUCH ON RELAXING YOUR BODY THAT YOU FORGET YOUR FACE

Once, I taught a one-hour class on the standing meditation and a few other energetic exercises. A friend took some photos and I discovered something dismaying. Almost without exception, my face was pinched into a frown—even when I was performing an exercise supposedly relaxing me. This feedback inspired me to place more focus on my facial muscles and to imagine them relaxing.

Your face contains 43 muscles, which can get as tense as your lower back, neck or hamstrings. Here's a funny observation you can use to verify for yourself:

The next time you're in a grocery store or anywhere featuring magazines, find one about yoga or mindfulness, flip through it, and locate a photo of a model in a relaxed meditation pose. Perhaps cross-legged and basking in the outdoors. Note the peaceful, serene expression on the model's face.

You're seeing someone *pretending* to look relaxed, but a truly relaxed face appears different. It looks goofy. The expression is blank (how could it be anything else?), with an intent-less gaze. That comes from ridding your facial muscles of tension, rather than arranging your expression to appear peaceful.

Become aware of your facial muscles. Notice any:

- Jaw clenching
- Eye squinting
- Forehead frowning
- Tension around your skull
- A pinch on the bridge of your nose, especially if you wear glasses
- Lips pursing

Relaxing your face is like the rest of your body. Breathe into it. You might feel a bit naked because facial expressions are part of the persona we wear.

E. STANDING IN AN UNEVEN WAY BECAUSE IT FEELS RIGHT

While touring the Tao Garden in Chiang Mai, Thailand, several years ago, I asked a couple to take some photos of me in the Immortal Post. They were happy to oblige and I was excited for a keepsake of me practicing under the domed canopy of an outdoor training hall, surrounded by colorful plants.

I settled in, did my best to relax into alignment, and they took a few shots. I thanked them and looked at my phone. The photos, with the beautiful background, looked great, but then I examined my posture. I looked...as if I was leaning to the left? Why was one arm lifted so much higher? At first, the image reminded me of a crab bustling along the ocean floor—but then I sighed and realized that'd be putting crabs in a bad light.

Well, I guess I still have plenty of work to do on my form.

I felt grateful for the wake-up call and learned not to trust my surface-level kinesthetic feedback. My sense of being aligned was anything but, which meant that true alignment would feel out of whack before my brain got used to it. After that, I discovered and eliminated deeper levels of tension in my hips and spine. My natural stance became more aligned.

As you relax your body, you might find yourself in a pleasant groove, feeling even and balanced...until you catch a glimpse of yourself in the mirror.

You might be surprised that you're leaning so far to the left, it's almost as if you're standing on one foot. Or your right shoulder is hitched a couple of inches higher than your left. Your head might tilt to one side. And yet, it doesn't feel as if your body's bent that way. You feel aligned because your body is so used to misalignment. Your only clue is seeing the misalignment in the mirror. When you relax more to correct the imbalance, you might feel off-kilter. Your perfectly-aligned head may feel awkwardly bent. As you keep practicing, the odd feeling will subside and your body will get used to true alignment. Check yourself in the mirror for objective feedback.

Don't feel bad for needing to adjust your posture. A study from New York University showed infants fall over 17 times per hour when they learn to walk during playtime.[61] If they took their falls as personally as adults take mistakes, the babies would stay on the floor.

A word of caution:

When your shoulders or hips are out of alignment, you might be tempted to force them into place. Instead, locate which body part needs to relax more and let the out-of-whack part glide back into whack. All misalignment is a symptom of something deeper. Resolve the deeper issue and alignment will occur. Forcing alignment without this step can make it worse.

F. STOPPING YOUR MEDITATION BECAUSE YOU FEEL UNCOMFORTABLE

Sharp pain is bad. If you feel any, stop and figure out the issue—which might require a physical therapist. However, when you begin practicing this meditation, your thighs and shoulders will burn, your hands will tremble, your feet will ache, and you'll feel tension in places on your body you didn't know existed—and you must withstand all of this.

One fall afternoon, I visited my friend Gary and asked him how his standing meditation practice was going. Nearly 70, he had a weight training program that, combined with his semi-refined pit bull nature (or, as he referred to it, his "pugnacious proclivity") kept him feeling young. I was curious how he handled the Immortal Post.

"Great," he said, "But I've got a question."

I grabbed a notepad and pen. Whatever he was about to ask would be valuable for the book in your hands.

"It's really tough when I first begin because there's so much effort and tension," he said. "I can definitely see how it increases focus, but it's tough to actually relax."

"You're absolutely right about the effort," I said. "I should have emphasized that more..."

When you begin your practice, your weakest link will be your physical strength, unless you're an athlete. As you progress and add time to your routine, the physical strain, especially in your legs, might still prevent you from relaxing. The Immortal Post might seem little more than a calisthenic exercise.

"But once you get up to eight minutes, things will start to change," I said.

When your muscles and tendons get strong enough, you'll be able to stand without straining. You can relax more and more. It will be effortless effort, but effort comes first.

ENDNOTES

1 Johnson PhD, J. A. (2019). *Yiquan Neigong Daoist Training*. The International Institute of Medical Qigong Publishing House. Pg. 30

2 Johnson PhD, J. A. (2020). *The Secret Teachings of Chinese Energetic Medicine Volume 1: Energetic Anatomy and Physiology* (1st ed.). The International Institute of Medical Qigong. Pg. 18

3 Johnson PhD, J. A. (2018). *Daoist Internal Alchemy* (Final ed.). International Institute of Medical Qigong Publishing House. Pg. 10

4 Oettingen, G., & Reininger, K. M. (2016). *The power of prospection: mental contrasting and behavior change*. Social and Personality Psychology Compass, 10(11), 591–604. https://doi.org/10.1111/spc3.12271

5 *Review of Evidence Suggesting That the Fascia Network Could Be the Anatomical Basis for Acupoints and Meridians in the Human Body*. (2020, October 16). PubMed Central (PMC) https://www.ncbi.nlm.nih.gov/pmc/articles/PMC3092510/

6 Minary-Jolandan, M. (2009, February 25). *Nanoscale characterization of isolated individual type I collagen fibrils: polarization and piezoelectricity*. PubMed https://pubmed.ncbi.nlm.nih.gov/19417467/

7 *Brief Report: Guided Migration of Neural Stem Cells Derived from Human Embryonic Stem Cells by an Electric Field*. (2012, February 1). PubMed Central (PMC). https://www.ncbi.nlm.nih.gov/pmc/articles/PMC4437764/

8 Keown, D. (2014). *The Spark in the Machine: How the Science of Acupuncture Explains the Mysteries of Western Medicine* (Illustrated ed.). Singing Dragon.

9 Radin PhD, D. (2013). *Supernormal: Science, Yoga, and the Evidence for Extraordinary Psychic Abilities* (1st ed.). Deepak Chopra Books

10 Johnson PhD, J. A. (2020). *The Secret Teachings of Chinese Energetic*

Medicine Volume 1: Energetic Anatomy and Physiology (1st ed.). The International Institute of Medical Qigong

11 *Memory transference in organ transplant recipients - Namah Journal.* (2011) Journal of New Approaches to Medicine and Health http://www.namahjournal.com/doc/Actual/Memory-transference-in-organ-transplant-recipients-vol-19-iss-1.html

12 Pearsall, P. (2000, March 21). *Changes in heart transplant recipients that parallel the personalities of their donors.* PubMed https://pubmed.ncbi.nlm.nih.gov/10882878

13 Johnson PhD, J. A. (2020). *The Secret Teachings of Chinese Energetic Medicine Volume 1: Energetic Anatomy and Physiology* (1st ed.). The International Institute of Medical Qigong. Pg. 18

14 Johnson PhD, J. A. (2020). *The Secret Teachings of Chinese Energetic Medicine Volume 1: Energetic Anatomy and Physiology* (1st ed.). The International Institute of Medical Qigong. Pg. 242

15 Tzu, L., & Dale, R. A. (2017) *The Tao Te Ching: 81 Verses by Lao Tzu with Introduction and Commentary (Sacred Texts)* (Translation ed.). Watkins Publishing. Pg. 201

16 *A reed before the wind lives on, while mighty oaks do fall.* (2009) Oxford Reference https://www.oxfordreference.com/view/10.1093/acref/9780199539536.001.0001/acref-9780199539536-e-1822

17 Watson, L. S. A. S. L. B. (1993). *Tao Te Ching (Hackett Classics) by Lao-Tzu Stephen Addiss Stanley Lombardo Burton Watson (1993-10-15).* Hackett Publishers. Pg. 131

18 *Tao Te Ching.* (1996). Tao Te Ching. http://www.wright-house.com/religions/taoism/tao-te-ching.html

19 Martin, W. (2004). *A Path and a Practice.* Amsterdam University Press. Pg. 59

20 Martin, W. (2004). *A Path and a Practice.* Amsterdam University Press. Pg. 114

21 Yang, J. (2020). *The Dao De Jing: A Qigong Interpretation* (1st ed.). YMAA Publication Center. Pg. 415

22 Johnson PhD, J. A. (2019). *Yiquan Neigong Daoist Training.* The International Institute of Medical Qigong Publishing House. Pg. 30

23 Martin, W. (2004). *A Path and a Practice.* Amsterdam University Press. Pg. 113

24 https://science.nasa.gov/science-news/science-at-nasa/2001/ast01oct_1

25 Hartig, M. (2020, July 31). *Capacitively coupled electric fields accelerate proliferation of osteoblast-like primary cells and increase bone extracellular matrix formation in vitro.* PubMed https://pubmed.ncbi.nlm.nih.

gov/11156291/

26 French, D. P. (2020, July 31). *An intervention to increase walking requires both motivational and volitional components: a replication and extension.* PubMed https://pubmed.ncbi.nlm.nih.gov/21745028/

27 Zhang, Y. (2011). *Using a combined motivational and volitional intervention to promote exercise and healthy dietary behaviour [sic] among undergraduates.* PubMed https://pubmed.ncbi.nlm.nih.gov/22055834/

28 Milne, S. (2002). *Combining motivational and volitional interventions to promote exercise participation: protection motivation theory and implementation intentions.* PubMed https://pubmed.ncbi.nlm.nih.gov/14596707/

29 Clear, J. (2018). *Atomic Habits: An Easy & Proven Way to Build Good Habits & Break Bad Ones* (1st ed.). Avery

30 *Just think: The challenges of the disengaged mind.* (2014, July 4). PubMed Central (PMC). https://www.ncbi.nlm.nih.gov/pmc/articles/PMC4330241/

31 Tzu, L. Tao Te Ching (Tarcher Cornerstone Editions) Penguin Publishing Group. Kindle Edition Pg. 31

32 *Effectiveness of Acceptance and Commitment Therapy on Anxiety and Depression of Razi Psychiatric Center Staff.* (2018, February 15). PubMed Central (PMC). https://www.ncbi.nlm.nih.gov/pmc/articles/PMC5839459/

33 Malmir, T. (2017). *Determining the Effectiveness of Acceptance and Commitment Therapy (ACT) on Life Expectancy and Anxiety Among Bereaved Patients.* PubMed https://pubmed.ncbi.nlm.nih.gov/29284992/

34 Martin, W. (2004). *A Path and a Practice.* Amsterdam University Press. Pg. 88

35 Tzu, L., & Dale, R. A. (2017) *The Tao Te Ching: 81 Verses by Lao Tzu with Introduction and Commentary (Sacred Texts)* (Translation ed.). Watkins Publishing. Pg. 117

36 Bermudez, M. A., & Schultz, W. (2014). *Timing in reward and decision processes.* Philosophical Transactions of the Royal Society B: Biological Sciences, 369(1637), 20120468

37 Wassum, K. M., Ostlund, S. B., Loewinger, G. C., & Maidment, N. T. (2013). *Phasic mesolimbic dopamine release tracks reward seeking during expression of Pavlovian-to-instrumental transfer.* Biological Psychiatry, 73(8), 747-755

38 Martin, W. (2004). *A Path and a Practice.* Amsterdam University Press Pg. 57

39 Perciavalle, V. (2016). *The role of deep breathing on stress.* PubMed https://pubmed.ncbi.nlm.nih.gov/27995346/

40 Johnson PhD, J. A. (2019). *The Hidden Teachings of Christian Mysticism (Vol. 2): Psychic Influences & Spiritual Protection* (1st ed.). The International Institute of Medical Qigong Publishing House. Pg. 51

41 Verduyn, P. (2015). *Passive Facebook usage undermines affective well-being: Experimental and longitudinal evidence.* PubMed https://pubmed.ncbi.nlm.nih.gov/25706656

42 Less Facebook use—*More well-being and a healthier lifestyle? An experimental intervention study.* (2020, July 1). ScienceDirect https://www.sciencedirect.com/science/article/pii/S0747563220300868

43 Allcott, H. (2020). *The Welfare Effects of Social Media.* American Economic Association. https://www.aeaweb.org/articles?id=10.1257/aer.20190658

44 Social Media Lab. (2019, November 20). *Social media use and psychological well-being: A Meta-analysis.* Stanford Social Media Lab https://sml.stanford.edu/pubs/2019/social-media-use-and-psychological-well-being-a-meta-analysis

45 Kramer, A. D. I. (2014, June 17). *Experimental evidence of massive-scale emotional contagion through social networks.* PNAS https://www.pnas.org/content/111/24/8788

46 Tzu, L. *Tao Te Ching* (Tarcher Cornerstone Editions) Penguin Publishing Group. Kindle Edition Pg. 62

47 Tzu, L., & Dale, R. A. (2017) *The Tao Te Ching: 81 Verses by Lao Tzu with Introduction and Commentary* (Sacred Texts) (Translation ed.). Watkins Publishing. Pg. 201

48 Martin, W. (2004). *A Path and a Practice.* Amsterdam University Press. Pg. 75

49 Tzu, L., & Dale, R. A. (2017). *The Tao Te Ching: 81 Verses by Lao Tzu with Introduction and Commentary (Sacred Texts)* (Translation ed.). Watkins Publishing. Pg. 220

50 Tzu, L. *Tao Te Ching* (Tarcher Cornerstone Editions) Penguin Publishing Group. Kindle Edition Pg. 38

51 Tzu, L., & Dale, R. A. (2017) *The Tao Te Ching: 81 Verses by Lao Tzu with Introduction and Commentary (Sacred Texts)* (Translation ed.). Watkins Publishing. Pg. 135

52 Tzu, L., & Dale, R. A. (2017) *The Tao Te Ching: 81 Verses by Lao Tzu with Introduction and Commentary (Sacred Texts)* (Translation ed.). Watkins Publishing. Pg. 156

53 Martin, W. (2004). *A Path and a Practice.* Amsterdam University Press. Pg. 44

54 Saunders, L. (2018, April 6). *Top 20% of Americans Will Pay 87% of Income Tax.* WSJ https://www.wsj.com/articles/top-20-of-americans-will-pay-87-of-income-tax-1523007001

55 Tzu, L., & Dale, R. A. (2017) *The Tao Te Ching: 81 Verses by Lao Tzu with Introduction and Commentary (Sacred Texts)* (Translation ed.). Watkins Publishing. Pg. 156

56 *Habit formation.* (2016, March 1). PubMed Central (PMC) https://www.ncbi.nlm.nih.gov/pmc/articles/PMC4826769/

57 Watson, L. S. A. S. L. B. (1993). *Tao Te Ching (Hackett Classics) by Lao-Tzu Stephen Addiss Stanley Lombardo Burton Watson* (1993-10-15). Hackett Publishers. Pg. 113

58 *Effects of mindful-attention and compassion meditation training on amygdala response to emotional stimuli in an ordinary, non-meditative state.* (2020, July 31). PubMed Central (PMC) https://www.ncbi.nlm.nih.gov/pmc/articles/PMC3485650/

59 Sahdra, B. K. (2011). *Enhanced response inhibition during intensive meditation training predicts improvements in self-reported adaptive socioemotional functioning.* PubMed https://pubmed.ncbi.nlm.nih.gov/21500899/

60 Tzu, L. *Tao Te Ching* (Tarcher Cornerstone Editions) Penguin Publishing Group. Kindle Edition Pg. 186

61 *How Do You Learn to Walk? Thousands of Steps and Dozens of Falls Per Day.* (2020, August 2). PubMed Central (PMC) https://www.ncbi.nlm.nih.gov/pmc/articles/PMC3591461/

ACKNOWLEDGMENTS

Thank you, Dr. Jerry Alan Johnson, Dr. Erika Johnson, Dr. William Welch Jr., Dr. Diego Sanmiquel, Dr. Kelly Ryan Lake, Dr. Chris Holder, and Peter Ragnar, for guiding me on the Daoist path. Thank you Mike, for introducing me to Daoism.

Thank you, Maury Cohen. I still remember the night when I paced back and forth, phone pressed to my ear, as you gently explained I needed to be less of a marketer and more of an author. Thank you for helping me through three or four rewrites of my first chapter while you looked for the perfect editor, and for your help after that.

Thank you, Steve Singular. I knew I'd found an amazing editor when, after I returned home from our first meeting excited about the notes you gave me, I realized you had convinced me to scrap my entire manuscript and start over. After ten drafts (but who's counting?) it got there.

Thank you, Jill Wisehart and Ryan Healy for helping with the book description.

Thank you, Lindsey Tschappat, Harinder Singh Sabharwal, Greig Veeder, Dr. Christine Sanmiquel, Gianna Bandoni, Jill Wisehart, Rex

Wisehart, and Emily Lark for giving me notes for how to improve this book.

Thank you, Jason "Wally" Waldron for reading a draft of this book, for your feedback, and for saying I'd graduated.

Most of all, thank you, Dina—love of my life. I'm glad you found our mutually relentless editing of this book sexy.

ABOUT THE AUTHOR

NATE RIFKIN has prospered by combining ancient mystical practices with modern strategies for living. As a spiritual explorer, he dedicates himself to the Daoist mystical tradition. As a leader in the field of business, he has written marketing campaigns that have generated tens of millions of dollars in sales. Nate lives in Golden, Colorado with his lovely wife. He publishes articles on *www.NateRifkin.com.*

Printed in Great Britain
by Amazon

65325019R00215